Project management based on PRINCE2® 2009 Edition

Other publications by Van Haren Publishing

Van Haren Publishing (VHP) specializes in titles on Best Practices, methods and standards within four domains:
- IT management
- Architecture (Enterprise and IT)
- Business management and
- Project management

Van Haren Publishing offers a wide collection of whitepapers, templates, free e-books, trainer material etc. in the **VHP Knowledge Base**: www.vanharen.net for more details.

VHP is also publisher on behalf of leading organizations and companies:
ASLBiSL Foundation, CA, Centre Henri Tudor, Gaming Works, Getronics, IACCM, IAOP, IPMA-NL, ITSqc, NAF, Ngi, PMI-NL, PON, Quint, The Open Group, The Sox Institute

Topics are (per domain):

IT (Service) Management / IT Governance	Architecture (Enterprise and IT)	Project/Programme/ Risk Management
ABC of ICT	Archimate®	A4-Projectmanagement
ASL	GEA®	ICB / NCB
BiSL	SOA	MINCE®
CATS	TOGAF®	M_o_R®
CMMI		MSP™
CoBIT	**Business Management**	P3O
ISO 17799	CMMI	*PMBOK® Guide*
ISO 27001	Contract Management	PRINCE2®
ISO 27002	EFQM	
ISO/IEC 20000	eSCM	
ISPL	ISA-95	
IT Service CMM	ISO 9000	
ITIL® V3	ISO 9001:2000	
ITSM	OPBOK	
MOF	Outsourcing	
MSF	SAP	
SABSA	SixSigma	
	SOX	
	SqEME®	

For the latest information on VHP publications, visit our website: www.vanharen.net.

Project management based on PRINCE2® 2009 Edition

Bert Hedeman

Gabor Vis van Heemst

Hans Fredriksz

Van Haren
PUBLISHING

Colophon

Title:	Project management based on PRINCE2® 2009 Edition
Series:	Best Practice
Authors:	Bert Hedeman (Hedeman Consulting)
	Gabor Vis van Heemst (Intrprimus)
	Hans Fredriksz (ISES)
Reviewers (Dutch edition):	- Ernst Bosschers (ISES International)
	- Arthur Coppens (Getronics)
	- Francisca Kouwen (Getronics)
	- Mark Kouwenhoven (PMcoaching)
	- Joost Nuyten (Rabobank)
	- Arie den Ouden (Ambidexter)
	- Henny Portman (ING)
Reviewers (English edition):	- Pierre Bernard (Pink Elephant Canada)
	- Guy Eastoe (Snap Tech SA)
	- Rubina Faber (Regal Training and Consultancy Ltd)
	- Julie Grabb (Enhancing Project Performance)
	- Dave Jones (Pink Elephant UK)
	- Eddie Kilkelly (ILX)
	- Marianna Ruocco (Pink Elephant Canada)
English translation:	DaVinci Vertalingen b.v.
Text editor:	Steve Newton
Publisher:	Van Haren Publishing, Zaltbommel, www.vanharen.net
ISBN:	978 90 8753 496 7
Print:	First edition, first impression, March 2010
	First edition, second impression with improvements, June 2011
Layout and type setting:	CO2 Premedia, Amersfoort - NL
Copyright:	© Van Haren Publishing 2009, 2010

Preface

An increasing number of organizations are working in a project-like manner, using the PRINCE2® project management method. For these organizations the advantages of using one uniform standard method are obvious: a uniform method of working and terminology makes projects comparable, transferable and orderly. Moreover, PRINCE2 has additional qualities, such as the standard 'no go'/'go' decision with each stage, the Business Case at the centre of the project and clear agreements about who is responsible for what.

This book is intended for everyone doing projects in real world. It is written for Project Managers, Project Leaders and Team Managers and all others who are involved with the starting up and management of projects.
It aligns with the 2009 Edition of the PRINCE2 methodology, with many lists serving as reference material for all project types and sizes. As this book illustrates, PRINCE2 is quite logical and this title demonstrates why why it is often referred to as a structured best practice for project management.

In addition, the contents of this book meet the majority of the theoretical requirements set for successfully passing the PRINCE2 Foundation exam. It also provides a good reference title as part of the wider reading and practical experience required from those taking the Practitioner exam.

In this book, the authors have successfully combined their long experience in project management and PRINCE2 training. Using this background they explain the PRINCE2 approach in a structured manner, complemented with useful examples to help bring the theory alive. The Themes, Processes, techniques and Management Products as defined in PRINCE2 are explained in an easy-to-read, concise text. In the appendices you will find an example of a Project Brief and a paragraph on how to deal with lessons learned in a project. Additionally, PRINCE2 templates can be obtained via the web site www.vanharen.net.

Finally we would like to thank all reviewers who have kindly contributed with their comments to the quality of this book. We very much appreciate their help and their time.

March 2010, The Publisher

Contents

1 Introduction to project management **1**
1.1 Why project management? 1
1.2 What is a project? 1
1.3 What is project management? 3
1.4 What is the job of the Project Manager? 4
1.5 What aspects are managed? 4
1.6 What is a successful project? 5
1.7 Why do projects fail? 6
1.8 Why PRINCE2? 7

2 Introduction to PRINCE2 . . . . **9**
2.1 What is PRINCE2? 9
2.2 The structure of PRINCE2. 9
2.3 Relationship to other OGC guidelines 9
2.4 What is not in PRINCE2? 10
2.5 PRINCE2, benefits. 11
2.6 Differences in PRINCE2 v2009 versus v2005 11
2.7 Spelling of PRINCE2 words. 15
2.8 About this book 16
2.9 Preparation for exams 16

3 PRINCE2, principles **19**
Principle 1 19
Principle 2 20
Principle 3 20
Principle 4 21
Principle 5 21
Principle 6 22
Principle 7 22

I Introduction to PRINCE2 themes

25

4 Business Case **27**
4.1 Introduction. 27
4.2 Conceptual framework 27
4.3 Business Case, types 28
4.4 Business Case, PRINCE2 approach 29
4.5 Business Case, content 32
4.6 Business Case, roles&responsibilities. 33

5   Organization **35**
    5.1   Introduction. 35
    5.2   Conceptual framework 35
    5.3   Project management structure. 36
    5.4   Project Management Team (PMT) 37
    5.5   Size of the Project Board. 42
    5.6   Involving stakeholders 42
    5.7   Preparing the Communication Management Strategy. 43

6   Quality. **45**
    6.1   Introduction. 45
    6.2   Conceptual framework 45
    6.3   Quality management 45
    6.4   PRINCE2 quality approach 47
    6.5   Quality planning 48
    6.6   Quality control. 51
    6.7   Quality review 52
    6.8   Quality, roles&responsibilities 55

7   Planning. **57**
    7.1   Introduction. 57
    7.2   What is a plan?. 57
    7.3   Benefits of drawing up a plan 57
    7.4   Elements of a plan 57
    7.5   Plan approach. 58
    7.6   Planning levels 59
    7.7   Planning, PRINCE2 approach 61
    7.8   Planning, roles&responsibilities 72

8   Risk **73**
    8.1   Introduction. 73
    8.2   Conceptual framework 73
    8.3   Risk 74
    8.4   Risk Management Strategy 75
    8.5   Risk Register. 76
    8.6   Risk management procedures 76
    8.7   Risk owner and risk actionee. 82
    8.8   Risk budget 82
    8.9   Risks, roles&responsibilities 83

9   Change. **85**
    9.1   Introduction. 85
    9.2   Conceptual framework 85
    9.3   Approach to change 86
    9.4   Configuration management procedures 89
    9.5   Issue control procedures and change control procedures 90

9.6   Change Authority and change budget 91
9.7   Roles and responsibilities 92

10 Progress **93**
10.1   Introduction 93
10.2   Conceptual framework 93
10.3   Management by exception 94
10.4   Progress, control 95
10.5   Roles and responsibilities 101

II Introduction to processes **105**
II.1   Why a process-based approach? 105
II.2   Four management levels 105
II.3   The management processes 106
II.4   PRINCE2 processes in a temporal framework 106
II.5   The structure of the process descriptions 107

11 SU, Starting up a Project **109**
11.1   SU, basic principles 109
11.2   Context 110
11.3   SU, process description 111
11.4   Overview of SU activities 115

12 IP, Initiating a Project **117**
12.1   IP, basic principles 117
12.2   Context 118
12.3   Process Description 118
12.4   Overview of IP activities 123

13 DP, Directing a Project **125**
13.1   DP, basic principles 125
13.2   Context 125
13.3   DP, process description 126
13.4   Overview of DP activities 131

14 CS, Controlling a Stage **133**
14.1   CS, basic principles 133
14.2   Context 134
14.3   CS, process description 135
14.4   Overview of CS activities 141

15 MP, Managing Product Delivery **145**
15.1   MP, basic principles 145
15.2   Context 146
15.3   MP, process description 146
15.4   Overview of MP activities 149

16 SB, Managing a Stage Boundary **151**
16.1   SB, basic principles 151
16.2   Context 152
16.3   SB, process description 152
16.4   Overview of SB activities 156

17 CP, Closing a Project **159**
17.1   CP, basic principles 159
17.2   Context 160
17.3   CP, process description 160
17.4   Overview of CP activities 164

18 The Project Environment **167**
18.1   Project versus programme 167
18.2   Multi-project management 168
18.3   Managing a project portfolio 168

19 Tailoring **171**
19.1   Introduction 171
19.2   Projects within programmes 174
19.3   Project, scale 175
19.4   Lifecycle models 179
19.5   Different kinds of projects 180
19.6   Project types 182

Appendix A Management products, set-up **187**

Appendix B Roles and responsibilities **211**

Appendix C Example of Product-based Planning **218**

Appendix D Health check **221**

Appendix E Glossary **229**

Appendix G Additional information **241**

Index **243**

1   Introduction to project management

1.1   Why project management?

Managing projects is as old as the hills. There are stories dating back to ancient times about activities we would now call projects. Just think of the challenges facing building the pyramids in Egypt and South America. Even the way our forefathers moved encampments from one hunting ground to another can be seen as a project.

The concept of a 'project', however, originated in the 1960s and was mainly applied to major infrastructure works. At that time, project management involved little more than planning the work. In the 1970s, attention switched to controlling the work and after that the personal skills of the Project Manager came under scrutiny. In the 1990s, attention shifted towards a process-based approach to project management. In recent decades, there has been more and more focus on the environment in which projects are implemented. More and more projects are (or are starting to be) part of portfolios or programmes within organizations.

Project management is increasingly becoming a profession. In the past project management was a task taken on in addition to regular work, whereas nowadays project management is a separate profession from which many people earn a living. However, despite the increased professionalism, projects still frequently fail. Some failed projects hit the headlines, but most are never heard of again. There is no simple reason why projects fail, but a lack of an effective method for managing projects is one of the major causes.

Without a project management method various stakeholders may have differing expectations for organizing and completing a project or the amount of responsibility and authority they have. Rarely are such projects delivered to the satisfaction of those involved. This particularly applies to projects with a long lead time or projects in a changing environment.

A good project management method should not be static. The environment and the market are subject to change, Executives and users take up new positions. In other words, projects have to be managed in a changing environment. It is still too often assumed that a project can be managed in a 'frozen' environment. This may make things easy, but it is just not how things are in the world of today.

An effective project management method helps the Project Manager to organize and manage a project in a continually changing environment while still involving all the stakeholders. PRINCE2 is such a method and uses the fundamental principles of good project management.

1.2   What is a project?

It is important to recognize the difference between a project and the 'business as usual' of an organization. Lack of clarity as to what a project actually is can lead to a lot of friction and frustration.

Definitions of a project, PRINCE2 definition

One frequently used definition of a project is: "A project is a time and cost constrained operation to realize a set of defined deliverables up to quality standards and requirements." (Source: ICB version 3.0)

In the context of the above, PRINCE2 describes a project as:

> *A temporary organization that is created for the purpose of delivering one or more business products according to an agreed Business Case.*

A temporary organization entails staff temporarily being given a different set of responsibilities and authority. Line management has to delegate certain responsibilities and authority to the project organization, otherwise a project organization cannot function properly. Business products are products that provide added value for the customer. A Business Case is a justification for initiating and delivering a project. In a Business Case, the anticipated benefits and estimated costs for the project are recorded, as well as the time over which the benefits will be realized.

Why are projects important?

One of the most important reasons for working with projects is that the desired results simply cannot be achieved, or can be achieved only with difficulty, within the existing line organization or organizations. The existing (corporate) structures and processes are primarily geared toward efficiency and much less suited to dealing quickly and properly with change. The project organization is temporary. In other words, it has been created for the duration of the project and differs in that respect from the line organization. Unsurprisingly, the style and nature of projects differs from the line activities.

Working with projects is a good way of safeguarding support for and commitment to use the end result as early as possible by involving the different stakeholders in the initiation and delivery of the project. In this regard, projects have become an indispensable way of implementing changes within organizations.

What makes projects so 'different'?

Projects have specific characteristics compared to standard business operations work. These include:

- **Change** – A project always means a change from the status quo - sometimes a minor one, but sometimes also a major one - and this creates resistance to the change.. A temporary project organization provides a good way of developing and safeguarding support for and commitment to use the end result early in the development stage by involving the different stakeholders in the initiation and implementation of the project. In this way, a broad-based grounding in the line organizations involved is assured at an early stage.
- **Temporary** – This is a distinguishing feature of projects. Project have a defined start and end date. The project finishes as soon as the pre-agreed products and/or services have been delivered and handed over to the customer.
- **Cross-functional** – A project has an organization specially set up for this purpose. What characterizes a project organization is that it comprises the different competencies and roles required for the project. This renders the project organization effective. In this regard, it does

not matter whether the team members come from the same (line) organizations or different ones.

- **Unique** – Every project is different because every change is different. The result to be produced is different or there are different objectives. Different people are involved in the project organization, there are different stakeholders or the context is different. No two projects are the same.
- **Uncertainty** – All the specified characteristics of projects result in uncertainties. They can produce both opportunities and threats. There is no getting around this, but it is an inextricable fact with which projects are faced. In this regard, projects are often much more risk-laden than normal activities and risk management is an indispensable component of project management.

Relationship between projects and programmes

The need for a change in the organization can be defined from the perspective of the corporate objectives. To this end, projects can be initiated. In such cases, the project provides the necessary products and services required by the business organization in order for it to achieve its objectives and the benefits associated with these. However, achieving business objectives and benefits is, and remains, one of the business organization's responsibilities and is not the project's responsibility.

A programme is sometimes set up to develop one or more corporate objectives. In such cases, the programme serves to initiate the different projects. The products and services required for the programme are then produced in the projects in order to fulfill the agreed goals and benefits. A programme has a less well-defined path and also a much longer lead-time than the separate projects within the programme, for a programme must consciously be finished, whereas projects automatically come to an end on delivery of the output of the project. After all, if everything is running as it should, benefits will continue each year (see table 1.1). Consequently, programmes are not large projects but one of the operational management's own responsibilities. Projects are, of course, driven by the corporate or programme management.

Projects	Program
Driven by deliverables	Driven by vision of 'end state'
Finite - defined start and finish	No pre-defined path
Bounded and scoped deliverables	Changes to business capabilities
Deliver product or service	Realizing objectives
Ends by handing over output	Must be closed formally
Benefits accrue outside the project	Benefits realized as part of the program and afterwards
Shorter timescale	Longer timescale

Table 1.1 Projects versus programmes (Source: Managing Successful Projects with PRINCE2, produced by OGC)

1.3 What is project management?

Project management is planning, delegating, monitoring and controlling all aspects of a project and motivating all parties involved to achieve the project's objectives within the agreed targets pertaining to time, costs, quality, scope, benefits and risks (see figure 1.1).

Figure 1.1 Project management (source: Managing Successful Projects with PRINCE2, produced by OGC)

The goal of project management is to control all specialist work in such a way that the desired output of the project is produced. This can only be done when it is a matter of collective effort. Consequently, project management is a duty borne by all those involved, from the different members of the Project Board and the Project Manager to the Team Manager(s).

1.4   What is the job of the Project Manager?

The Project Manager is responsible, within the limits set by the Project Board, for the day-to-day management of the project. The Project Manager is therefore responsible for planning, delegating, monitoring and controlling the work within the project. In addition to this, the work consists of:

- Getting the stakeholders involved for the provision of input and reviewing the results to be delivered and generating support in order to mitigate any resistance;
- Planning and reviewing the benefits that are to be achieved together with the ultimate results of the project;
- Motivating project team members and other people involved in the project.

1.5   What aspects are managed?

There are six control aspects that have to be managed by the Project Manager during every project, these being:

- **Time** – This encompasses the end-to-end lifecycle of a project, including the handing over of the end result.
- **Costs** – This pertains to the costs involved in creating the products, including the project management costs.
- **Quality** – Staying within budget and delivering on time is not enough. The end result also has to satisfy the set requirements and wishes and be suitable for the goal for which it is intended.
- **Scope** – What is the end result? What is it exactly that is going to be delivered and what will not be? What work has to be done and what does not? All too often the people involved make assumptions and form images that are simply not correct, with all the negative consequences these entail.
- **Risks** – Every project has a degree of uncertainty and therefore contains risks. In itself this is not a problem, as long as it is managed well. Managing the threats - as well as the opportunities that present themselves during the project - is thus an absolute must.
- **Benefits** – Perhaps the most important questions in projects are 'why are we doing this?', 'what are we trying to achieve by doing this?', 'what advantages can be gained from the end result?' and 'are the costs still in the right proportion to the anticipated benefits?'

1.6   What is a successful project?

In the last few years there have frequently been discussions about the results gleaned using projects. Not so long ago, enormous investments were made in IT projects that were promising the earth. Many of these projects were unable to live up to their promises and there were increasingly strident calls for a critical eye to be cast over the results actually achieved.

But this is also the case in other sectors. Research results are regularly published showing that many projects are being completed late and/or are too expensive. Projects are also being closed prematurely without producing any results, or the output of the project is not used in practice. How does this happen? So much experience has been gathered regarding implementing projects. Where do projects go wrong? And furthermore, what are the factors that ought to be taken into consideration to complete a project successfully?

First of all, it is important to have a common definition of what constitutes project success. Opinion is divided on this. In the Nederlandse Competence Baseline (NCB version 3), project success is defined as "achieving the project objectives within the agreed constraints". Teun van Aken[1] offers a definition of project success as being "when all stakeholders are satisfied with the results achieved".

> *A project is successful when all stakeholders are satisfied with the results achieved.*

Teun van Aken's definition clearly goes further than the definition from the NCB. If, for example, the users are dissatisfied with the output of the project, they will not be well-disposed towards getting the maximum return out of the product (or service) delivered and the result produced will be used less or not at all. You cannot refer to such cases as being successful projects. For that reason we adhere to Van Aken's definition of project success.

A large number of parties are stakeholders. However, the most important parties are:
- Executive;
- Users;
- Suppliers;
- Project team.

The Executive is the one wishing to achieve certain benefits with the results of the project and the one paying for the project. The users are the ones faced with the end result. This could be end users, but also people responsible for the management and maintenance of the final product and direct stakeholders. The suppliers are the ones responsible for achieving the end result. The project team are the ones that actually deliver the output of the project. Practical experience shows that the users are the most important factor in determining the extent to which a project is successful.

Thus several parties determine the success of a project. For this reason, it is important throughout the project to look at these stakeholders and the criteria for success they are using. This could be completely different for each of them and could be different for each project. The lack of factors that are deemed important by some stakeholders could be a reason for loss of motivation and even for calling off the project. Possible success factors for the various stakeholders are:

- Executive: The benefits of the project output exceed the cost of the project and are in line with expectations (fit for purpose);
- Users: The output meets the criteria set in advance and is fit for use;
- Supplier: A positive return on expenditure;
- Project staff: The work is challenging and enjoyable and is appreciated.

1.7   Why do projects fail?

Some of the reasons often given for the failure of projects are:
- Lack of a clear Business Case;
- Lack of ownership by Executive;
- Lack of support from the top of the organization;
- Result to be produced not defined sufficiently or unequivocally;
- Lack of acceptance criteria and quality criteria;
- Lack of clarity on roles, responsibilities and authority;
- Lack of structure and specific checkpoints;
- Changing specifications or lack of a working change control;
- Lack of commitment from the users from the start of the project.

A clear Business Case forms the basis of a project. The fact is, this will incorporate the reasons why the Executive wants to implement the project and what the added value of the project output is for the organization in proportion to the costs and effort needed to achieve the project output. If it is not clear what the project will be contributing to the corporate organization, then support from the Executive and the management of the corporate organization will dwindle during implementation of the project. Important decisions will be delayed or not taken at all. There will be problems financing the project. Other projects and initiatives will suddenly seem more important. Without a good Business Case and without management support, there will certainly be resistance from the users as soon as they become aware of exactly what it is the project is going to signify for them. And with the decline in commitment from the Executive and the management and the increase in resistance from the users, the project staff will get the feeling that their efforts are not important and not wanted. They will look for other things to do or, worse still, become demotivated. Thus it can involve a dramatic chain reaction.

An inadequately defined output constitutes another risk. How can something be produced to the satisfaction of another person if the desired end result is not clear? In this regard it is not only important that the quality criteria are made known but also that the acceptance criteria are specified. The clearer the description of these criteria, the better the work to be carried out can be evaluated, the easier it will be to direct things toward the output ultimately to be achieved and the better user expectations regarding the final output can be managed.

Not managing the scope and the changes well could also play a significant role in the failure of projects. Every change for the good of one person has consequences for another. Changes not controlled well could result in frustration for the other parties involved and often have significant unforeseen consequences for the project as well. Managing the scope and controlling the changes is therefore a must.

Finally, sometimes it seems like an attractive option not to involve the users in the project: no nagging, the ability to make good progress and quick decisions are attractive prospects. However, not involving users from the beginning of the project can lead to incomplete specifications, no interim monitoring on whether you are on the right track, no interim indication that the project output to be delivered has to be adjusted and significant resistance as soon as the users become aware of what the project is going to signify for them. This latter invokes the old adage 'if you want something done properly, do it yourself'. Results in which you are involved yourself are always better, even if the output may be 'objectively' less. This could lead to the end result not being accepted, or it being accepted but then not being used, or (in the worst case scenario) a premature halt being called to the project after a great deal of frustration and expense for all parties concerned and the 'culprits' being stigmatized.

It is therefore better to have prior insight into the Business Case, to define the output well, to manage the process, control the changes and get the users involved. Even if this results in it becoming clear in the meantime that the project is no longer viable, the project can then be adapted or halted prematurely and in a professional manner, without unnecessary loss of capital and unnecessary damage to those involved.

1.8   Why PRINCE2?

The causes of project failure discussed in section 1.7 led to the development of the project management method PRINCE2. The method focuses on managing projects in a changing environment with the Business Case as a guiding principle, addressing the commitment of all stakeholders and the control of the process. PRINCE2 places more emphasis on controlling the process than on sticking to the original principles.

In this regard, project organization and risk management are important areas for attention. Within the project organization, the connection and interaction between the project and its environment are established. The uncertainties in and around the project are controlled using risk management. For in the PRINCE2 method, risk management constitutes an integral part of all the processes to be implemented.

2   Introduction to PRINCE2

2.1   What is PRINCE2?

PRINCE2 is a structured project management method based on best practice. PRINCE2 is process-based. In other words, its method assumes that a project is not so much implemented in a linear fashion as in terms of process. The method focuses specifically on the management aspect of projects. In 1996, PRINCE2 was introduced by the then CCTA (Central Computer and Telecommunications Agency), after which the methodology was modified several times, most recently in June 2009.

PRINCE2 stands for 'Projects in Controlled Environments' and is the de facto project management standard in the British government. These days PRINCE2 is controlled by the OGC (Office of Government Commerce), which has registered it as a trademark in the United Kingdom and other countries.

Throughout the world PRINCE2 is being used increasingly as *the* method with which to manage projects. The OGC holds the copyright to the PRINCE2 brand and to the PRINCE2 methodology, but the method can be used freely.

The method is generic, resulting in it being independent of the type of project. It creates a clear distinction between the intrinsic aspects and the management aspects within projects. Consequently the method is straightforward to use and can easily be introduced as a standard within organizations.

2.2   The structure of PRINCE2

The PRINCE2 method approaches project management from four angles:

* **Principles** – The fundamental principles to which any given project must adhere if it is to be a PRINCE2 project.
* **Themes** – The minimum management aspects that must be managed by the Project Manager throughout the project. Each theme describes the specific application and its necessity.
* **Processes** – The processes describe the entire course of the project step-by-step from commencement to closure. Each process describes the requisite activities, management deliverables and related responsibilities.
* **Tailoring the method** – PRINCE2 cannot be successful until it is applied 'sensibly'. Adjusting the method to the type of project and the project environment is therefore crucial.

2.3   Relationship to other OGC guidelines

The PRINCE2 project management method forms part of a set of guidelines developed by the OGC. Using these guidelines, both organizations and individuals can get better results from their projects, programmes and services (see figure 2.1).

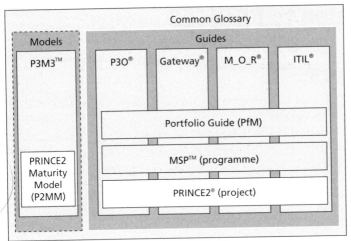

Figure 2.1 OGC best-practice guidance (Source: Managing Successful Projects with PRINCE2, produced by OGC)

P3M3 – Portfolio, Programme and Project Management Maturity Model. This is a set of best practice guidelines. This enables critical performance areas to be assessed and improved. P3M3 distinguishes five levels of maturity for organizations.

P2MM – PRINCE2 Maturity Model can be used as a tool to introduce PRINCE2 in organizations. It is a derivative of P3M3.

P3O – Portfolio, Programme and Project Offices provides practical tips on how to design, set up and use project offices.

Gateway – OGC Gateway Review Process is a a review process that examines programmes and projects at key decision points in their lifecycle, and looks ahead to provide assurance that they can progress successfully to the next stage. This process is mandatory for high-risk government projects in the United Kingdom.

M_o_R – Management_of_Risk expands on project risk management covered by PRINCE2 and provides guidance on how risk sits not just within the project environment but within the context of the entire organization.

ITIL – IT Infrastructure Library offers a comprehensive set of best practice guidelines for IT Service Management, and increasingly for service management in general.

PfM – Portfolio Management Guide explains the basic principles of portfolio management within organizations.

MSP – Management of Successful Programmes provides a structure for organizations that are running and managing programmes.

2.4 What is not in PRINCE2?

The PRINCE2 method does not describe every aspect in the field of project management. This does not mean that these aspects are unimportant. On the contrary, these aspects are indispensable to the projects, but have been omitted from the method deliberately. It is the strength of the PRINCE2 method, however, to indicate clearly what is and is not described. It does not involve the following three areas of interest:

- **Specialist work** – Thanks to the method's generic design, it is widely applicable. On the other hand, this means that specific intrinsic activities are not described for an industry or type of project. Obviously in this regard the method can easily be tailored accordingly.
- **Techniques** – Nowadays there are many kinds of planning techniques, planning software and other support technologies. Often these have already been described in detail by specialist companies. PRINCE2 does describe techniques that directly support the application of the method, such as the focus on products.
- **Leadership qualities** – No project can be completed without leadership, motivational and communication skills. However, this aspect has been described so well and so comprehensibly in other models and literature that reference is made to these as a supplement to the method. Even though PRINCE2 does not encompass any social skills, it does support the social conduct required to be able to manage projects effectively: a good structure supports the right conduct.

2.5 PRINCE2, benefits

PRINCE2 is a methodology that, thanks to its continuous application, has continued to develop to a mature level with many benefits. The most important of these are summarized below:

- **Best practice** – This means that the method has been created from practical experience of projects from many different backgrounds and industries, making it extremely recognizable and practicable. The recognizability is further reinforced by the uniform terminology and approach. Furthermore, no specific requirements are set for the type of project to which PRINCE2 can be applied. The method is generic.
- **Clearly defined organizational structure** – In PRINCE2 the tasks, responsibilities and authority are clearly described for all roles within a project. In addition to this, specific attention is paid to involving the stakeholders in the decision-making at the decision times during the project based on the principle of managing by exception.
- **Focus on rationale and products** – There is continuous focus on the project's viability. Is this project still worth the effort? Are the benefits still wanted and feasible? Are the costs and benefits still in equilibrium? As an extension to this, is continuous attention being paid to the project's deliverables?
- **Control** – The project is controlled throughout. The plans tie in with the needs of the different management levels within the project. The quality of both product and process are continually assessed and adjusted where necessary. Any changes, problems and also risks are assessed and followed up on.
- **Learning and developing** – Within projects it is important to keep learning and developing, thereby improving. There is something to be learnt from every experience in subsequent projects. PRINCE2 encourages the reuse of project products (e.g. documents), suggestions and lessons in order to be able to manage projects increasingly well.

2.6 Differences in PRINCE2 v2009 versus v2005

The fundamentals of the PRINCE2 method have not changed. The most important improvement is that the underlying principles of PRINCE2 are now explicit guiding principles for the content of the themes and processes as these are defined within the method (see figure 2.2). The principles are also emphatic guiding principles for tailoring the method to a specific project in a given context. It is explicitly stated that deviation from the use presented in the themes and processes is possible, but that if not all PRINCE2 principles are applied in a project, it can no longer be termed a PRINCE2 project.

The changes that have been implemented can be distinguished according to methodical changes, changes in the structure of the manual and smaller changes within a specific theme, product or process.

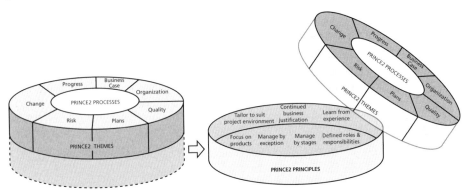

Figure 2.2 Differences in PRINCE2™ v2009 versus V2005 (Based on OGC PRINCE2 material)

Structural changes

The most important structural changes are:
- Firstly, of course, the new chapter that has been added in which the PRINCE2 principles are explicitly named and described.
- More attention has been paid to adapting the method to a specific project in a given context. This has now become a separate chapter called Tailoring PRINCE2.
- The method is less prescriptive. With regard to many subjects, it is stated that deviation from the approach described is possible. It is stated that it is better to work according to the spirit of the method than to adhere to the rules of the manual.
- The method is less bureaucratic. Sub-processes have been swapped for activities. Fewer management products have been defined.
- There is now greater emphasis on learning from experience. In the first PRINCE2 process, learning from experience gleaned from previous projects is expressly mentioned as an activity. Lessons now come up for discussion in all reporting and meetings. Conveying one's own experiences to the corporate or programme management is now included during stage boundaries too.
- There is a clearer link to other OGC methods, such as Management of Successful Programmes (MSP) and Management of Risk (M_o_R).
- Strategies have been introduced for risks, quality, configuration management and communication, all in line with MSP.
- There is more reference to techniques to be used. Reference is made to frequently-used techniques, not only in planning but also for risks and (for example) the Business Case.
- Delivery of the results in stages is pointedly assumed.

Changes to the manual
- First of all, the manual has been reduced from some 450 pages to around 330 pages, primarily by removing duplication of components and processes.
- The components have become themes and have been put before the processes. As themes they have also become what they are, namely areas for attention, without wishing to create an impression of being integral to a project - the term 'component' suggests.
- The eight components have been reduced to seven themes. Configuration management has now been integrated into the Change theme.
- Control aspects have now been renamed as the Progress theme.
- The Techniques section is now defunct. The techniques are now described in the relevant themes, alongside other important techniques.
- The number of processes has been reduced from eight to seven. The Planning process has now been included as a procedure within the Planning theme. This puts planning in line with other procedures, such as those of risk management and change control, which always used to be dealt with like procedures within the components/themes.
- There are more support and guidelines for the members of the Project Board and the senior management. To this end, the OGC has even published a separate manual with a separate exam associated with it.
- The appendix incorporating risk categories has become defunct.
- The health check has now been arranged according to the different steps in the project process.

Detailed changes
Themes
- **Business Case** – The Post-Project Review Plan is now called Benefits Review Plan. This plan is now created during initiation of the project and assessed by the Project Board during project authorization. For each stage, the Benefits Review Plan is brought up to date. Justification of the project is now based on whether the project is wanted, viable and achievable. The lifecycle of the Business Case is now subdivided into developing, verifying and confirming. The Business Case now also contains an Executive summary, dis-benefits and benefit tolerances. In the case of delivery in stages, benefits reviews can be held during the project.
- **Organization** – The four levels of management are now called corporate or programme management, directing, managing and delivering. The Change Authority has now been included in the organization chart. The configuration librarian is now part of the Project Support. In line with MSP, the Senior User is now responsible for identifying and defining the benefits and the operational or programme management holds this role responsible for demonstrating that the benefits forecasted are being achieved. The agreements on communication are now detailed in a Communication Management Strategy.
- **Quality** – There is now greater emphasis on the quality of the products. The quality path has been replaced by a quality audit path with overlapping paths for quality planning and quality management and quality control. The 'project product' has been introduced, which refers to the project's final product to be delivered. The Project Product Description contains the customer quality expectations, the acceptance criteria and the quality tolerances at project level. The Project Quality Plan has been replaced by the Quality Management Strategy. The Stage Quality Plan is no longer distinguished separately in the Stage Plan.

- **Plans** – The method now states that a Product Description is required for all products identified. In contrast to this, the technique focus on products, which is now explained within the Planning theme, is less prescriptive. Thus for external products they only 'advise' choosing an anomalous colour or shape, for example.
- **Risks** – This chapter has been completely revised and therefore ties in heavily with the Management of Risks (M_o_R) method from the OGC. The agreements on approach to risk are now set down in a Risk Management Strategy. The risk process has been modified. Risks are now distinguished according to opportunities and threats. The responsibilities of the risk-owner have been extended and the role of a risk-actionee is now recognized. The Risk Log has now become a formal Risk Register, which is created during the initiation of a project.
- **Change** – The Daily Log is now also used to record issues and risks that can be managed informally. The change procedure has been modified. Formal issues are now recorded in an Issue Register. The configuration management has been fully integrated into the Change theme. The approach to change control and configuration management is now recorded in the Configuration Management Strategy.
- **Progress** – The Progress theme replaces the Control component. This theme now concentrates entirely on the implementation of the project. The control aspects in the processes Starting up and Initiating a Project and Closing a Project are now no longer dealt with within this theme.

Processes
- **Starting up a Project (SU)** – Now also specifies the review of previous lessons. The project organization, the project approach and the Project Product Description have now been incorporated into the Project Brief. The Daily Log and Lessons Log are arranged in this process.
- **Directing a Project (DP)** – This process now begins at the end of the SU process in response to the request to commence initiation of the project. Apart from this, the DP process in itself has largely stayed the same. However, whereas in the past the Project Board requested initiation of the process Managing a Stage Boundary and premature closure of a project, this action is now the responsibility of the Project Board itself.
- **Initiating a Project (IP)** – The first activities of this process are now developing the different strategies for risk management, quality control, configuration management and communication management. The Risk Register is now arranged in this process too. The 'PID' is now defined as the Project Initiation Documentation. It now has to be explicitly recorded in the PID how the PRINCE2 method has been tailored to a project in this context.
- **Controlling a Stage (CS)** – This process has largely stayed the same. Only the sub-processes 'capture' and 'examine issues' have now been merged and extended into one activity: capturing and examining issues and risks.
- **Managing Product Delivery (MP)** – This process has largely stayed the same. Only the responsibility for recording the risks and the results of the quality reviews has now been returned to the Project Manager or (as the case may be) Project Support.
- **Managing a Stage Boundary (SB)** – The name of this process is now in the singular. The action 'update the Risk Register' is now part of the 'update Business Case' activity. The PID and the Benefits Review Plan are now being updated. The products completed in the project up until that point can already be delivered in stages and transferred to the customer. The formulation of a Lessons Report and recommendations for follow-on actions can now be part of this process.

- **Closing a Project (CP)** – New here are the activities prepare planned closure and prepare premature closure. Separate activities for handing over projects and recommending project closure have now also been defined. In principle, the Lessons Report and the recommendations for follow-on actions are now part of the End Project Report.

Tailoring PRINCE2

This is a new chapter. Whereas previously this aspect was addressed separately in the various processes, it has now been merged into one chapter. This subject has also been expanded considerably with regard to what had been set down in the 2005 version of the PRINCE2 manual. A distinction is made between implementing the method in an organization and tailoring the method to a specific project in a given context. The various aspects of the project and the environment that merit adaptation of the method to the project are examined. In addition to this, the differences between project and programme management are explained and the possible connections between the project and programme organization are examined. Finally it is explained how the method can be tailored to projects of different size and complexity.

Appendices

- **A. Arrangement of management products** – The number of products has been reduced from 36 to 26. Further explanation is now given for each product. How the different management products can best be presented has been added.
- **Governance** – This is an entirely new appendix in which it is shown how and to what extent the PRINCE2 method covers governance of the principles of project management as published by the British Association for Project Management (not included in this book).
- **B. Roles and responsibilities** – The role Change Authority has been added. The role project office has become defunct. The requisite competencies for the various roles have been added.
- **C. Example of product-based planning** – This example has moved from the previous technique focus on products to the appendix. A Project Product Description and an example of a product breakdown structure in the form of a mind map have been added.
- **E. List of terminology** – This has been expanded in relation to the previous version.
- **F. Other information** – This contains a brief explanation of the various methodologies supported by the OGC.

2.7   Spelling of PRINCE2 words

PRINCE2 recognizes specific management products and roles. These are the products and roles described in Appendix A and B. For the purposes of identification, these words are always written with a capital letter. All other management products and roles are not recognized as specific PRINCE2 words and are not written using capitals:

- With capital letter: Executive and Business Case (for example).
- Without capital letter: product breakdown structure (for example).

The verbs and nouns pertaining to the PRINCE2 processes are also written with a capital letter. Activities within a process, however, are not characterized by capitals:

- Process: Starting up a Project.
- Activity: plan the initiation stage.

2.8   About this book

This book has been based on the manual 'Managing Successful Projects with PRINCE2®' from the OGC, which was fully revised in 2009. It is by no means the intention to 'translate' the manual, but rather to make the methodology more accessible to the reader and to 'enrich' it with additions, practical tips and examples. It provides insight into how PRINCE2 can be used to manage projects and thus serves as a practical reference work for the experienced Project Manager. Thanks to its accessibility, the book is also extremely well suited to being used by anyone wishing to acquaint himself/herself with the method or working on a team engaged in projects (PRINCE2 or otherwise).

- **Chapter 1 Introduction to Project Management** – This chapter provides the reader with insight into what a project is or is not, why projects are 'different' and what managing projects entails.
- **Chapter 2 Introduction to PRINCE2** – This chapter specifically examines what the PRINCE2 method encompasses, the structure of the method, its relationship to other OGC guidelines, what is not included in the method's scope, the benefits of the method and the differences between the 2005 version and the 2009 version.
- **Chapter 3 Principles** – This chapter examines the fundamental principles to which any given project must adhere if it is to be a PRINCE2 project.
- **Section I Themes** – In separate chapters, this section examines the management aspects that must be applied as a minimum throughout the lifecycle of every project. For each theme the goal, the terms, the approach and the responsibilities of the relevant management aspect are described.
- **Section II Processes** – In separate chapters, this section examines the various processes that can be identified in a project lifecycle. For each process the underlying activities, the accompanying responsibilities and the management products that are required and that are to be delivered are described.
- **Section III** – This section describes the context within which projects are carried out and how the PRINCE2 methodology can be tailored to the specific characteristics and the given context of a project. This section also looks at the connection between project, programme, portfolio and multi-project management, the characteristics and setting up of programmes and change management.
- **Appendices** – These contain a description of the various management products and the responsibilities and required competencies for the different roles recognized within the PRINCE2 method. An example is also given of the technique focus on products, and a project health check, a list of terminology and a translation list have been included.

2.9   Preparation for exams

In the PRINCE2 method, a PRINCE2 Foundation and PRINCE2 Practitioner exam can be taken based on Managing Successful Projects with PRINCE2™.

The PRINCE2 Foundation exam is aiming to measure whether a candidate could be act as an informed member of a project management team on a project using the PRINCE2 method. The PRINCE2 Practitioner exam is aiming to measure whether a candidate could apply PRINCE2 to the running and managing of a non-complex project within an environment supporting PRINCE2.

This book 'Project Management Based on PRINCE2' provides a good basis for both exams..

3   PRINCE2, principles

PRINCE2 offers a project management method independent from the specific characteristics and the context of a project. This is possible due to the fact that PRINCE2 is based on a number of principles that a project must satisfy and not on a prescribed set of specific rules and precepts.

These principles have been shown to be effective over the years, and they are universal and can be used in any project. These principles also serve to motivate the users of the method, because it offers these users the opportunity of organizing and moulding the project, tailored to the project's specific characteristics and context. For a PRINCE2 project, however, application of these principles is not optional. If you do not think and act from the perspective of these principles, you cannot call it a PRINCE2 project!

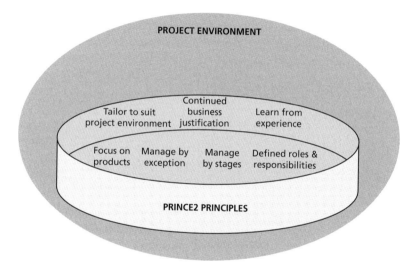

Figure 3.1 The seven principles of PRINCE2 V2009 (Based on OGC PRINCE2 material)

The seven principles are (see figure 3.1):
1. Continued business justification.
2. Learn from experience.
3. Defined roles and responsibilities.
4. Manage by stages.
5. Manage by exception.
6. Focus on products.
7. Tailor to suit the project environment.

Principle 1

Business justification is continually tested during a PRINCE2 project.

For every PRINCE2 project there must be a business reason to commence it. This reason is the project's business justification and is indispensable as a foundation for making decisions with regard to the project. Although the business justification can change during the course of the project, it will still have to remain valid and thus be tested continually. This justification is set down in the Business Case, formally approved and then subjected to formal change control. Even the so-called 'mandatory' projects require justification in order to make the reason why they have been selected transparent, for there are always several options to choose from in order to satisfy the same requirement. If, for whatever, reason the justification ceases to be valid, then calling a halt to the project is the only correct option in order to avoid wasting resources (human and otherwise).

Principle 2

PRINCE2 project team members learn from experience. Lessons are not only sought but also recorded and applied during projects.

Project management is a profession. It is a trade that must primarily be learned by applying it. Every project is unique and for that reason there will always be new and unexpected challenges, risks, mishaps and strokes of luck. It is therefore important to discover and apply lessons as early as possible. During the preparation stage of a project you can learn from previous experience in similar past projects. If no experience of similar projects has been acquired internally, then external experience can be called upon. During the implementation of a project you can learn from experience being acquired. The challenge is to apply these lessons as quickly as possible so that the benefit of these lessons can be enjoyed whilst the project is still being implemented.

In this regard, learning is more than just the individual learning of the project staff; rather, it is a matter of team learning. Team learning is the process by which a team as a whole develops competencies necessary to perform certain tasks. Without these shared competencies teams can be highly incompetent in their way of working, in spite of the fact that individual members of the team may well be competent in their own right. Team learning starts with dialogue, by means of which the members of a team learn to think together rather than to proceed from their own bias.

Principle 3

A PRINCE2 project has clearly defined roles and responsibilities organized in such a way that the interests of the business, user and supplier are represented.

There is a famous saying: 'A ship is only as strong as its crew.' This particularly applies to projects. The characteristics of a project demand the 'right' crew and not just those people that happen to be 'available'. A project can be compared with an organization within an organization. A temporary organization is required for the purposes of delivering the result, including the accompanying tasks, responsibilities and authority. These can sometimes be profoundly different to the normal agreements and cultures in this regard.

PRINCE2 distinguishes three stakeholders in the project organization. First of all the business interest must be represented, with focus on 'am I getting value for money?' In addition to this, the interests of the user(s) and supplier(s) are crucial in order to indicate what the result must satisfy and how and with whom this will subsequently have to be achieved. This project management team has to be put together evenly, so that a common goal can be pursued with clarity on what the team members expect from each other.

Principle 4

A PRINCE2 project is divided into stages. As a result of this, the project can be planned, monitored and managed for each stage.

Thanks to the use of stages, a project stays manageable. It provides the opportunity for directing the project step-by-step or stage-by-stage. Each stage boundary provides a formal checkpoint allowing approval of the (interim) products already assessed (and possibly already deliverable) as well as detailed planning of the next stage on the basis of this. Working in stages also provides an opportunity for checking progress in a planned fashion and deciding to continue according to planning, perhaps adjusting course or even ceasing the project prematurely. PRINCE2 uses a Project Plan to oversee the entire project and various Stage Plans to be able to monitor the operational implementation of the work. In every project there is at least one initiation stage and one implementation stage.

Principle 5

PRINCE2 operates on the principle of management by exception.

This allows PRINCE2 to offer higher management the option of retaining control over the project without continually having to devote significant amounts of time to it. It is an efficient way of controlling things, because decision-making is done at the right level and thus the progress of the project is rendered certain. Within the project, PRINCE2 uses three management levels for directing a project, managing a stage and delivering the products respectively.

For each level, specific agreements are made on freedom of action (tolerances) with regard to the different control aspects. These are the aspects of time, cost, quality, scope, benefits and risks. The principle assumes you have your own responsibilities within the tolerances agreed in advance. If it is anticipated that tolerances will be exceeded, escalation to the next higher management level is required. Thus reporting is only done where this is necessary or desirable. Meanwhile management will be informed using Highligh Reports and at stage boundaries. However, this does not mean that (regular planned) consultation cannot take place.

Principle 6

> A PRINCE2 project is geared toward delivering products, including satisfying the agreed quality criteria.

According to PRINCE2, results-oriented working is an essential and fundamental principle for projects. Each activity has to deliver 'something'. This philosophy ensures that it is clear to each stakeholder what the project will deliver and whether this meets expectations. The combination of products also provides insight into the scope of the project: what is and is not being achieved?

An important tool in this regard is the technique of product-based planning and the use of Product Descriptions. With the aid of these things it is made transparent what the project will deliver and what the aim, composition and sources of the individual products will be. What is also crucial in this regard is that the quality criteria are recorded as well as how and by whom the quality of the individual products will be tested.

The focus on the delivery of products supports many aspects of the methodology, such as planning, organization, progress, quality and risks.

Principle 7

> PRINCE2 is tailored to each project.

What is special about PRINCE2 is that the method can be used irrespective of the nature of the project and irrespective of the context within which the project is being implemented. A direct consequence of this is that the method does have to be used 'sensibly', i.e. not slavishly sticking to prescribed activities and products, but also not ignoring every suggestion or recommendation in the method. The aim is to tailor the method in such a way that it 'suits' the specific project in its environment. This requires an active attitude on the part of both the Project Board and the Project Manager. For this reason, the fundamental attitude in tailoring the method has to be:
• It is necessary to receive information, not necessarily documents;
• It is necessary to make decisions, not necessarily to have meetings.

The way in which the method is tailored to the specific circumstances must be described explicitly in the Project Initiation Documentation, so that everyone is aware of how the basic processes and procedures have been adapted for this project.

Section I   Themes

I Introduction to PRINCE2 themes

The PRINCE2 themes describe those aspects of project management that have to be continuously and integrally addressed throughout the course of every project (see figure ʜ1).

Business Case	➤ Why?
Organization	➤ Who?
Quality	➤ What?
Plans	➤ How, how much, when?
Risks	➤ What if?
Change	➤ What's the impact?
Progress	➤ Where are we now?
	➤ Where are we going?

Figure I.1 PRINCE2 Themes (Based on OGC PRINCE2 material)

Business Case – This theme describes mechanisms to assess whether there is and continues to be a business justification to implement and continue with a project. This theme describes how the justification for the project is recorded in the Business Case and how this is developed further, updated, assessed and corroborated throughout a project's lifecycle. This theme also describes the development, updating and application of the Benefits Review Plan and the respective responsibilities for the different roles therein.

Organization – A project is an aggregate of activities in a temporary organization. This theme describes the roles and responsibilities necessary to direct and manage the project and to deliver the results, and how the project organization is related to the existing organizations of the customer and the suppliers. This theme also describes how stakeholders must be involved in the project and how communication from and to stakeholders must be organized.

Quality – The Quality theme is geared toward defining and implementing the resources with which the project will be able to complete and assess the products that are fit for purpose. This theme also describes how management can ensure compliance in this regard.

Planning – PRINCE2 projects are performed on the basis of a series of approved plans. This theme describes the procedure necessary to develop and update the plans and the product-based planning technique that can be used in this regard. This theme also describes the different plans and how these tie in with what the different management levels require in this regard.

Risks – Generally speaking projects entail more risks than normal corporate activities. This theme describes how risks in projects are managed and how these are integrated into the management of the overall project.

Change – This theme describes identification, assessment and control of each possible and approved change with regard to the approved objectives. Included here are specification changes, off-specifications, and general problems and concerns requiring attention from management. Configuration management in projects is also described in this theme.

Progress – Progress describes the continuing viability of the approved plans. This theme describes the process of approving plans, monitoring progress, drawing up the forecast for the work yet to be done, corrective action to be taken and escalating concerns on progress if the agreed tolerances are at risk of being exceeded.

Other themes such as health and safety and environment, together with new areas for attention like doing business in a socially responsible manner, are not addressed explicitly but can be included within the themes described above.

4   Business Case

The purpose of the Business Case theme is to establish mechanisms to judge whether the project is or remains desirable, viable and achievable to start or continue with the project.

4.1   Introduction

The Business Case provides the business justification for a project. It is essential to know how the project's costs relate to the returns, what the Executive is aiming to achieve with the project outputs and benefits and how great the risks are in this regard. If the costs and risks do not weigh up against the expected benefits, then there is no valid Business Case and there is no reason to start or continue the project.

If it emerges during implementation of the project that there is no longer a valid Business Case, then the project should be stopped for the time being. In such cases, the project may be continued in an alternative form, assuming there is a positive Business Case for this.

The Business Case must be formulated at the start of the project and must regularly be updated over the course of the project, at least at the end of each management stage. It is expected of all a project's stakeholders that they supply information that may be important for the Business Case or for achieving the Business Case objectives.

By unequivocally developing, maintaining, assessing and verifying the Business Case throughout the project's lifespan, the Business Case will contribute directly to the principle of continued business justification and will support the principle of managing by exception.

4.2   Conceptual framework

What is a Business Case?

The Business Case provides the information required to be able to establish whether a project is and continues to be advisable, viable and achievable, thereby showing whether it is and continues to be a project which meets corporate or programme objectives and which the organization should invest in. It is a basis for the initial financing of the project, but throughout the project it must be continually updated with current costs, scheduling, risks and estimates regarding the benefits to be achieved.

The Business Case clarifies which corporate objectives are being supported with the products to be developed and what added value is expected for the company. In this regard, it is important that this is done in an unequivocal manner so that the Business Cases of the various projects can be compared with one another and so that, at the level of corporate or programme management, an assessment can be formed as to which projects will and will not continue.

Output, outcome and benefits

Within this framework it is also important to use an unambiguous conceptual framework. In this regard, PRINCE2 employs the following definitions:

- **Output** – Every specialist product or specialist service of the project being delivered.
- **Outcome** – Effect of a change stemming from the use of the project's output.
- **Benefit** – A quantifiable change as a result of the outcome which is deemed positive by one or more stakeholders.
- **Dis-benefit** – A quantifiable change as a result of the outcome which is deemed negative by one or more stakeholders.

The output of projects enables the organization to implement changes that will yield a desirable result, that will produce benefits and with which the organization will be able to achieve its strategic goals. However, the implementation of change and the end result desired can in themselves entail side effects too, which in turn could produce benefits, but also dis-benefits (see figure 4.1).

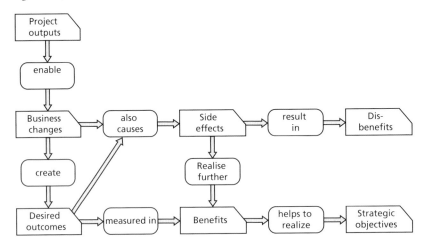

Figure 4.1 Realization of benefits and the implementation of changes (Based on OGC PRINCE2 material)

4.3 Business Case, types

To a large extent, the type of project determines the way in which it will have to be assessed whether it is advisable to invest in a project, as in:

- Compulsory projects;
- Not-for-profit projects;
- Evolving projects;
- Multi-organization projects.

Are we faced with compulsory projects, involving us having to implement statutory orders? Are we dealing with a not-for-profit project, in which predominantly non-financial benefits are playing a role? Is it a question of an investment project, where we have to look primarily at the 'return on investment'? Is it a case of a project being implemented by several organizations pooling the risk? In all cases it will have to be considered whether it will be prudent to invest the money in this project or to opt for another project or another approach. Even in the case of compulsory projects it will have to be decided whether you want to go for gold or if silver or bronze will suffice. Will that golden solution produce so much more added value that it really is the best option? In other words, irrespective of the type of project a cost-benefit analysis will have to be produced for each project, even if it will not always be possible to quantify the benefits in hard currency.

4.4 Business Case, PRINCE2 approach

The Business Case has to be developed prior to and/or at the outset of the project and has to be maintained during the project's lifecycle. The Project Board will have to assess the Business Case during the go/no go decision points, such as at the end of a stage. Finally, the benefits to be achieved in the Business Case will have to be tested and confirmed during the benefits reviews (see figure 4.2).

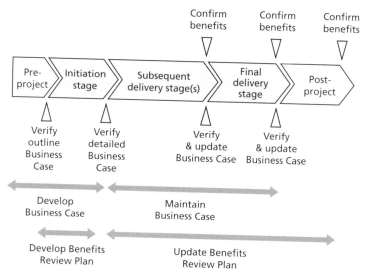

Figure 4.2 The development path of the Business Case (based on OCG PRINCE2 material)

Alongside the development and maintenance of the Business Case, a Benefits Review Plan will also have to be developed, maintained and assessed. The Benefits Review Plan forms a basis for assessing the Business Case and measuring the benefits forecast.

In a project lifecycle it is possible for some project outputs to be delivered during the project i.e. at the end of a stage and not just at the end of the project. In these cases the benefits from the early project deliverables can be assessed, perhaps even as early as during the next stage. This is also the reason why the Benefits Review Plan has to be developed as early as the initiation stage of the project and has to be maintained during the project.

Note: the benefits reviews can even be part of the project. However, achieving these benefits falls outside the scope of the project.

Developing the Business Case

The Executive owns the Business Case on behalf of the customer. However, the Executive can delegate development of the Business Case to a corporate analyst or to the Project Manager. In this regard it is also the responsibility of the Executive to assure the other stakeholders that the project remains advisable. Furthermore, the Executive should consider the use of a Project Assurance role to assist the Project Manager in the development of a viable Business Case (see also section 5.4).

The first Business Case is often developed in an early stage of the product's lifecycle, usually within the framework of a feasibility study. Such studies involve various alternatives being produced and compared to one another. In principle these are different outline Business Cases. The results of such feasibility studies are presented to the corporate or programme management. On the basis of this, the project mandate is finally issued and the Starting up a Project process is set in motion.

During this process, the outline Business Case is brought up to date or (if that point has not yet been reached) produced and included in the Project Brief, which is submitted to the Project Board for approval. During the Initiation Stage the Business Case is expanded in sufficient detail to allow the Project Board to make an informed decision on whether or not to go ahead with the project.

If an external supplier is involved in a project, then there are two different Business Cases: one for the customer and one for the supplier. The Business Case in the project is that of the Executive.

Maintaining the Business Case

Within the project, the Project Manager is responsible for maintaining the Business Case, even if they do not have to carry out the work personally. Project Assurance should ensure, on behalf of the Executive, that this is done and take care that the impact of the various issues and risks is included in the Business Case.

During every impact analysis the Project Manager must check what will be the impact on the Business Case. Furthermore, the Project Manager should update the Business Case at the end of each management stage and the Business Case should be reviewed/updated when creating/updating any plans..

Assessing the Business Case

Within the project, the Business Case is assessed by the Project Board, however it is ultimately the Executive who will need to confirm that a valid Business Case exists. The Business Case is assessed by the Project Board for the first time at the start of the project to authorize the project intiation. At the end of the initiation stage, the Project Board assesses the Business Case to authorize the start of the delivery of the project. Subsequently the Project Board must reassess the Business Case with each go/no go decision in order to check whether the project is still viable and whether continuing with the project is still justified.

> The management of the department was enthusiastic about the new telephone switchboard. The new switchboard is going to cost € 50,000, but the Project Manager had calculated that each member of staff would save at least five minutes a day with the new switchboard, and this is equal to two man-years for the whole organization. However, it was not the intention that two persons should be released and do other work; the profit was purely theoretical. Therefore, apart from the fact that working with a new switchboard is convenient, there was no business justification for this investment.

A similar decision has to be made at the end of each management stage, in order to authorize the Stage Plan for the next stage. Similarly, a decision must also be made following escalation of an exception, to authorize the Exception Plan after the Project Board has asked the Project Manager to produce such an Exception Plan.

The Executive should assess the Business Case at the end of the project, in order to establish whether the Business Case is a sufficient and fair basis on which to review the forecast benefits after finishing the project. Finally, on completion of the project the corporate or programme management will have to assess the project's success as part of the benefits reviews to be held.

Confirming added value

In order to be able to review benefits, it is necessary for:
- Benefits to be identified and quantified;
- Objective measurements to be selected which are genuinely able to demonstrate that the benefits have been achieved;
- A baseline measurement to be carried out. This should be done at the start of the project, before the project is authorized, but must be repeated prior to the go/no go points during the project and at the end of the project in order to re-establish the forecast values;
- A decision to be made on how the benefits will be measured, when and by whom.

The extent of the long-term benefits is recorded in the Business Case. How and when the expected benefits can be assessed is recorded in the Benefits Review Plan.

The Executive is usually responsible for holding the benefits reviews. This responsibility can also be placed upon the corporate or programme management. The Senior User is usually the one that has to show that the forecast benefits are being achieved.

Developing and maintaining the Benefits Review Plan

The Benefits Review Plan describes:
- The scope - what benefits have to be measured;
- Who is responsible for measuring the expected benefits;
- How and when the expected benefits can be measured;
- The baseline measurement, on the basis of which the improvements are to be measured;
- How performance of the project product itself will be assessed.

The Benefits Review Plan is produced by the Project Manager in the Initiation Stage and assessed and approved by the Executive at the point of the project being authorized. The Benefits Review Plan should be brought up to date at the time of each go/no go decision during the project *and* at the end of the project. The benefits achieved during the project must be reported to the Executive by the Project Manager in the End Stage Report. The Senior User may be made accountable for measuring and realizing those benefits that must be achieved post project. The Executive should have their approval of the Benefits Review Plan confirmed by the corporate and programme management.

4.5   Business Case, content

The Business Case typically contains:

- **Executive summary** – Usually limited to a few pages.
- **Reasons** – Why the project is necessary and how the project will contribute to the corporate or programme strategies and objectives.
- **Business options** – Options in terms of 'what are we going to deliver?' and not in terms of 'which approach or supplier shall we choose?'. At the very least, business options must contain the zero option (doing nothing) and a minimum and maximum variable. Many use the gold-silver-bronze metaphor. All business options should be compared with the zero option.
- **Expected benefits** – Both financial and non-financial. An attempt should be made to quantify all non-financial benefits financially. At the very least, all benefits must be quantified, be linked to the strategic objectives that have to be fulfilled and be linked to the project results that have to be delivered. It should also be stated for each benefit who is responsible for achieving the benefit in question (benefit owner).
- **Expected dis-benefits** – Along with the benefits, the dis-benefits also have to be specified. In this regard, owners must also be appointed that will endeavour to minimise these dis-benefits.
- **Timescale** – Here both the time over which the investments will be made and the time over which the benefits will be achieved must be indicated.
- **Costs** – The costs of producing the deliverables and the assumptions on which these have been based, as inferred from the Project Plan, the costs of management and maintenance of the deliverables and the financing agreements.
- **Investment appraisal** – Assessment of the development costs versus maintenance and usage costs during the forecast economic lifespan.
- **Major risks** – Indicate here both what the most important business risks are and what the overall aggregate risk profile of the project is.
- **Advice** – Conclusions and recommendations to the Executive or (as the case may be) corporate or programme management as to whether the project should be implemented, halted or adapted.

An investment appraisal can be performed on the basis of different techniques:

$$\text{Return on investment (ROI)} = \frac{\text{Total net return}}{\text{Total investment}} \text{ x } 100\%$$

Payback period = The number of years or months after delivery over which the investment costs are recovered.

Net present value = The total of the net income minus the investments at present value. Money now has a value, known as present value. However this has to be offset against benefits which will be received in the future. The idea of net present value is to use a 'discount rate/percentage' to represent the devaluation of the 'present value' of money in the future and hence give a more accurate assessment of the value of benefits in the future. For example, if the company's profit margin is at 12%, the present value of money is twice as much as in year 6. So, if a project is forecasting a €300,000 benefit to accrue in year 6, then it is in fact only worth €150,000 in today's money.

Break-even point = The point at which the cost spent is equalled by the value of benefits received.

The most common techniques are calculation of the net present value in combination with the internal rate of return. On the basis of the latter value, investments can be compared with one another in a straightforward manner based on profitability.

4.6 Business Case, roles&responsibilities
See table 4.1 for a description of the roles and responsibilities for the Business Case theme.

Corporate / programme management • Provide mandate and define any standards for development of the Business Case (BC) • Hold Senior User to account for realizing the benefits • Accountable for Benefits Review Plan (post-project)	**Project Manager (PM)** • Prepare the BC on behalf of the Executive • Conduct impact analyses on issues and risks that may affect project's viability • Assess and update the BC at the end of each management stage • Assess and report on project performance at project closure
Executive • Own Business Case for duration of project • Approve Benefits Review Plan • Ensure alignment of project with business strategies • Secure funding	**Project Assurance** • Assist in development of the BC • Ensure viability of the BC is constantly reassessed • Monitor changes to the Project Plan to identify any impact on the BC • Verify and monitor BC against issues and progress • Review impact assessments on Project Plan and BC • Monitor project finance on behalf of the customer • Ensure project stays aligned with corporate or programme strategy • Verify and monitor Benefits Review Plan for alignment to corporate or programme management
Senior User • Specify the benefits upon which the BC is approved • Ensure the desired project outcome is specified • Ensure that project produces products which deliver the desired outcomes • Ensure the expected benefits are realised • Provide actual versus forecast benefits statement at benefits reviews	
Senior Supplier • Approve supplier's Business Case (if any) • Confirm that the products required can be delivered within expected costs and time	**Project Support** • Keep the Business Case under configuration • Advise PM about changes that may affect the Business Case

Table 4.1 Roles and responsibilities of the Business Casetheme

5 Organization

The aim of the Organization theme is to define and establish roles and responsibilities.

5.1 Introduction

PRINCE2 assumes a customer-supplier relationship. The customer is a person or group that commissions the assignment to implement the project and that benefits from the end result. The supplier produces the actual results of the project and makes people and resources available for this purpose. The customer and supplier may be part of the same organization or from different organizations

PRINCE2 distinguishes between the management of the project and those people producing the actual specialist products. PRINCE2 is a project management methods and, as such, focuses on the management of the project. PRINCE2 further presupposes that the Project Manager is part of the customer organization. Incidentally, this is not always the case. A similar division of roles is also possible if the Project Manager is part of the supplier's organization. In the latter case, though, the customer will less frequently assign responsibility for putting together the customer's Business Case to the Project Manager. If that is the case, however, the Project Manager will also continue to be responsible for monitoring the Business Case during the project on behalf of the Executive.

What is typical of a project is that it comprises a temporary management environment. Several disciplines from different functional units are often involved in the implementation of the project. Often several people and parties in the customer organization or the environment have a stake in the output of the project. To be able to make a project succeed, it will come as no surprise that what is needed is a broad-based understanding and experience of the line organizations involved, a clear and effective structure of roles and responsibilities and good communication between the project organization and the stakeholders. Moreover, it is important to assess the roles in the project on a regular basis so as to ensure that they are still being filled effectively.

5.2 Conceptual framework

A project is a temporary organization whose aim is to produce pre-defined products or services. For that reason, a project organization cannot be linked to permanent positions in a company; rather, in a project organization it is always a matter of roles that can be filled by different people in different projects. Sometimes it is also possible that several people fill a specific project role jointly. Sometimes one person can combine several project roles, even if this is not possible for every role.

Three project parties can always be discerned within a project (see figure 5.1). All three parties must be involved in directing the project in order to ensure that the project succeeds.

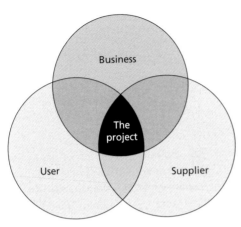

Figure 5.1 The three project parties (Source: Managing Successful Projects with PRINCE2, produced by OGC)

- **Business** – For the corporate or programme management, the added value that can be achieved with the products being delivered justifies starting up the project and investing in it. The interests of these parties must be represented in the project. The project's Executive represents the interests of the corporate and programme management in the project.
- **Users** – Those who will benefit by using the project outputs or be impacted by the outputs. This may, where appropriate, include those who will need to maintain the product outputs once they are in operational use.
- **Suppliers** – Everyone having (joint) responsibility for producing the deliverables. These are the people and parties responsible for designing, developing, facilitating, producing and implementing the output of the project. Suppliers can be internal departments and/or external parties.

The users

A new printer is being installed in the Sales department at Xanta. The printer will be placed in the corridor next to *Rita's room*. She has asthma. The printer is to be used by the *departmental secretaries*. The *account managers* in the department needed this new printer so as to be able to present their proposals more professionally. *Xanta's customers* had indicated that they did not like using the documentation they were receiving from Xanta. The ink ran and made your hands dirty, even after a long time. The new printer will be maintained by the company's own *general and technical services department*. All these parties should be seen as users. The representative of the users who was involved in the purchase and installation of the new printer had to take all the interests of these users into account. Due to his active participation, the installation was ultimately completed to the satisfaction of all parties.

5.3   Project management structure

The four levels of management within the project management structure comprise the corporate or programme management, the Project Board, the Project Manager and the Team Managers (see figure 5.2).

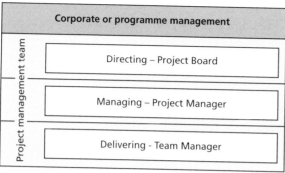

Figure 5.2 The four levels of management within the project management structure (Source: Managing Successful Projects with PRINCE2, produced by OGC)

The corporate or corporate management is responsible for establishing the corporate strategies, the project mandate, ensuring that the different projects are attuned to one another and fulfilling the benefits and the ultimate corporate objectives. The corporate or programme management appoints the Executive and also has to ratify the appointment of the Project Manager and the other members of the project management team.

The Project Board is responsible for directing the project. The Project Board is responsible to the corporate or programme management for the success of the project and is accountable for the project within the mandate set out by corporate or programme management. The Project Manager is responsible for day-to-day management of the project within the framework provided by the Project Board. The Team Manager is responsible for supervising the specialists and producing the specialist products.

5.4 Project Management Team (PMT)

The project's Project Management Team comprises the Project Board, the Project Manager and the Team Managers. The project organization comprises the Project Management Team plus the team members.

It is important that the roles in an organizational structure are described clearly and unequivocally and that they do not overlap. Each role in a project entails its own duties, authority and responsibilities and interfaces with the other roles (though it should be noted that some roles can be shared). Overlap of roles means lack of clarity and inefficiency. An unclear structure can cause a lot of confusion and loss of time, particularly in a project. The project management team structure is shown in figure 5.3.

The Project Board – Comprises the roles Executive, Senior User and Senior Supplier and is the project's decision-making body. The seniority of the members of the Project Board is highly dependent on the size and type of the project. However, it is important that each of the members truly does have the authority to decide for the group they are representing. It should not be the case that the Project Board makes decisions that then have to be confirmed repeatedly by a higher management level. The Project Board must be given sufficient authority to be able to make decisions and implement them of its own accord.

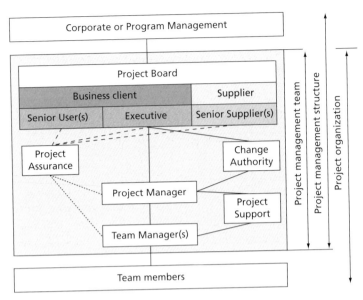

Figure 5.3 Project management team structure (based on OGC PRINCE2 material)

The members of the Project Board are appointed by the corporate or programme management. The Project Board is judged by the success of the project and is responsible for the project within the limits set by the corporate or programme management. They have to bring unequivocal direction and leadership to the project, make the required resources available and provide unambiguous decision-making. The Project Board must be seen to support the Project Manager and must ensure that the project stays within the agreed tolerances and that the products are delivered in accordance with the agreed specifications. Finally, the Project Board must ensure that there is effective communication, both within the project and with external stakeholders.

It is important that the Project Board is given sufficient authority within the corporate or programme management so as to be able to make strategic decisions. Furthermore, it is important that the Project Board is prepared to delegate the day-to-day management of the project to the Project Manager, and is also capable of doing so, and that the members of the Project Board should be available to direct the Project Manager and to make the necessary decisions.

In unusual cases, the roles of Executive and Senior User or the roles of Executive and Senior Supplier can be combined. From the perspective of the customer-supplier relationship, it is not possible to combine the roles of Senior User and Senior Supplier. If this is possible due to the nature of the work, then it will be deemed a task within the day-to-day business and not a project.

The Executive – Is accountable for the project. From the perspective of this responsibility within the Project Board, the Executive makes the final decisions on the project. The Executive is chairman of the Project Board and is owner of the Business Case. This role is supported by the Senior User and the Senior Supplier. The Executive must ensure that the project delivers 'value for money' and that the objectives as phrased in the Business Case can be fulfilled by the output of the project. In this regard, the Executive has to try and maintain equilibrium between the interests of the customer, the users and the suppliers.

The Executive is also accountable for setting up a good project organization and the formation of planning. This means that the Executive is involved in the start-up stage and initiation stage of the project. During the project, the Executive will be involved in possible issues and problems on a strategic level. This role is responsible for making the accompanying decisions and for the communication or escalation of them to higher corporate or programme management. It is the Executive who formally closes the project and discharges the Project Manager. The Executive chairs the benefits reviews and will communicate the outcome to the stakeholders. The Executive role cannot be shared so there should only be one Executive on a Project Board.

The Senior User – Represents the interests of the users. The Senior User is responsible for ensuring that the specifications and accompanying acceptance and quality criteria are defined unequivocally and in full, and that the product is fit for purpose. From the perspective of the users, the Senior User is responsible for ensuring that the products are tested to the appropriate quality standards and methods and will also have to indicate which users will be involved in the tests.

The Senior User is also responsible for communicating with the users or their management and for the deployment of people and resources from the users, if these are required in the project (e.g. for drawing up specifications and for testing). In the event of a conflict of interests among the users, the Senior User will have to make the final decision. This role is responsible for approving the change proposals from the point of view of the users. Usually the Senior User is designated as Change Authority within the Project Board.

The Senior User is also responsible for identifying and defining the benefits and is responsible for demonstrating to the corporate or programme management that the forecast benefits are being achieved. The role of Senior User can be filled by several people within a Project Board. Alternatively, the organization may choose to have a user forum and select a member of this to be the representative on the Project Board.

The Senior Supplier – Represents the interests of those people designing, securing, producing and implementing the output of the project. The Senior Supplier is responsible for ensuring that the specialist products are being produced in accordance with the agreed criteria. In drawing up the product specifications, the Senior Supplier is responsible for checking the technical feasibility. In addition to this, the Senior Supplier contributes to creating the planning and the estimating of the costs, and the role is responsible for freeing up sufficient people and resources to achieve the output of the project in accordance with specifications and within budget and planning. The role of Senior Supplier can be filled by several people within a Project Board. Alternatively, it may be decided to have a supplier forum and select a member of this, if there is a lead supplier, to be the representative on the Project Board.

In an organization that is directed in a highly functional manner, it will often be tricky for the Project Manager to gain agreement on the deployment of required resources and on solving the issues that have arisen. In such situations, the Project Manager will need to exert their authority in order to free up the required resources from the different functional departments and to resolve the issues.

In the event of no supplier having yet been given the assignment, it may be the case that a representative from purchasing or procurement takes on the role as Senior Supplier. After issuing the assignment(s), the representative from purchasing or procurement will normally be replaced in the role of Senior Supplier on the Project Board by a senior representative from the contracted organization. In such cases, it might be a good idea to have the representative from purchasing or procurement assume the role of Project Assurance for the remainder of the project.

The Project Assurance – Represents the responsibility of the individual members of the Project Board in order to provide reassurance to the Project Board that what has been agreed to be delivered as per the PID etc. is being conducted appropriately. This supervisory task can take up a lot of time and often requires specific qualities and is therefore usually delegated to one or more persons outside the Project Board. The members of the Project Board continue to be accountable for this supervision, however. In addition to this, Project Assurance must ensure that the Project Board receives the right information as well.

Anyone delegated to take on a Project Assurance role reports to the Project Board member who appointed them. The role of Project Assurance for the Executive is often filled by someone with a finance background as they have responsibility for the Business Case. The role of Project Assurance for the Senior User is often filled by the customer's Quality Manager. The role of Project Assurance for the Senior Supplier is often filled by a Controller and the supplier's Quality Manager. The role of Project Assurance cannot be combined with the role of Project Manager.

> It is essential that there is a common idea on how the project is to be directed and what the tasks and responsibilities of the different people in the team will be. It is possible for there to be significant differences of opinion on this among the different members of the Project Board and the Project Manager. Should this be the case, then it is advisable to run a joint workshop so as to attune the different ideas on these matters to one another.

Change Authority – Is also a responsibility derived from the Project Board. The Change Authority is the person or group to whom the Project Board has delegated the responsibility to assess, authorize and deal with change requests and off-specifications within the agreements made on these things. If the changes and off-specifications are at risk of exceeding the agreed tolerances, then the Change Authority must escalate this to the Project Board using an Exception Report.

Often a Senior User is the Change Authority, but even the Project Manager can be authorized as a Change Authority. The role of Change Authority can also be allocated to people or groups from the corporate or programme management, such as a Change Advisory Board. A Change Authority is usually allocated their own change budget, from which the agreed actions have to be financed.

The Project Manager – Is responsible for the day-to-day direction of the project within the tolerances as these have been agreed with the Project Board. In this regard, the Project Manager is responsible for planning the work, authorizing the Work Packages, monitoring progress and taking corrective action. If the agreed tolerances are at risk of being exceeded, the Project Manager must escalate this to the Project Board using an Exception Report.

People are the most important factor in the project's success. It will come as no surprise that the Project Manager has to do a lot more than organize the processes and procedures and monitor and control progress. The person fulfilling the role will have to motivate the team and ensure that the team cooperates effectively to achieve the planned results. It is important when designing the team that both the skills and social competencies of individuals be balanced to ensure that the team can be effective. A key factor here is to ensure that all the team members understand the project together with the associated roles and responsibilities for the activities within it.

It is the primary responsibility of the Project Manager to ensure that the project produces the agreed products, in line with the agreed standards of quality, on time and within budget. In this regard, the Project Manager cannot lose sight of the fact that delivering results is not an end in itself; rather, there is an ultimate situation that is desired and that has to be accomplished by means of the results delivered. The Project Manager is not responsible for accomplishing this ultimate situation, but does have to ensure that the Business Case in question is still realistic and (if necessary) update the Business Case or have it updated. The role of Project Manager cannot be shared.

The Team Manager – Is responsible for producing the specialist products. The role of Team Manager is optional. The Project Manager can decide to direct the work personally. Team Managers are responsible for the Managing Product Delivery process and with it the production of one or more specialist products in accordance with an agreed Work Package. Included in this Work Package are the agreements on what output has to be delivered in accordance with which specifications and within which planning and which budget. This Work Package is agreed with the Project Manager on the basis of the approved Stage Plan and is accepted by the Team Manager.

When putting together the teams, the availability of the required people and resources must be taken into account. Involving a large number of part-time employees can complicate the planning and performance of the work. In those cases building a team is more difficult as well, which can be a clear disadvantage. Furthermore, a fragmented deployment of resources will increase costs and have a negative effect on lead-time.

Project Support – Is the responsibility of the Project Manager. This role can be delegated to a separate entity. This could be one of the project staff, a supporting department within the Project Management Team or a department set up for this purpose within the corporate or programme organization. This responsibility encompasses (among other things) the administrative support, and advice and guidance in the use of project management procedures and templates and any applications. Administrative handling of the configuration management procedures in particular falls under the remit of Project Support.

Within some organizations a permanent Project Office has been set up that can take over part of the Project Support's tasks for a project. Often the procedures and standards to be employed are also set by such an office. Moreover, this kind of Projects Office is frequently set up to provide coordination between projects (e.g. in a programme) and to assign critical resources.

For an additional summary of the tasks and responsibilities of the different roles in the Project Management Team, see appendix B.

5.5   Size of the Project Board

The Project Board must represent all the stakeholders in the project. This can lead to several people having to fill the role of Senior User and Senior Supplier. However, this can seriously undermine the sharpness of the Project Board. If there are several users and/or suppliers, then it is advised that these parties organize themselves separately at their own discretion (e.g. as groups or forums) and that only the representatives of such groups be members of the Project Board (see figure 5.4). The Project Board is not a consultative body but a decision-making platform.

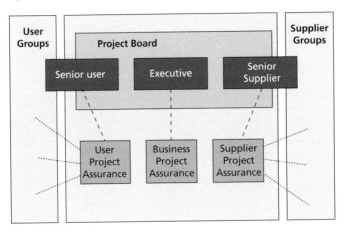

Figure 5.4 Possible reporting structure using user and supplier groups (Based on OGC PRINCE2 material)

Members from the individual groups can (if possible) take on the role of Project Assurance.

5.6   Involving stakeholders

Involving stakeholders and generating support for and commitment to the project and its output are often critical success factors in organizing and managing projects. In this regard, the Project Manager has an explicit responsibility within the accountability of the Project Board in general and that of the Executive in particular. This goes far beyond just informing the various parties.

When involving parties, you must not only look at those that are involved directly but also at all internal and external stakeholders. In this respect, stakeholders are also much more than just the decision-making parties in a project. The term concerns all internal and external parties that have an interest (positive or negative) in the project's completion or outcome (see figure 5.5).

When analyzing stakeholders, a distinction should be made between the project's impact on the stakeholders and the stakeholders' effect on the project. Stakeholders can not only be informed or simply consulted, but can also be involved in drawing up the specifications, the implementation, the assessments or in the decision-making. This makes a huge difference to their effect on the project and the extent to which support can be generated among the parties. The choices in this regard should be considered carefully.

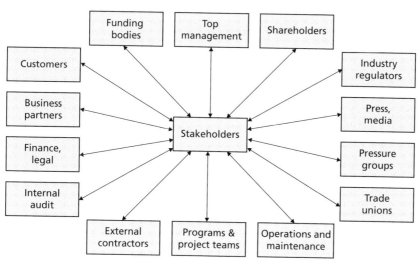

Figure 5.5 Stakeholders

As early as the start-up stage it is necessary to carry out a sound analysis of the stakeholders. This analysis should form the basis for putting together the Project Management Team. This analysis will have to be expanded in more detail during the initiation stage and will have to form the basis for preparing the Communication Management Strategy. The communication activities must then be included in the Project Plan in connection with preparing the control aspects.

During the Stage Boundaries, the Communication Management Strategy selected must be evaluated and (if necessary) modified and the communication activities for the next stage must be fleshed out and recorded in the Stage Plan for the next stage. At the end of the project, the Communication Management Strategy and the communication activities for the entire project should be evaluated.

5.7   Preparing the Communication Management Strategy

The aim of the Communication Management Strategy is to establish a framework that will enable effective internal and external communication with stakeholders. The Communication Management Strategy encompasses a description of the way in which, and the frequency with which, stakeholders are provided with information. The strategy also encompasses the results of the stakeholder analysis and the information that the different stakeholders require. Finally, the communication procedures and the requisite files and techniques that will be used are documented in the strategy.

In this regard, communication is not just providing information, but a two-way process. What information do the stakeholders require? What information can/must they supply to the project and how will the project deal with this? Finally, how the effectiveness of the communication strategy itself will be measured should be documented. The Communication Management Strategy is produced during the Initiation Stage.

6 Quality

The aim of the Quality theme is to define and implement the resources by means of which the project will be able to produce and assess products that are fit for purpose.

6.1 Introduction

The Quality theme describes the PRINCE2 approach to ensure that the project delivers products that fulfill the customer quality expectations and by means of which the benefits desired can be achieved.

Quality is product-based within PRINCE2: what does the project have to deliver, what criteria do these products have to fulfill and what methods of measuring will be used to ensure these criteria are fulfilled? Because of PRINCE2's product focus, this theme makes a direct contribution to the focus on product principle.

The Quality theme describes the quality methods, procedures and responsibilities for specifying, developing, completing and approving the specialist products and the management products.

Finally, the Quality theme describes the quality cycle of continuous improvement within the project and within the relevant existing organizations by recording, applying and passing on lessons. In so doing, the Quality theme contributes directly to the principle of learning from experience.

6.2 Conceptual framework

Quality – Defined as the aggregate of intrinsic and ascribed characteristics and properties of a product, person, process, service and/or system contributing to a capacity to fulfill certain expectations that have been made known, are obvious or have been imposed.

Scope – The aggregate of products to be delivered and activities to be carried out. PRINCE2 describes the scope as the aggregate of products to be delivered and the requirements these must satisfy. The scope is described by a plan's product breakdown structure and the accompanying Product Descriptions. In order to be able to define a scope well, however, it also needs to be established what work that is required to produce the various products does or does not fall within the scope of the plan.

6.3 Quality management

Quality management – The combination of coordinated activities to direct and manage an organization with regard to quality.

Quality management system – The complete set of quality standards, procedures and responsibilities for a site or an organization.

Within the context of PRINCE2, a site or organization is seen as the corporate or programme organization within which the project is being carried out. According to this definition, a quality management system is thus linked to that corporate or programme organization and not to a project. A project has a Quality Management Strategy, which is in fact an adaptation of the corporate or programme organization's quality management system. A project's Quality Management Strategy can be derived from both the customer's and the supplier's quality management system.

Quality planning – The aspect of quality management focussed on determining the quality objectives and specifying the necessary operational processes and resources to fulfill these quality objectives. Quality planning encompasses defining the requisite products and the accompanying quality criteria, assessment methods and responsibilities as well as how quality will be ensured and assured in the project.

Quality control – The aspect of quality management focussed on fulfillling the quality requirements. Quality control encompasses all activities geared toward checking the implementation process and the deliverables, and the activities that will increase chances of project success by eliminating causes of error and inadequate performance.

Quality assurance – The aspect of quality management focussed on ensuring there is confidence in the quality requirements being satisfied. Quality assurance is a process-oriented approach, most familiar in the form of the Deming Cycle, developed by Dr. W. Edwards Deming: Plan – Do – Check – Act.

Within PRINCE2, quality assurance is defined as being a responsibility of the corporate and programme management alone, thereby placing quality assurance in PRINCE2 firmly outside of the scope of the project. In PRINCE2, the responsibility for assuring quality in a project is viewed as being part of the wider responsibility of Project Assurance (see table 6.1).

Project Assurance	Quality Assurance
Assurance to the project's stakeholders that the project is being conducted appropriately and properly and complies with the plans and standards agreed	Assurance to the corporate or programme management that the project is conducted appropriately and properly and complies with the relevant corporate or programme standards and policies
Must be independent of the Project Manager and project team	Must be independent of the project management team
Responsibility of the Project Board	Responsibility of the corporate or programme organization
Corporate or programme quality assurance function can be used by the Project Board as part of the Project Assurance regime (e.g. to conduct quality audits)	Proper Project Assurance can provide confidence that the relevant corporate or programme standards and policies are met.

Table 6.1 The relationship between Project Assurance and quality assurance

6.4 PRINCE2 quality approach

The specific quality approach of PRINCE2 results in the following quality audit path (see figure 6.1):

- Quality planning – Encompasses the development of the Project Product Description, the Quality Management Strategy, the individual Product Descriptions and organizing the Quality Register.
- Quality control – Encompasses the implementation of the quality activities, establishing and maintaining the quality and approval records, updating the Quality Register and obtaining acceptance of the project output.

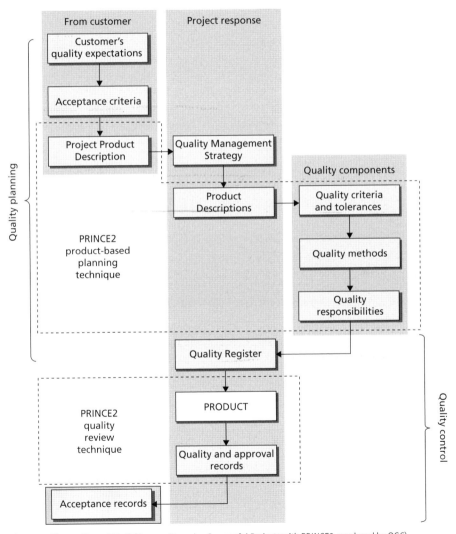

Figure 6.1 The quality audit trail (Source: Managing Successful Projects with PRINCE2, produced by OGC)

6.5   Quality planning

Customer quality expectations – Describe the following:

- The quality expected of the project product;
- The standards and processes required to achieve this quality;
- The extent to which the customer's and supplier's quality management system must be used in the project;
- The measurements to assess whether the quality expected is being achieved.

These expectations of quality are set down in the Starting up a Project process after discussions with the (Senior) Users and other stakeholders and recorded in the Project Product Description. Sometimes these expectations of quality are already offered through the project mandate. In that case, it will have to be tested whether these expectations are current and complete and represent a good reflection of what is required.

These expectations of quality are often described in general terms, such as 'user-friendly' and 'easy-maintenance'. However, where possible, they should be defined/ measurable to ensure that these expectations can be met. It is also advisable to indicate a priority in the expectations of quality relating to the final product.

Acceptance criteria – A (prioritized) list of measurable quality criteria to which the characteristics and properties of a set of products are to comply in order to be accepted by the most important stakeholders. If all acceptance criteria are satisfied, then the project can be concluded.

> A well-known way of prioritising quality criteria is the MoSCoW method:
> - **Must have** – essential to the success of the project;
> - **Should have** – is highly desirable, but a similar property would also suffice;
> - **Could have** – this requirement should only be included if there is sufficient time;
> - **Won't have for now** – this requirement will not enter the discussion for the time being, but could well be interesting for the future.

The acceptance criteria must be agreed during the Starting up a Project process and are also recorded in the Project Product Description.

'Safe', 'easy to use' or 'sustainable' are all examples of possible expectations of quality. Possible acceptance criteria could then be:

- Safe – no loose components;
- Easy to use – can go in the dishwasher;
- Sustainable – complies with a specific NEN-ISO standard.

Project Product Description – The Project Product Description describes everything that has to be delivered at the end of the project, this being the project output or the project product. The Project Product Description is produced during the Starting up a Project process as a result of an initial scoping session for the project and is itself part of the Project Brief. After approval from the Project Board with the authorization to commence the project, the Project Product Description shoud be subject to formal change control.

The Project Product Description encompasses:
- The purpose that the project's product fulfills and who will use it;
- The set of products that the project is to deliver;
- The products that are to be used to achieve the project's output (e.g. an existing system) and the documents upon which the achievement and assessment of the project's output have to be based (e.g. specifications, floor plans, etc.);
- The requisite skills to develop and achieve the project's output or an indication as to who will have to deliver the requisite resources;
- The customer quality expectations;
- The acceptance criteria, including possible quality tolerances;
- The way in which the acceptance criteria for the project's output as a whole will be tested and who is responsible for ultimate acceptance of the project's output.

The Project Product Description is expanded in more detail when the Project Plan is being produced during the Initiating a Project process and is given final approval as part of the Project Plan - and thus as part of the Project Initiation Documentation - by the Project Board when authorizing the project. If necessary, the Project Product Description is updated during the Managing a Stage Boundary process and reformulated during the authorization of a Stage or Exception Plan by the Project Board.

Quality Management Strategy – The project's adaption of the corporate or programme organization's quality management system that defines the quality techniques and standards to be used and the quality responsibilities required to be able to fulfill the requisite quality criteria for the project's deliverables. If existing processes and standards are adapted for the project, this must be stated explicitly in the strategy.

The Quality Management Strategy encompasses:
- The procedures pertaining to quality planning, quality control and quality assurance, the latter including the responsibilities of the Project Board, the compliance audits and the reviews from the corporate or programme management;
- Quality techniques and applications;
- Quality records that will be kept up to date and the form and composition of the Quality Register;
- Quality reports; aim, frequency, form and addressee;
- Times at which quality activities - such as inspections and reviews - will be carried out;
- Roles and responsibilities for quality within the project and the relevant quality responsibilities of the corporate or programme management.

The Quality Management Strategy is produced during the Initiating a Project process and approved by the Project Board. The Quality Management Strategy is updated at the end of a management stage, as part of the PID, when preparing the next Stage Plan in the Managing a Stage Boundary process.

Product Descriptions – Intended to ensure that all parties involved have a common understanding as to what is required to produce the product, what requirements it must satisfy, who is responsible for producing it and how and by whom the product will be tested and approved.

For each identified product a Product Description must be prepared. A Product Description has to be prepared as soon as the product is identified, even if only in rudimentary form. A Product Description should be baselined as soon as the Stage Plan in question is approved.

A Product Description encompasses:
- Aim, composition and sources/products that have to be used in the development, production and assessment of the product.
- Form and presentation regarding how the product has to be delivered. A report can be produced in digital format or in Word and should be done according to a certain layout. A product can be packaged and prepared for air transport.
- The competencies required to develop and achieve the project's output or an indication as to who will have to supply the requisite resources. The person ultimately responsible for producing the project will often not be known until during preparation of the Stage Plan.
- Quality criteria, these being the quality requirements the product has to satisfy and the way in which it will be measured, and whether these are being satisfied by the parties assessing the finished product.
- Quality tolerance – the accepted exception to a quality criterion.
- Quality method – the quality control (e.g. quality review) to be used during the development and delivery of the product in question.
- Competencies required for performing the various quality reviews or who will be supplying the resources for performing the quality reviews. The person(s) ultimately responsible for reviewing the product will often not be known until during preparation of the Stage Plan.
- Those responsible for quality – the ultimate names of those responsible for preparing, assessing and approving the product.

Quality Register – A formal document in which all quality reviews planned and completed are recorded, including a reference to where the quality and approval documents in question have been stored (see table 6.2).

Quality activity ID	Product ID	Product	Quality method	Producer	Reviewer(s)	Approvers	Target review date	Actual review date	Target approval date	Actual approval date	Result
1	121	Test plan	Inspection	Ali	Paulo	John, Rita	14-Feb	21-Feb	21-Feb	28-Feb	Approved
2	124	Water pump	Performance test	Paulo	Ali, Bob	John	20-Mar	20-Mar	27-Mar	n.v.t	Rejected
3	124	Water pump	Maintenance test	Paulo	Ali, Amir	Rita	21-Mar	21-Mar	27-Mar	27-Mar	Approved
9	124	Water pump	Performance test	Paulo	Ali, Bob	John	14-Jun		21-Jun		

Table 6.2 Example of a Quality Register (Source: Managing Successful Projects with PRINCE2, produced by OGC)

The Quality Register is created during the Initiating a Project process, at the same time as preparing the Quality Management Strategy. The planning data in the Quality Register is initially added when approving the Stage Plan in question and updated when authorizing the Work Package in question. The data from the quality reviews performed is completed as a result of the current reviews and approvals. It is customary that management of the Quality Register is placed with Project Support, with accountability for it residing with the Project Manager.

6.6   Quality control

Quality methods – The resources and activities for checking the implementation process and the deliverables and the activities for eliminating causes of error and inadequate performance.

For quality methods, the following can be distinguished:
- In-process methods – the means by which quality resources are included in the development and implementation process itself, such as use of calibrated instruments and automated processes, but also interim inspections and reviews or a simple 'management by walking around'.
- Appraisal methods - the means by which completed products are assessed for completeness and fitness for purpose.

Interim or final assessments can be distinguished as follows:
- Testing: whether the quality criteria can genuinely be qualified objectively;
- Inspecting: if a certain degree of professional judgement is required;
- Quality review – if a customer opinion is also required.

Quality documents – Documents showing that the planned quality reviews have been carried out and that the products satisfy the quality criteria, as these have been set down in the Product Descriptions concerned. Quality documents assure the Project Board that the agreed quality procedures have been implemented and that the most important stakeholders are satisfied with the project's output.

The quality documents substantiate the details as these have been set down in the Quality Register. Among other things, quality documents contain references to quality inspection documentation such as test plans, statistics on errors, a record of corrective action to be taken and quality reports such as audits.

It is customary for the Project Support to archive the quality documents. Quality documents are a valuable source for evaluating the project and recording lessons.

Approval documents – The documents which record that the products delivered have been approved. Such approval can be provided in many ways. It could be a decision recorded in a meeting report, an officially signed document, or a straightforward e-mail. It is important to archive such documentation centrally for reference.

Acceptance documents – Documents in which the official acceptance of the project product has been recorded at the end of the project. Usually a separate acceptance of the project product is required from both the end user and the parties responsible for control and maintenance prior to the handing over of the project product to the customer.

6.7   Quality review

A quality review is a structured procedure performed by a team of people involved that has been invited to carry it out. Its purpose is to assess the conformity of a product with a set of quality criteria. In a quality review, the emphasis is on recording errors and improvements and not on solving the problems on the spot.

In a quality review, the most important parties involved are invited to assess a product based on the accompanying Product Description. The core of the review is a meeting in which those involved must form a collective opinion of the product and/or how to proceed.

The aims of a quality review are:
- Ascertaining conformity;
- Involving all those with current interests;
- Extending ownership and obtaining commitment;
- Being able to confirm that a product can be approved;
- Creating a baseline for change control.

Four roles can be distinguished in a quality review:
- **Chairperson** – Responsible for performing the entire review process.
- **Presenter** – The person that introduces the product into the review on behalf of the people that have produced the product, and the one that is also responsible for dealing with any corrective action. Often the Team Manager is the presenter.
- **Reviewer(s)** – The person(s) assessing the product from the perspective of their specific expertise or interest.
- **Administrator** – The person providing administrative support and taking the minutes of the review meeting.

Meeting preparation – The chairperson prepares the meeting, checks whether the product is ready for review and establishes whether the stated reviewers are available. If everything is in place, the presenter then sends a copy of the product and the relevant Product Description to the reviewers. The reviewers assess the product on the basis of the quality criteria, create a list of questions with faults and issues identified and send it to the chairperson. They also note small errors (e.g. language errors) on the copy of the product and send this back to the presenter. Finally the chairperson draws up a consolidated questionnaire and sends this to the presenter in preparation for the meeting.

Meeting – In the review meeting the presenter will (after an initial round of introductions if necessary) provide a brief explanation of the product. Then, under the direction of the chairperson, the general faults and issues will be discussed. Afterwards, again under the direction of the presenter, those present will go over the product in detail section by section, discussing specific faults and issues. The administrator records all agreements made during the meeting and will reconfirm these agreements at the end of the meeting. Finally, the chairperson will assess the outcome of the review and draw the meeting to a close. In a review, the product can be approved, partially approved or rejected. In the case of the latter, the review will have to be held again after the product has been corrected.

Follow-on maintenance – After the review the chairperson will inform the stakeholders. The administrator sends the meeting report to Project Support. The presenter initiates the corrective actions and has them signed off by the allocated reviewers. Once all actions have been completed, the chairperson approves the product and the administrator will send the quality documents in question to Project Support. The presenter requests approval from those people required to sign off the product as approved.

If the action(s) cannot be completed within the agreed tolerances, then the chairperson has to report this to the Project Manager as an issue. If the person that has to sign off the product attends the review, then it will be possible to sign the product off immediately as part of the review.

Important success factors for a quality review are:
- Review the product, not the person;
- Mobilise reviewers according to their own expertise;
- Error identification, NOT correction;
- Avoid conflict. If need be, agree to disagree. In such cases the chairperson will have to report this to the Project Manager as an issue;
- Invite reviewers according to their role in the project and not according to their position;
- Make a Product Description available;
- Select an independent chairperson; as Project Manager it is possible that you are not impartial;
- Ensure that all parties are represented within the project.

A good quality review:
- Reinforces stakeholder commitment and fosters team building;
- Reinforces the Project Manager's leadership through focus on quality rather than only focussing on costs and lead-time;
- Enables early identification of errors and desirable changes, thereby providing a platform for improvement;
- Offers objective and measurable control of progress;
- Encourages individuals to develop;
- Sees to it that results are recorded in quality documents;
- Contributes to the culture of quality in the project management team and among the stakeholders.

File structure
It is important to maintain a set file structure for drawing up and archiving project documents. This prevents documentation stored being difficult to find at a later point in time. Furthermore, a set file structure makes it possible to take over the work of colleagues should circumstances necessitate this.

A distinction is made between a management file and a specialists' file. A management file contains all documents required for managing the project. A specialists' file contains all documents for delivering the output of the project, such as a provisional or definitive design.

The arrangement of a specialists' file will depend firmly on the project product to be delivered. For a management file a general arrangement can usually be adhered to. In this regard, the following things are discerned:

- Quality file – All management documents directly related to controlling the quality of the project's deliverables, such as the Quality Management Strategy and Configuration Management Strategy, the Product Descriptions, the Quality Register and Issue Register, the Issue Reports and the Lessons Log.
- Project file – Contains all other documents pertaining to the project as a whole, or:
  - All project start-up and final documents, such as the Project Brief, the PID and the End Project Report;
  - All Project Board authorizations, such as project authorization and authorization of a Stage or Exception Plan;
  - All other management products that must be brought up to date throughout the project, such as the Project Plan, the Business Case, the Risk Register and the Benefits Review Plan.
- Stage file – Contains all other management products for each stage.

This arrangement fits in with ISO 9000, in which it is prescribed that all quality documents must be archived together.

6.8 Quality, roles&responsibilities

For an overview of the roles and responsibilities for the Quality theme, see table 6.3.

Corporate / programme management	Project Manager (PM)
• Approve application of corporate/ programme Quality Management Strategy (QMS) • Bring into action Quality Assurance	• Document CQE and AC • Prepare Project Product Description • Prepare Quality Management Strategy • Prepare and maintain PDs • Ensure TMs implement agreed quality control measures
Executive • Approve Project Product Description • Approve Quality Management Strategy • Confirm acceptance of project product	**Team Manager (TM)** • Implement agreed quality control measures • Produce products consistent with PDs • Manage quality controls for Work Package products • Assemble quality records • Advise PM about product quality status
Senior User • Customer quality expectations (cqe) • Acceptance criteria (AC) • Approve Project Product Description • Approve Quality Management Strategy • Approve Product Descriptions (PD) for (key) products • Provide user resources for quality activities • Communicate with user stakeholders • Provide project product acceptance	**Project Assurance** • Advise Project Board and PM on Quality Management Strategy • Assist Project Board and PM on reviewing PDs • Advise PM on suitable quality reviewers • Assure Project Board on implementing strategies
Senior Supplier • Approve Project Product Description • Approve Quality Management Strategy • Approve quality methods, techniques & tools • Approve PD for key specialist products • Provide supplier resources for quality activities • Communicate with supplier stakeholders	**Project Support** • Provide administrative support of quality controls • Maintain Quality Register & quality records • Assist with project quality processes

Table 6.3 Roles and responsibilities of the Quality theme

7 Planning

The aim of the Planning theme is to facilitate the implementation, communication and management of achieving a specific goal or set of goals by defining the required resources.

7.1 Introduction

To a significant extent, project management is based on designing and developing a plan. Without a good plan, there is no common idea regarding the work to be carried out, there is no basis upon which the work's progress can be measured and there is no basis for managing the implementation.

The Planning theme describes the framework for designing, developing and updating the various plans in a project.

In the PRINCE2 approach, drawing up a plan is product-based. Consequently, the Planning theme makes a direct contribution to the principles of focusing on the product, learning from experience, managing by stages and managing by exception.

7.2 What is a plan?

A plan is a description of the way to get from the current position to a future position. Plans are usually recorded in a document. A plan thereby becomes a document that describes how, when and by whom a specific goal or set of goals is to be fulfilled.

Planning is the activity of drawing up or (as the case may be) updating a plan.

7.3 Benefits of drawing up a plan

Drawing up a plan forces the parties involved to reflect in advance on what has to be delivered, in what order and what work is required to achieve this. A good plan can ensure that agreement is reached beforehand on how to tackle the implementation. With a clear and well-organized plan, support can be generated among the parties involved in a straightforward manner. Everyone will be clear about what their individual input will have to be in order to achieve the plan. It will also become clear what the mutual dependencies are between the various duties and the various parties. With the help of a plan, progress can be monitored, the implementation can be controlled and the course can be adjusted in a structured manner.

A plan forms the basis for the implementation of the work. A good plan also forms the basis for the authorization of the implementation of this work by the next higher level of management.

7.4 Elements of a plan

A plan not only encompasses a schedule, but also the combination of elements required to fulfill the objectives that have been set:

- Plan description – A brief description of the scope to which the plan pertains (the entire project, a stage, a Work Package or an exception) and an outline description of the way in which the output will be realized.
- Plan conditions – What has to be available, or what conditions have to be met <u>before</u> implementation of the plan can be commenced.
- External dependence – Upon what external factors is proper implementation of the plan dependent. This could be timely delivery of other projects, but also (for example) whether a necessary permit is issued.
- Planning assumptions – Such as the availability of certain experts, access to certain office space and the skills of the staff available.
- Recorded lessons – What specific lessons from previous projects have been incorporated in this plan.
- Monitoring and controlling – Details of the way in which progress will be monitored, the method and frequency of the various instances of reporting, and the progress and decision-making meetings to be held.
- Budgets – Available budgets, including any risk and change budgets.
- Tolerances – Time, money and scope tolerances.
- Product Descriptions – These should be included for all identified products within the plan's scope, including the quality tolerances therein.
- Scheduling – In the form of a bar chart, network planning or product checklist and (if possible) supported by a product breakdown structure and product flow diagram.
- Resources – Requisite and available resources (human and otherwise) within the timeframe.

A plan provides the opportunity of anticipating and analysing implementation risks at an early stage. So, alternatives should be identified in the planning stage if certain risks materialize. Such alternatives can be incorporated into the plan as back-up provisions (commonly referred to as contingency plans).

7.5   Plan approach

Drawing up a plan is an iterative and cyclical process. Often several people will work on a plan, with everyone developing one or more elements. In such cases, it is necessary to exchange information regularly and to jointly consider the consequences for the plan as a whole. Harmony with the next higher level of management and other stakeholders is necessary to ensure that the plan stays in line with the objectives of the parties involved.

Furthermore, it is important to discuss the plan with the people and parties that have to carry out the actual work as well as with the management who have to make the required resources (human and otherwise) available for implementation of the plan. Involving these parties increases the quality of the plan and the commitment and the support coming from the various parties required to implement the plan successfully.

7.6 Planning levels

PRINCE2 has three planning levels to satisfy the needs of the various management levels in the project, these being the <u>Project Plan, the Stage Plan and the Team Plan</u>. In the Stage Plan, a distinction can be made between the Stage Plan for the initiation stage and the Stage Plans for the respective management stages during implementation of the project.

When there is a risk of exceeding the agreed tolerances, an <u>Exception Plan must be produced (if required)</u>. The Project Manager is responsible for preparing the Exception Plans for both the project and individual stages. When there is a risk of deviating from a Team Plan, it is the responsibility of the Team Manager to produce an Exception Plan. However, this falls outside of the scope of the PRINCE2 method and as such is not included here (see figure 7.1).

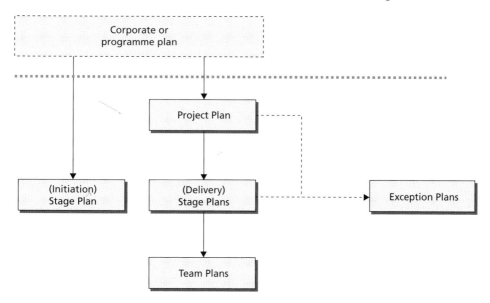

Figure 7.1 PRINCE2's planning levels (Source: Managing Successful Projects with PRINCE2, produced by OGC)

Each planning level <u>must tie in with the next higher planning</u> level. The Project Plan has to tie <u>in with the corporate or programme plan</u>. The Stage Plan has to tie in with the Project Plan. The Team Plan has to tie in with the Stage Plan. The lower the planning level, the shorter the duration, but the more details the plan will include.

Project Plan

The Project Plan <u>is the baseline for the Project Board to monitor</u> and direct the project stage <u>by stage</u>. The Project Plan outlines how the project product will be realized within the given objectives of time, money, scope and quality, the agreed management stages and the most important deliverables, activities, milestones and required resources within the timeframe.

The Project Plan is prepared by the <u>Project Mana</u>ger in the initiation stage and is approved by the Project Board as part of the Project Initiation Documentation. Prior to the end of each intermediate management stage, the <u>Project Plan is updated and approved with the authorization</u> <u>to proceed with the next stage</u>. During the Closing a Project process, the Project Plan is updated using the details from the previous implementation stage as a basis for preparing the End Project Report.

The Project Plan provides input for the Business Case with regard to the necessary investments and the period over which these investments have to be made.

Stage Plan

A Stage Plan serves as the baseline for the Project Manager for the day-to-day management of the relevant stage. A Stage Plan describes the products to be delivered and the Work Packages to be implemented during a stage. The Stage Plan is prepared by the Project Manager and approved by the Project Board.

A Stage Plan is required for each individual management stage. For that reason there are at least two Stage Plans: the Stage Plan for the initiation stage and the Stage Plan for the delivery stage. If there is only one delivery stage then the relevant Stage Plan can be amalgamated with the Project Plan.

The Initiation Stage Plan is prepared at the end of the initiation stage. The Stage Plan for the initial delivery stage is prepared at the end of the initiation stage. The Stage Plans for the other management stages are prepared as part of the Managing a Stage Boundary process at the end of the previous management stage. This enables a Stage Plan to be produced within the period for which it is possible to plan accurately (the planning horizon) and to plan using the knowledge gleaned from the achievements in earlier stages.

Team Plan

A Team Plan serves as the baseline for the Team Manager for implementation of one or more Work Packages. A Team Plan describes the deliverables and the work to be carried out in order to be able to implement and deliver the relevant Work Packages. A Team Plan is prepared by the Team Manager and must be approved by the Project Manager in the project and by the Senior Supplier in the line (outside of the project).

In cases where a Work Package is implemented by another department or by an external supplier it is not always desirable to have the (customer's) Project Manager peruse all details of the Team Plan. In such cases, the plan as it is presented will be restricted to those details that provide the Project Manager with sufficient insight to be able to verify the progress of the delivery of the Team Plan.

A Team Plan is not arranged in a set way. Suppliers do not necessarily work based on the PRINCE2 method and even the foregoing may lead to other arrangements of such plans.

A Team Plan is prepared by the Team Manager, at the same time as the Project Manager is preparing the Stage Plan: during the Managing a Stage Boundary process at the end of the previous management stage, or adopting a Work Package at the start of the Managing Product Delivery process.

A Team Plan is optional. If no separate Team Plan is prepared for the various Work Packages, then the relevant Team Managers will have to be involved more emphatically in preparing the Stage Plan. The Stage Plan will also have to contain more details than it would if a separate Team Plan was being prepared for the various Work Packages.

Exception Plan

An Exception Plan is a plan that describes what is needed to correct the effects of exceeding the tolerances or the resulting threats. In terms of arrangement, an Exception Plan is the same as the plan it is replacing, and in terms of timeframe it relates to the time left for the plan it is replacing. An Exception Plan is approved by the management level one level higher than the management level for whom the original plan was intended.

If there is a risk of a Work Package's tolerances being exceeded, then the Team Manager will have to escalate this to the Project Manager as an issue. The Project Manager will investigate this issue and take corrective action and (if necessary) agree a new/modified Work Package with the Team Manager.

If there is a risk of a stage's tolerances being exceeded, then the Project Manager will have to escalate this issue to the Project Board by means of an Exception Report. Based on the alternatives presented in such an Exception Report, the Project Board can decide to continue with the project nonetheless, to finish the project prematurely, or to instruct the Project Manager to produce an Exception Plan.

If there is a risk of the project's tolerances being exceeded, then the Project Board will have to escalate the Exception Report in question to the corporate or programme management.

7.7   Planning, PRINCE2 approach

In PRINCE2, when preparing a plan the principle focus is on the product; first and foremost it must be clear what has to be delivered, in what order, before the requisite activities can be planned so as to produce the deliverables. In itself this is perfectly logical. And so the focus on the product provides the basis for virtually all planning techniques.

First of all it has to be established what conditions a plan must satisfy. Then it has to be determined what has to be delivered and in what order. Only then can it be established what activities have to be carried out to achieve this, so that estimates can be formed on the basis of the defined activities, a schedule produced and the plan documented. Whilst preparing a plan, continuous attention should be paid to the possible risks that the implementation of the plan could pose (see figure 7.2).

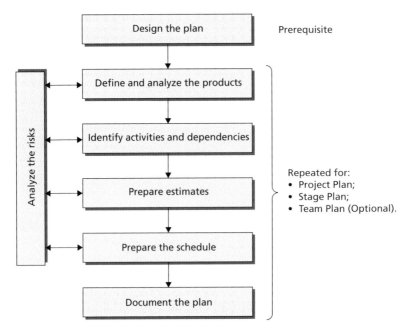

Figure 7.2 The PRINCE2 approach to plans (Source: Managing Successful Projects with PRINCE2, produced by OGC)

Plan design

Before the content of a plan can be prepared, the following must be agreed with the parties involved:

- What planning or budgetary packages or methodology will be used?
- How the elements of the plan such as planning and budgeting will be presented?
- What estimating methods will be used (function point analysis?)?
- How many planning levels will be adopted?
- What level of detail will the plan incorporate?
- What monitoring methodology will be employed?

All these aspects can affect the way in which the plans in a project are produced. Each project-specific deviation from corporate or programme standards must be explicitly approved and specified in the Project Initiation Documentation.

 Designing a plan is usually done in the initiation stage. Where necessary, it will be updated when Managing a Stage Boundary.

Define and analyse the products

For the purposes of defining and analysing the products required and to be delivered in a plan, PRINCE2 uses the product-based planning technique. First of all the Project Product Description (PPD) is prepared during Starting up a Project to specify what has to be delivered (project product). Next a product breakdown structure of this project product is developed. Then the Product Descriptions are prepared for the individual products identified and finally a product flow diagram is produced for these products. Within the PRINCE2 method, the final deliverable is known as the project product (see figure 7.3).

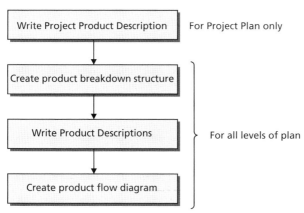

Figure 7.3 Product-based planning technique (Source: Managing Successful Projects with PRINCE2, produced by OGC)

Benefits of focus on products

Focus on products enables any potential differences in expectations to be prevented or resolved. By initially focussing on the products, the parties reach agreement in advance on what has to be delivered, in what order, what requirements this product has to satisfy, and how and by whom this will be assessed.

Focus on products increases user commitment. Users often have little affinity with the activities to be performed, but they do have affinity with the products required and to be delivered. As a result of this, there is likely to be greater acceptance of the final product.

Focus on products makes it clear what is part of the project (scope) and what is not (exclusion). Requisite (external) deliverables are established and allocated. An early view is taken of the work to be carried out, together with the interim assessments of the (intermediate) products. Finally, focus on products provides a good basis for defining the Work Packages to be implemented. By defining the deliverables, better distribution of responsibilities between different parties in a project team is possible.

Write the Project Product Description

The Project Product Description is the Product Description for the final product. For the position of the Project Product Description in the project's lifecycle and an explanation of the components of a Project Product Description, see the Quality theme (section 6.5).

The Senior User is responsible for specifying the project product. In practice, the Project Product Description is written by the Project Manager in consultation with the Executive and the Senior User.

Create the product breakdown structure

The project product to be delivered usually consists of several products that have to be completed, assessed and delivered separately. Hence it is reasonable to firstly create a hierarchical breakdown of the project product into the separately required deliverables. This prevents any individual deliverable from being forgotten.

The product breakdown structure begins with the project product. Do not break it down further than to the level of the individual products being commissioned and controlled within the relevant plan. A further division can be included under the heading 'assembly' in the Product Description itself. The breakdown can be further divided (if necessary) into an underlying planning level. A product breakdown structure is required for each individual Stage Plan.

> Between the owner of the car and the garage it is probably a matter of tyres, brake system and the engine. Between the mechanic and the warehouse it is probably a matter of the different filters and the various nuts and bolts. The extent of the breakdown of products in a plan therefore depends on who the plan is intended for.

In a product breakdown structure, ensure that each sub-product is only linked to one product above it (see figure 7.4 (A)). Avoid one-to-one relationships (see figure 7.4 (B)). This is not a breakdown. Do not use arrows or a temporary sequential breakdown of the project product (see figure 7.4 (C)). This is done in the product flow diagram. It is precisely the intention that a hierarchical and a temporary sequential breakdown be developed alongside one another to prevent products being forgotten. If divisions have to be placed under one another due to lack of space, the individual products must not be linked to one another but only to the intermediate products above (see figure 7.5).

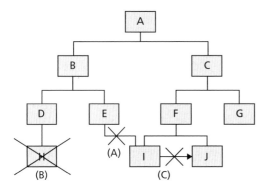

Figure 7.4 Drawing product breakdown structure

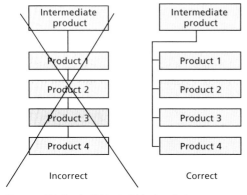

Figure 7.5 Notation for linking individual products

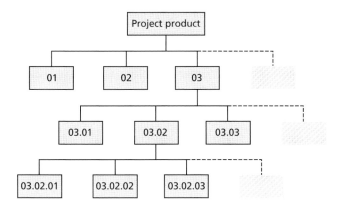

Figure 7.6 Utilizing codes in a product breakdown structure

The breakdown comprises products (nouns) and not activities (verbs). Do not use the same nouns in multiple locations in the breakdown, not even in the different layers of the breakdown or in the different groups. This leads to confusion and errors.

It is also sensible to allot a code to the different products in a breakdown. In this regard it is common to add an extra digit or digit group to the code for each layer in the breakdown (see figure 7.6).

A distinction should be made between the products, groups and external products to be produced:
• **Groups** – A set of products having no other function than to enable a structured clustering of products. A group does not have to be assessed in itself.
• **External products** – Products that already exist or are being created or updated outside of the scope of the project.

Groups can be represented in a parallelogram, external products in an oval shape, and proprietary products in a rectangle (for example). Different colours can also be selected, but this is often not as clear. It is recommended that this distinction is made so as to avoid misunderstandings later on. It is also advisable to include external products as a separate risk in the Risk Register.

Furthermore, distinguish between different product development phases if possible, such as a provisional and a definitive design, or the different phases during transportation, particularly if responsibility for the transportation is being transferred from one party to another.

Product breakdown structures can also be depicted in various ways: both in the traditional form, such as in figure 7.5, like in a mind map, but also (for example) simply in lists with different sub-levels. What is important in this regard is to ensure compliance with the standards within the corporate or programme organization and what the 'users' of the breakdown prefer. Standardized product breakdown structures are available within certain product models.

Do not forget to include the management products in the breakdown as well. Producing management products costs time and money and should certainly not be forgotten. Usually the specialist products are planned first and the management products added to these later on. For an overview of management products see appendix A. The number of management products in a specific project can be much more limited though.

Write the Product Descriptions

A Product Description has to be produced for all identified interim and final products in a product breakdown. Naturally no Product Descriptions whatsoever are required to be prepared for groups. Although it is not required for external products, preparing a Product Description is recommended.

A Product Description must be prepared as soon as an individual product is identified. The first Product Description is often no more than a title and an identification code, entered in a pre-printed template. Yet it is essential that this is done to prevent the Product Descriptions concerned being forgotten.

A Product Description has to be baselined as soon as the Stage Plan for the stage in which the product to be produced has been approved. A Product Description is often the first document included in the Configuration Item Record. Furthermore, each change to the Product Description immediately requires an adjustment to the Configuration Item Record.

The Project Manager or the Team Manager is responsible for preparing the Product Descriptions, though they must involve the users and product specialists in this. The users and product specialists are responsible for the quality criteria and the other quality aspects that have to be recorded in the Product Description.

Just as with the product breakdown structure, a Product Description does not have any prescribed format, though this is recommended (see section 6.5 and appendix A). What is important is that the required information is recorded, not how it is recorded. A detailed programme of requirements often contains the required information as well. What is important is that this is specifically tested. Missing aspects can lead to significant problems later on.

For small projects, sometimes just the Project Product Description will suffice. For management products, often standardized Product Descriptions already available within the organization can be used.

Create the product flow diagram

As a foundation for the ultimate planning, it is necessary to know in what order the products are to be produced and used. To this end a product flow diagram is prepared as a final step in the focus on the product. In this flow diagram, all products from the product breakdown structure are depicted in a temporary sequential mutual relationship.

The rules for creating a product flow diagram are simple. The flow diagram is drawn from top to bottom or from left to right. All products from the product breakdown structure are shown with the same names and preferably also drawn in the same way as in the product breakdown structure. The order in which the products are produced is shown using arrows. In principle, products can only be produced simultaneously or after one another. The flow diagram culminates in the project product.

In the product flow diagram the specialist products and the event-driven management products are depicted, such as the end stage products and test plans to be produced. Periodic management products, such as Checkpoint Reports, Highlight Reports, logs and registers, are not included in the flow diagram.

During preparation of the product flow diagram new products are frequently identified for the plan. These products have to be added to the product breakdown structure in order to be certain that both diagrams continue to match one another. Product Descriptions also have to be prepared for these 'forgotten' products.

When preparing a product flow diagram it is advisable to fill in the flow diagram both from the perspective of the plan's starting point (from front to back) and also from the perspective of the plan's end (from back to front). This yields the best results. It is also advisable when preparing the product flow diagram to enlist the people who will be carrying out the work and who will be using the project's output.

The sequential or simultaneous relationships depicted in a product flow diagram are usually just a rough sketch of the reality. In a product flow diagram for a Project Plan, products are often shown that are further divided up later on in a Stage Plan or a Team Plan. Nonetheless, dividing the Project Plan up further or defining more complex relationships is not recommended. It is better to accept a straightforward flow diagram for the Project Plan and not to expand the products and product relationships further until during the underlying Stage Plans and Team Plans.

Work breakdown structure (WBS)
An alternative for a product breakdown structure is the work breakdown structure. The term work breakdown structure (WBS) comes from the Project Management Body of Knowledge (PMBoK) and, as such, is not a PRINCE2 –technique. In PMBoK the work breakdown structure is described as:

'A deliverable-oriented hierarchical decomposition of the work to be executed by the project team to accomplish the project objectives and create the required deliverables. It organizes and defines the overall scope of the work for the project. Each descending level represents a definition of the project work with an increasing degree of detail. The WBS is made up of Work Packages. The product-based nature of the hierarchy contains both internal and external deliverables.'

With this description the work breakdown structure fits in perfectly with the product breakdown structure as it is defined with a focus on the product. Unsurprisingly, the tension between those who see the product breakdown structure as an ideal basis for preparing a plan and those who see the work breakdown as the best basis for this is no more than a war of words. Both terms are intrinsically the same. And so the question as to whether it is reasonable to prepare a work breakdown after a product breakdown does not form part of the discussion.

Obviously after a product breakdown the Work Package (as lowest level of the breakdown) does have to be fleshed out. Usually several activities have to be performed in order to be able to deliver a Work Package. A Work Package contains activities and milestones so as to be able to accomplish delivery of the Work Package. This is the case both in a product breakdown structure and in a work breakdown structure.

WBS dictionary
A WBS dictionary is a document describing every component of the WBS, with the components of the WBS encompassing all entities in the WBS, including both the final product at the highest level and the intermediate products like the Work Packages. This dictionary accompanies the WBS. For each WBS component, the WBS dictionary contains an ID number, a declaration of the work, the responsible organization and a list of planned milestones. Other information for each WBS component could be: contract information, quality requirements and technical references, activities to be performed, the planned start and finish dates, requisite resources and planned costs. Every WBS component contains cross references to other WBS components in the WBS dictionary.

This results in significant correspondence between a Work Package description in a product breakdown structure and a WBS component in a work breakdown. The WBS dictionary shows significant similarity to the Configuration Item Records in the configuration management database.

Identify dependencies and dependencies
Having a product flow diagram is often not sufficient to be able to form a proper estimate of the work to be carried out and the resources and time required to fulfill the plan. Activities can be interdependent, thereby affecting lead-times. For this reason it is usually necessary for the individual projects to also identify the activities required to deliver the product in question. In fact this is an instance of planning within the individual Work Packages that have to be implemented and delivered. In this regard, network planning is used for complex projects.

These activities must also encompass the management and quality activities, such as the activities needed to assess and purchase the external products. In addition to this, a record is made of the interdependencies between the activities and the dependencies on external events and products, such as placement of a purchasing order by the Purchasing Department or a decision from the programme management.

Network planning and the critical path
In a network plan, the various activities in a mutually sequential connection are shown. A frequently used method in this regard is the precedence chart, in which the activities in the junctions are represented using sequential arrows between the junctions (see figure 7.7). For each junction (activity or task) a record is made of the earliest possible start (ES), latest possible start (LS), earliest possible finish (EF), latest possible finish (LF) and finally the overall margin. Based on this, the critical path can be calculated by working out the ES and the EF from start to finish through the various chains. The critical path is the longest path in a network, which in turn can identify the minimum time that the whole project will take

to complete. The overall margin can be calculated by working back from the end to start by calculating the LF and EF through the various chains. The overall margin is the total quantity of time that an activity can be delayed by without a plan's longest lead-time being extended.

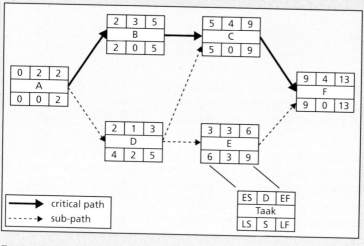

Figure 7.7 Example of a precedence chart

Prepare estimates

Based on the defined activities and dependencies, estimates can be prepared as to the resources required and the necessary lead-times.

There are a few basic rules that should be taken into consideration when preparing estimates:
- Never work in single hours, instead use blocks of four hours.
- Assume a maximum of 44 weeks a year, in some organizations even less.
- Take into account the fact that people are usually only 80 percent productive, so we ought to plan in 25 percent more resources than is arithmetically necessary based on 100 percent productivity.
- Factor in time for meetings, preparing reports and analyzing issues.
- Also plan time for assessing the completed products *and* time and resources for repair work. Hardly anything is right first time.

When preparing estimates it is important to identify the various people and tools required, and to then prepare a separate estimate for each type of resource. This can be done on the basis of an expert opinion, or on previously collected data. Estimates are at their most accurate if made both top-down and bottom-up and then compared with one another. Involve the people that are going to carry out the work in preparing the estimates. With the Delphi method, for example, the opinions of several experts are used as a first step, with a series of questions answered independently.

For critical estimates it is advisable to use a list with three points and to average these: what is the most probable resource requirement or lead-time (W), what is an optimistic estimate (O) and what is a pessimistic estimate (P). The expected value to be adhered to is then:
$$\mu = (O + 4xW + P)/6.$$

Prepare the schedule

First of all, the order of the activities to be performed has to be determined, together with the most important decision points and milestones. The next thing to identify is what people and tools will be available for implementation of the plan. Following on from this the available resources must be allocated to the various activities, and then the schedule should be calculated on the basis of the allocated resources and a presumed level of productivity.

The resultant lead-time or delivery date is then compared with the desired or recorded lead-time or delivery date. If this results in a negative discrepancy, then the time plan will have to be optimized. This can be done by removing the non-critical activities or postponing them, or by stretching them out over a longer period so that less resources will be needed for each unit of time. If this still does not suffice, then it will have to be decided whether other people and resources can be mobilised in order to make up the required resources, or whether additional resources can be freed up. Sometimes it is possible to perform activities in a different order. Ultimately the resource planning will have to be balanced. Beware of wishful thinking in this regard. If this does not work, then the problem will have to be fed back to the management as an issue.

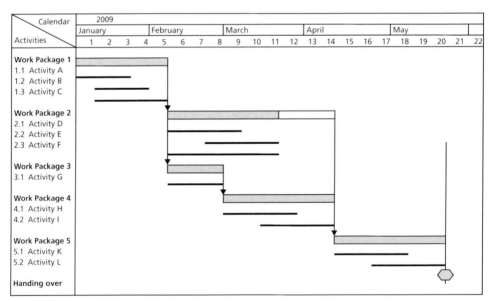

Figure 7.8 Example of a bar chart

In the case of simple plans, the above can be carried out manually using a bar chart or a basic spreadsheet. For more complex plans, it is better to use a network plan, as already indicated.

Based on the definitive resources and the costs associated with these, the final estimate of the plan's costs can be prepared. Do not forget the costs for the management and quality activities. These costs can be further supplemented by a contingency sum, the expected monetary value of the risks identified and an estimate for any change requests. All this serves as input for the budget that ultimately has to be set.

Product identifier	Product title	Product Description approved		Draft ready		Final quality check completed		Approved		Handed over	
		Plan	Actual	Plan	Actual	Plan	Actual	Plan	Actual	Plan	Actual
...											
121	Test plan	02/01	02/-11	07/02	07/02	14/02	21/02	21/02	25/02	N.A.	N.A.
122	Pump	02/01	02/01	13/03	13/03	14/05		30/05		14/07	
...											

Table 7.1 Example of a product checklist (Source: Managing Successful Projects with PRINCE2, produced by OGC)

Based on the ultimate order of the activities and resources, the definitive schedule can then be prepared. It is advisable to visualize the schedule through the use of a bar chart (see figure 7.8) or a product checklist (see table 7.1).

Risk, analyse

Preparing a plan involves constantly having to weigh up the various risks that the different choices entail. Every deployment of resources and every order of activities contains opportunities and threats. So it is important to continually take account of the risks associated with the various choices in the decision-making. Thus a plan is not prepared in a simple series of steps but in an iterative and cyclical process that usually has to be gone over several times in order to arrive at an acceptable optimum that will be supported by the different stakeholders.

Examples of risks that frequently occur in the act of planning are:
- Deployment of a lot of resources at the same time;
- Plan does not contain allocated resources or contains untested suppliers;
- Plan relies heavily on external factors;
- Plan depends on new technologies;
- Plan contains little or no management decision points;
- Plan contains little leeway;
- Plan contains several critical paths, or paths that are almost the same as the critical path.

Document the plan

Finally, the various elements of the plan are combined into one document, and the approach selected and the plan's prerequisites, external factors and assumptions are written down.

Without this information the plan is of little value. Unsubstantiated plans can lead to significant differences of opinion in the event of subsequent changes to these plans. Without substantiation, the management level being reported to is not capable of assessing the plan and any alternatives, and the Project Manager or Team Manager is not able to monitor the plan's progress properly either.

7.8   Planning, roles&responsibilities

For an overview of roles and responsibilities for the Planning theme, see table 7.2.

Corporate / programme management	Project Manager (PM)
• Provide corporate/ programme planning standards • Define project tolerances in mandate • Approve project Exception Plans	• Develop Project and Stage Plans • Design management and technical stages • Instruct corrective actions when Work Package tolerances are forecasted to exceed • Prepare stage and project Exception Plans
Executive • Approve Project Plan • Define stage tolerances • Approve Stage and Exception Plans • Commit business resources to Stage Plans	**Team Manager (TM)** • Create and update Team Plans • Prepare schedules for each Work Package • Escalate to PM when Work Package tolerances are forecasted to exceed
Senior User • Ensure Project and Stage Plans remain consistent from user perspective • Commit user resources to Stage Plans	**Project Assurance** • Monitor changes to the Project Plan on impact to the Business Case • Monitor stage and project progress against agreed tolerances
Senior Supplier • Ensure Project and Stage Plans remain consistent from supplier perspective • Commit supplier resources to Stage Plans	**Project Support** • Assist with Compilation plans • Contribute with specialist expertise • Baseline and store plans

Table 7.2 Roles and resposnsibilities relevant to the Planning theme

8　Risk

The aim of the Risk theme is to identify, assess and control uncertainties, thereby improving the capacity of a project to be successful.

8.1　Introduction

Every project has its risks. Risks cannot be avoided. Due to the temporary nature of a project and the large number of stakeholders often involved, projects can attract a higher degree of risk than the activities involved in day-to-day operations. Projects yield results necessary to implement change and achieve new benefits. These results are commonly surrounded by uncertainties. Unsurprisingly, these uncertainties do not have a direct impact on the project output to be delivered, but they do have a direct impact on the business justification for the project. From this perspective, these 'business risks' also have to be included in the project management.

Risk management should not be an incidental action at the start of the project, but rather an integral aspect of managing projects throughout their life span, which should include both the project risks and the business risks linked to these. The aim of risk management is to manage the uncertainties in the internal and external project environments proactively so that the project has the maximum opportunity to succeed.

The Risk theme makes a direct contribution to the principle of continued business justification.

8.2　Conceptual framework

Risks and issues

A risk is an uncertain event or set of events that, should it occur, will have an affect on the achievement of the objectives. An issue is any relevant and unplanned event that has happened and that requires management attention. Both terms are often confused. Whereas a risk is an uncertain event that, if it occurs, will have consequences for the project, an issue is a relevant event that has happened and that was not planned and that requires the attention of the management.

Whereas with an issue you have to solve the problem or produce the opportunity, with risks you have to introduce measures to control the uncertainty *and* plan responses in case this uncertainty becomes an actuality. See the Changes theme for the management of issues.

> Today we went on holiday to France. It was announced on the radio that there were long traffic jams on all major roads heading south. Consequently it is (pretty much) certain that we will not make it to our hotel on time this evening and that the rooms will be given away (issue). How do we resolve this?

> Tomorrow we are heading south on holiday. There is a significant chance that there will be long traffic jams, as a result of which we will arrive late at our hotel tomorrow evening, resulting in the rooms being given away (risk). How can we best anticipate this?

Opportunities and threats

Risks comprise a combination of opportunities and threats *and* the impact these opportunities and threats have on the objectives that are to be fulfilled:

- **Opportunity** – An uncertain event or circumstance, the occurrence of which would have a positive effect on the objectives to be fulfilled.
- **Threat** – An uncertain event or circumstance, the occurrence of which would have a negative effect on the objectives to be fulfilled.

Within PRINCE2, the aspects of time, money, scope, quality, risks and benefits are defined as the objectives to be fulfilled. Aspects like health, safety, security and the environment are not mentioned individually by PRINCE2, but can of course be incorporated into the project as separate objectives.

The majority of uncertain events and circumstances entail both opportunities and threats. And so it is important that opportunities and threats are managed integrally as risks.

8.3 Risk

Risk management is the systematic application of procedures to the tasks of identifying and assessing risks, and then planning and implementing risk responses. In order to manage risks effectively, the risks have to be identified, assessed and controlled.

Principles for good risk management are:
- Understand the context of the project;
- Involve stakeholders in the identification, assessment and control of the risks;
- Set clear project objectives as a reference for managing the risks;
- Develop a Risk Management Strategy and organize risk management procedures;
- Report regularly on any new risks and the status of existing risks;
- Establish clear roles and responsibilities for managing risks;
- Create an open culture to make the discussion of risks possible;
- Define and monitor warning indicators that indicate whether certain risks could arise;
- Evaluate the management of risks regularly and look for points for improvement.

Risks have to be managed within an organization on an operational, tactical and strategic level. Risks in projects are often tactical risks pertaining to the implementation of changes in the organization. It is important to realize that risks on the different levels in an organization have an effect on each other and that managing risks in projects must be attuned to managing the risks in the corporate and programme organization (see figure 8.1).

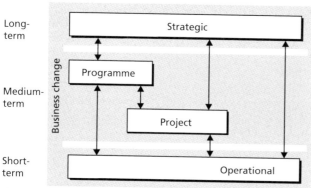

Figure 8.1 Organizational perspectives (Source: Managing Successful Projects with PRINCE2, produced by OGC)

PRINCE2 recommends the development of a Risk Management Strategy and the setting up of a Risk Register for each project.

8.4 Risk Management Strategy

The aim of developing a Risk Management Strategy is to establish a framework on the basis of which an effective risk management procedure can be set up and risk management can be embedded in the regular project management activities.

The project's Risk Management Strategy must be derived from the risk management policy and the corporate or programme organization's risk management manual. In the policy document it is stated how risk management will be implemented in the organization for the purposes of supporting the fulfillment of the business strategies, including the organization's risk appetite, and the risk tolerances and procedures to be adhered to. In the manual the steps and necessary activities are given for how the risk management procedures have to be implemented.

The Risk Management Strategy describes:
- The risk management procedures, controls, techniques and records to be used;
- Risk techniques and applications;
- Records to be used;
- Roles and responsibilities with regard to managing risks;
- When risk management activities such as risk analyses will be performed;
- How risks are reported and to whom;
- The categories to be used for probability, impact and proximity of risks;
- Risk categories such as operational, corporate and project risks;
- Risk response categories to be used for opportunities and threats;
- Warning indicators to be used;
- Risk appetite and risk tolerances to be used;
- Any approved risk budget.

Generic warning indicators for project risks are:
- Percentage of Work Packages not yet completed;
- Percentage approvals still outstanding;
- Number of issues being submitted monthly/average time that issues remain outstanding;
- Number of corrective actions resulting from quality reviews;
- Cost and schedule performance index in the earned value analysis;

Specific warning indicators for risks in a project include customer satisfaction, staff turnover, non-attendance at meetings and the number of team changes.

What is important is not only the absolute value of these indicators but also whether the values are increasing or decreasing.

Risk appetite is the attitude of an organization with regard to taking risks, which subsequently determines the degree of risk acceptance. Risk tolerance is the threshold level of risk exposure which, if a risk crosses this threshold, necessitates an Exception Report being produced.

The Risk Management Strategy is developed by the Project Manager in the initiation stage and is approved as part of the Project Initiation Documentation by the Project Board during authorization of the project. The Risk Management Strategy is evaluated and (if necessary) updated, at least at the end of each management stage.

8.5   Risk Register

The aim of the Risk Register is to create a central record of information pertaining to all identified opportunities and threats concerning the project.

The following things are recorded in the Risk Register:
- Who registered the risk and when;
- Risk category and description of the risk;
- Probability, impact and possibly the expected financial value of the risk;
- The proximity of the risk and its progress over time;
- Risk responses and to which category these belong;
- Status of the risk (active or closed);
- The person responsible for the individual risk (risk owner) and the person responsible for implementing the risk responses (risk actionee).

The Risk Register is set up at the same time as the development of the Risk Management Strategy, during the Initiating a Project process. Risks that had already been identified in the initiation stage are similarly registered. The Project Manager is responsible for setting up and maintaining the Risk Register.

8.6   Risk management procedures

PRINCE2 has a risk management procedure comprising five steps (see figure 8.2).

Figure 8.2 Risk management procedure (Source: Managing Successful Projects with PRINCE2, produced by OGC)

Identify

The identification of the risks can be further divided into:

- **Identifying context** – This involves gathering information about the project itself, the context and the objectives plus the development of the Risk Management Strategy.
- **Identifying risks** – This involves identifying and recording the individual risks, identifying possible warning indicators and understanding the vision of stakeholders regarding risks identified.

Common techniques for the identification of risks are:
- Reviewing lessons from previous projects or one's own Lessons Log;
- Brainstorming sessions with stakeholders and material experts;
- Reviewing checklists. These checklists are often depicted in the form of a fishbone diagram (see figure 8.3);
- Cause-effect diagrams (see figure 8.4).

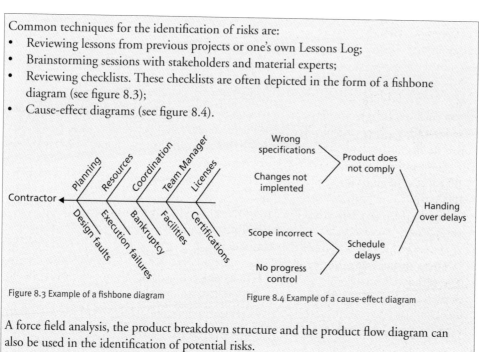

Figure 8.3 Example of a fishbone diagram

Figure 8.4 Example of a cause-effect diagram

A force field analysis, the product breakdown structure and the product flow diagram can also be used in the identification of potential risks.

It is important for the identification of risks that they are recorded in an unambiguous way. It obviously makes a difference if an error will lead to rejection of a batch with a loss of €10,000 or users possibly being poisoned, thereby putting the survival of one's own organization at risk. In such cases it is strongly recommended that risks be identified on the basis of a defined risk cause and the possible risk effect: a risk is that ...<event/condition>... as a result of which ...<result>... with the effect of ...<consequence>... (see figure 8.5).

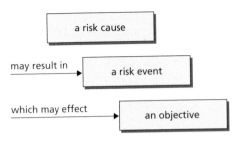

Figure 8.5 Risk cause, event and effect (Source: Managing Successful Projects with PRINCE2, produced by OGC)

In terms of the identification of a risk, simply stating 'breaking down on the road' is not sufficiently explicit. Breaking down on the road, as a result of which you have to call the breakdown service and only have a few hours delay to the journey is one thing; breaking down on the road with the engine exploding and costing you thousands of Euros is completely different. Both cases of breaking down should be considered as separate risks. Each of these risks also has its own perceived value for the person involved. It would not be the first time that parties are talking at cross-purposes because one is thinking of the 'breakdown service' scenario and the other the 'engine exploding' scenario.

In addition to identifying the risk cause and the risk effect, the relevant risk category and a provisional risk owner have to be recorded when identifying the risks. Finally, the risks identified and the accompanying facts are set down in the Risk Register.

Project risks are the risks that have an impact on the project output and the project objectives like time, money, scope and quality. Corporate or commercial risks are risks that have a direct impact on the forecast benefits and thereby their effect on what the customer wishes to achieve through the project output.

Assess
Assessing the risks can be further divided into:
- **Estimating** – Estimating for each individual risk the chance of the risk occurring, the impact of the risk on the project's objectives and the time in which the risk could occur if no risk measures are implemented. Also establishing the risk owner for each individual risk.
- **Evaluating** – Reviewing the net effect of the aggregate of risks for the project. This makes it possible to assess whether the composite risk still falls within the risk tolerance for the project as a whole and thus whether there is still a business justification to implement or continue the project (as the case may be).

When estimating the individual risks, it is also important to look at how the probability and impact vary during the course of the project.

Common techniques for estimating risks are:
- Probability tree – (see figure 8.6);
- Pareto analysis – Here the various risks are classified in order of size. The Pareto principle is that 20 percent of the risks cause 80 percent of the overall net effect of the risks on the project. And thus it is also the intention that most of the attention is focussed on that first 20 percent of the risks (see figure 8.7);
- Probability impact matrix – Here the risks are depicted in classes of probability and impact (see table 8.1);
- Expected financial value – Same as the chance-effect matrix, but the impact is now expressed as the expected financial effect of the risk on the project (see table 8.2).

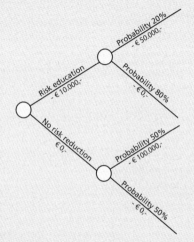

Figure 8.6 Probability tree

Figure 8.7 Pareto analysis

Risk	Opportunity	Impact	Priority
A	1	4	4
B	2	3	6
C	3	5	15
D	3	4	3
E	4	4	16
F	4	3	12

Table 8.1 Probability impact matrix

Risk	Opportunity	Impact	Expected monetary value
A	30%	€50.000	€15.000
B	60%	€25.000	€15.000
C	20%	€100.000	€20.000
Total			€50.000

Table 8.2 Expected financial value

To obtain an overview of all individual risks together, plotting the risks in a risk profile is recommended. In the risk profile, the risk tolerance line can also be shown. For all risks above the risk tolerance line, a risk response must be implemented. For risks under the risk tolerance line the risk responses are optional. Risks that are virtually certain to occur have to be treated like issues (see figure 8.8).

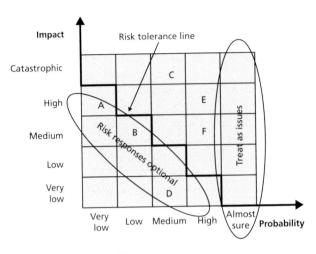

Figure 8.8 Summary risk profile

Plan

After reviewing the risks, the manual risk response are identified. Here a distinction has to be made between risk responses for opportunities and threats (see figure 8.9).

Effect	Threat Responses	Opportunity Responses
High	Avoid	Exploit
	Reduce	
	Fallback	Enhance
	Transfer	
	Share	
Low	Accept	Reject

Figure 8.9 Threat and opportunity responses responses (Based on OGC PRINCE2 material)

- **Risk response, avoid** – Seeing to it that the risk cannot reoccur at all. In order to achieve this, a completely different approach usually has to be selected.
- **Risk response, reduce** – Selecting a response that will reduce the probability, the impact or both.
- **Risk response, fallback** – A special form of reduction: planning a response that is not deployed until the risk actually occurs or (as the case may be) threatens to occur. The probability remains the same, but the impact decreases.
- **Risk response, transfer** – A special form of reduction: the negative financial effect of transferring a risk to someone else. Thus, for example, the negative financial impact can be placed upon a supplier or transferred to an insurance company.
- **Risk response, share** – Here the opportunities and threats are shared. In this regard, attention must be paid to the no-claims schemes with suppliers.

- **Risk response, accept** – A deliberate decision not to implement any risk responses to a threat on the assumption that taking action will not be effective until the threat actually occurs.
- **Risk response, exploit** – Ensuring that the opportunity is seized and that the impact will be realized.
- **Risk response, enhance** – Enhancing the probability and/or positive effect of the opportunity. This can also be done by developing a plan that can be set in motion as soon as the opportunity arises or (the opposite of fallback) by participating in a venture (the opposite of transfer).
- **Risk response, reject** – A deliberate decision not to implement any responses on the assumption that taking action will not be effective until the opportunity actually occurs.

For each of the various risk responses it must be indicated what the possible effectiveness of the response is and to what extent the response is cost-effective. The proposed response (with substantiation) must be presented to the relevant decision-makers. For risks falling below the risk tolerance limit this can be the Project Manager. Risks above the risk tolerance limit have to be escalated to the Project Board. After a decision has been made, the agreed actions must be incorporated into the plans in question. Often a combination of risk responses is implemented for several risks simultaneously.

Implement

In order to implement the risk response it must be ascertained that risk owners and risk actionees have been appointed for all individual risks. Look at whether the agreed risk responses are being implemented. Check whether the risk responses are effective and the risks are actually decreasing and the opportunities increasing. Possibly take corrective action if the anticipated effect is not forthcoming.

After implementation, the inherent risk will not usually disappear completely. The latter will only occur if the threat has genuinely been avoided or the opportunities have genuinely been exploited. If, after implementing the agreed risk responses, the residual risk is still over the risk tolerance line, the risk will have to be escalated once again and additional risk responses will be required. As a last resort the project will have to be stopped or (as the case may be) not started.

Communicate

For the effective management of risks it is necessary to have frequent communication on any new risks identified and the status of known risks. A risk analysis should not only be performed during the start-up stage and the initiation stage but each time a plan is prepared or updated, each time the Business Case, risks is updated and each time the impact of an issue is considered. Risk management is a continuous process throughout the project.

Communicating, risks must be done in every report and during every consultation. A separate section is dedicated to risks in the Checkpoint Reports and the Highlight Report. In the End Stage Report and End Project Report, risks form part of the report on the Business Case. In an Exception Report it must be indicated both for the present situation and for the options what the effect on the risks is.

During the project team consultation, risks have to be addressed. This can best be done by including risks in the separate agenda items and only addressing risk as a whole. Is the aggregate risk level still acceptable or not for all the agreed actions?

The Team Manager must escalate new risks and every threat of exceeding a risk tolerance to the Project Manager by means of an issue. If at the stage level the risks threaten to exceed the risk tolerance, then the Project Manager will have to escalate this to the Project Board by means of an Exception Report with proposals for new risk responses. If at the project level there is a possibility of the risk tolerance being exceeded, then the Executive will have to escalate this to the corporate or programme management.

During the Project Board meetings, the most significant risks *and* the aggregate risk level for the entire project will remain a subject for discussion when reviewing the continued viability of the project.

Finally, the application and the effectiveness of the risk management will have to be evaluated regularly. This will have to be done at least at the end of each management stage and at the end of the project. Points for improvement are to be included in the Lessons Log and in the Lessons Report.

The management of risks is therefore not a separate activity but an integrated component of project management. To a very large extent, project management is risk management.

8.7   Risk owner and risk actionee

A risk owner is the person responsible for managing, monitoring and controlling all aspects of a specific risk, including implementation of the risk responses. In respect of the risk, the risk owner reports to the Project Manager.

If the implementation of a risk response does not fall within a risk owner's remit, then a separate risk actionee will have to be appointed. A risk actionee is the person responsible for implementing a specific risk response. The risk actionee reports on the implementation to the relevant risk owner or owners (as the case may be).

8.8   Risk budget

A risk budget is a budget to finance costs relating to risk responses *and* the possible costs of the impact of the risks, should they materialize.

When estimating the possible costs of the impact of the risks, it is best to use the aggregate expected financial value of all risks.

It is much more cost-effective to allocate such a risk budget separately with the Project Manager than to fully incorporate the anticipated costs associated with risks straight into the budgets of the individual Work Packages. In the latter case, these funds will always get used up. With a risk budget, only costs for genuine risks will be incurred. This is often not more than 30 percent of the costs that would otherwise be incorporated straight into the budgets of the individual Work Packages.

For those risks that have not yet been foreseen it is best to include a contingency sum.

8.9 Risks, roles&responsibilities

For an overview of the roles and responsibilities for the Risk theme, see table 8.3.

Corporate / programme management	Project Manager (PM)
• Provide risk management policy • Provide risk management process guide **Executive** • Approve Risk Management Strategy • Responsible for business risks • Escalate risk to corporate or programme management **Project Board** • Inform PM about external risks • Take decision on risks **Senior User** • Ensure user aspects of risks are managed **Senior Supplier** • Ensure supplier aspects of risks are managed	• Create Risk Management Strategy • Create and maintain Risk Register • Responsible for management of risks **Team Manager (TM)** • Participate in identifying, assessing and controlling risks **Project Assurance** • Review risk management practices • Ensure alignment with strategy **Project Support** • Assist PM in maintaining Risk Register **Risk owner** • Management of individual risk **Risk actionee** • Carry out risk response action

Table 8.3 Roles and responsibilities relevant to the Risk theme

9 Change

The aim of the Change theme is to identify, assess and control any potential and approved change to the baseline.

9.1 Introduction

Changes in specification can hardly be prevented and often are even desirable. The different stakeholders often do not realize until the project is underway and the final product is becoming clearer, what it was they asked for and what the consequences will be. The customer's needs often change during the project. Stakeholders change. The project's internal and/or external environment change. All of these are reasons why changes have to be implemented during the project.

In addition to this there are also aspects during a project that require attention from the management so as to be sure the project is successful - a supplier going bankrupt, certain specialists being off sick, completed products being rejected, and so on. The likely impact on the project will have to be considered for all these issues, and a decision taken on what the most appropriate action should be.

The aim of issue and change control is thus not to prevent change happening or issues arising but rather to identify issues and (proposed) changes and have them assessed and managed. You cannot prevent issues; at most you can negate them.

Effective issue and change control is necessary to:
* Prevent surreptitious expansion of the scope;
* Be able to manage the effect of issues and changes on the rest of the project;
* Ascertain the effect on the practicability and viability of the project;
* Ensure acceptance by stakeholders.

Good configuration management is a condition for effective change control.

Effective issue and change control directly supports the principle of managing by exception. The principles of defined roles and responsibilities and focus on products support effective issue and change control.

9.2 Conceptual framework

Issue and change control is the procedure that ensures that all issues and changes which could have an effect on the project's objectives are identified and assessed, and are approved, rejected or adhered to. In this regard, changes are a specific type of issue.

An **issue** is any relevant and unplanned event that occurs and requires action from the management. A **change** is a change to a baseline, in which a baseline is defined as the point of departure based on which a product, process or status is monitored and controlled. A baseline can be an approved report or approved drawing. A baseline can also be a recorded status of a product or item.

PRINCE2 distinguishes three issues:
- **Request for change** – A proposal for a change to a baseline of a product, process or status.
- **Off-specification** – A product that does not satisfy, or that obviously will not satisfy, the agreed specifications.
- **Problem or a concern** – Any other issue that has to be resolved or has to be escalated by the Project Manager.

Configuration management is the management of the configuration items, encompassing the technical and administrative tasks required to manage them, such as identification, maintenance, the controlled change, the status justification and the verification of these configuration items.

The goal of configuration management in a project is to ensure that:
- Everyone always works with the right products;
- All products are easily traceable;
- It is always known what the actual status of the various products is;
- These products do not get changed without authorization.

A **configuration** is the aggregate of a product's functional and technical properties, as described in the technical documentation and carried over into the product. The configuration of an organization is the aggregate of all the properties of that organization. The configuration of a project is the aggregate of the products to be delivered in a project.

A **configuration item** is a product managed using configuration management, or a product that is or should be managed (as the case may be). In a project this concerns all specialist products used or created during the project.

If wanted, management products can also be managed under configuration management. Usually, however, the management documents are only managed under information or document control.

9.3   Approach to change
The management products through which issues and changes can be controlled are:
- Configuration Management Strategy;
- Configuration Item Records;
- Product Status Account;
- Daily Log;
- Issue Register and Issue Reports.

Configuration Management Strategy
The Configuration Management Strategy describes how and by whom the products in a project will be controlled and protected. The Configuration Management Strategy must be derived from the corporate or programme organization's configuration management policy and configuration management processes.

The Configuration Management Strategy describes:

- The configuration management procedures;
- The issue and change control procedures;
- The records that have to be managed;
- The tools and techniques to be used;
- Categories to allow classification of the priority and severity of issues;
- The way of reporting on the status of the configuration items and the issues;
- Roles and responsibilities with regard to configuration management and issue and change control and the appointment of any Change Authority and the possible allocation of a change budget;
- The timing of configuration reviews and audits.

The Configuration Management Strategy is developed during the initiation stage and approved by the Project Board as part of the Project Initiation Documentation. The Configuration Management Strategy is evaluated at the end of each management stage and updated (if necessary).

A frequently used way of prioritizing the urgency of changes is the MoSCoW method. See also 'quality planning', section 6.5.

Configuration Item Records

A Configuration Item Record is a record in which all aspects of a configuration item to be controlled are set down, such as status, version and variants of a configuration item and the interrelations with other configuration items. Nowadays these are usually stored digitally. The aggregate of Configuration Item Records constitutes the configuration management database (CMDB).

The configuration management database is set up at the same time as developing the Configuration Management Strategy. However, not until the various plans are being developed and the relevant product breakdown structures and Product Descriptions are being produced can the details be entered into the individual Configuration Item Records. Every time the status or one of the other aspects of a configuration item changes, the relevant Configuration Item Record has to be modified (e.g. if the configuration item can be put into production when authorizing a Work Package or if the configuration is approved following a quality review).

It is important to organize the Configuration Item Records in such a way that the configuration database can be transferred to the customer organization in a straightforward manner when the project is closed.

Product Status Account

A Product Status Account is an account that describes the status of the configuration items. The status list can be prepared for the whole project's configuration items, but also for a stage or a Work Package. A Product Status Account is primarily used by the Project Manager to check the status and the version numbers of the configuration items. Such a Product Status Account is put together for the purpose of assessing a stage's status as part of the Managing a Stage Boundary process and during preparations for closing the project.

Daily Log

The Daily Log is the Project Manager's log. In it, the Project Manager records the various notes from discussions and meetings and all other issues that are worth noting and/or require follow-on during the day-to-day activities. Records can be set down in the relevant management documents from the Daily Log. For other issues that do not require a formal record, the Daily Log serves as a reference.

The Daily Log is organized as soon as the Project Manager starts work on the (future) project, i.e. as early as the start-up stage, as soon as the Project Manager is appointed for the project by the Executive.

Issue Register and Issue Reports

An Issue Register is a report in which all issues are recorded and which has to be formally monitored and acted on and in which the status of these issues is kept up to date. The Issue Register is created by Project Support at the same time as the Configuration Management Strategy is being prepared by the Project Manager. The Project Manager, however, is responsible for recording and updating the issues in the Issue Register. Formal issues originally entered in the Daily Log should be transferd to the Issue Register once the Issue Register is created.

The Issue Report is a file in which a record is maintained of all information that pertains to an issue, that must be acted on formally and that is therefore recorded in the Issue Register. In the Issue Report the issue is described in more detail than in the Issue Register. The Project Manager is responsible for preparing and updating the Issue Report.

The Issue Register and the Issue Report have to be updated as soon as an issue's impact and possible corrective actions have been established, as soon as it has been decided what corrective action has to be taken and as soon as it has been established that these actions have been implemented and the issue can be closed.

The following are recorded in the Issue Report:
- Identification number and type of issue;
- Date and the person that reported the issue;
- Description of the issue;
- Impact analysis, possible corrective action and recommendations;
- Priority and severity of the issue;
- Who drew up the Issue Report;
- Decision, date of decision and who took decision;
- Date issue closed.

The following are recorded in the Issue Register for each issue:
- Identification number and type of issue;
- Date and the person that reported the issue;
- Brief description of the issue;
- Priority and severity of the issue;
- Current status of the issue and the date on which the status was last updated;
- Date issue closed.

9.4 Configuration management procedures

The configuration management procedures in different projects can differ considerably from one another. Even within the very same project the configuration management procedures can differ considerably for the individual products. Obviously it still makes a difference whether the various components to be managed are from, for example, a plane or a new house that is being built.

However, for each project, more or less formal configuration management procedures are always required. It will not be the first time or the last time that project members on the shop floor use drawings or other documents that have not yet been approved, or that have been replaced by new versions. Configuration management is, therefore, not an option. Configuration management has to be utilized in every project. The only question is how detailed and how formal the configuration management should be.

Five steps are distinguished within the configuration management procedures:

- **Configuration management, planning** – Establish which products will be managed under configuration management, down to what level of detail configuration items will be split up and what details will be recorded in the individual Configuration Item Records.
- **Configuration management, identification** – Current identification and definition of the individual configuration items. Establishing a coding system and recording the collected data in the relevant Configuration Item Records in the configuration database.
  Identifying and defining the individual configuration items is what is described in the Planning theme as preparing a product breakdown structure and defining the relevant Product Descriptions.
- **Configuration management, control** – Controlling the configuration items *and* the Configuration Item Records. Baselining the approved products. Implementing changes upon authorization of the changes. Saving old versions. Receiving, storing and protecting configuration items. Releasing configuration items to authorized people. Updating the Configuration Item Records.
  For physical products, control of the configuration can encompass intake, storage and distribution from the warehouse.
- **Configuration management, status accounting** – Recording and reporting on the current and historical status of the configuration items and the changes implemented through Product Status Accounts.
- **Configuration management, verification and audit** – Reviewing the extent to which the current status of the configuration items corresponds with the official status recorded in the Configuration Item Records and assessing whether the set configuration management procedures are being complied with and are effective. Such reviews are primarily done at the end of a stage and at the end of the project.

For each of these stages and underlying activities individual procedures have to be established.

A proportion of the current desktop PCs no longer meet the requirements set by new software. For this reason, the management of Xantia has decided to launch a project to replace the oldest PCs and to upgrade the storage capacity of the newer PCs. They have asked

Els to manage the project. Els sets off briskly and uses the company's configuration database. However, at the implementation stage it emerges that the new software does not work on all upgraded PCs. It turns out that there is a greater quantity of different 'new' type PCs than is featured on the list. It also emerges that a proportion of the employees are using their 'own' applications on their PC. The new PCs, however, do not seem to support these applications. More detailed investigation reveals that the configuration database was far from up-to-date. An expensive affair, as a result of which work is lost and many orders have to be cancelled.

9.5 Issue control procedures and change control procedures

The issue and change control procedures also have five stages (see figure 9.1).

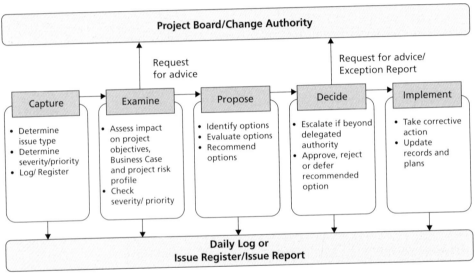

Figure 9.1 Issue and change control procedure (Source: Managing Successful Projects with PRINCE2, produced by OGC)

- **Capture** – Specify whether an issue can be dealt with informally or not. Specify the type of issue and an initial indication of the severity and priority of the issue. Record the issue in the Daily Log or in the Issue Register. For the latter, an Issue Report should also be produced. Inform the person that reported the issue that it has been recorded. Inform stakeholders involved in line with the agreements in the Communication Management Strategy.
  It is often sensible to ask the person that reported the issue to prepare the Issue Report. It can also be agreed that all formal issues must be reported using an Issue Report.
- **Examine** – Investigate what the impact of the issue is on the stage and project objectives, on the individual risks and on the risk profile of the stage and the overall product, on the Business Case, and on the interests of the individual stakeholders. Use the knowledge and experience of the team members. If necessary, ask members of the Project Board for advice and/or consult with the members of the Project Assurance. Determine the severity and priority of the issue. Update the Issue Report and the status in the Issue Register. Inform the person that reported the issue and the stakeholders concerned.

- **Propose** – Identify and evaluate the possible measures. Weigh up the costs and the added value of the different measures and the interests of the different stakeholders. Draw up a recommendation. Record the possible corrective action and the recommendation in the Issue Report. Update the status in the Issue Register.
- **Decide** – Present the issues to the person authorized to decide on them. Escalate the issue if there is a risk of the agreed tolerances being exceeded. Ensure that the necessary decisions are made. Record the decisions made in the Issue Report. Update the Issue Register. Inform the person that reported the issue and the stakeholders concerned.
- **Implement** – Implement the agreed measures or prepare an Exception Plan, by order of the Project Board. Close the issue, as soon as the measures have been implemented. If the measures implemented do not lead to the desired effect, record this as a new issue or re-open the existing issue. Inform the person that reported the issue and the stakeholders concerned.

A Project Board (or a Change Authority) can approve or reject a change request, but can also postpone the decision, request further information, or request that an Exception Plan be produced. With regard to an off-specification, the Project Board (or a Change Authority) actually has the same options, even though they may talk of accepting an exception to a specification rather than approving it. A concession is an off-specification accepted by a Change Authority or Project Board without corrective action (see figure 9.2).

Request for change	**Off-specification**
• Approve change	• Concession
• Reject	• Reject
• Defer decision	• Defer decision
• Request more information	• Request more information
• Ask for Exception Report	• Ask for Exception Report
Problem/concern	
• Provide guidance	
• Ask for Exception Report	

Figure 9.2 Responses of the Project Board to possible issues

9.6 Change Authority and change budget

It is the responsibility of the Project Board to assess change requests and off-specifications and to decide on these. This can take up a lot of time, however. It often requires a considerable degree of knowledge and insight into the situation and has to be considered in-depth with other parties outside the project in order to arrive at a correct decision. In view of these considerations and in view of the principle of managing by exception, it is therefore often reasonable to delegate the authority for making such decisions to a Change Authority, who can make such decisions on behalf of the Project Board.

Small changes and slight off-specifications can even be left to the Project Manager. For more important decisions, the authority can often be delegated to a separate Change Authority, with critical changes and off-specifications always having to be passed back to the Project Board. All changes and off-specifications that result in tolerances possibly being exceeded should always be escalated to the Project Board.

In order to have a little room for manoeuvre, it is sensible to give a Change Authority their own budget. The benefit of this budget is that costs relating to changes do not have to be at the expense of the operational budget or that the Executive does not have to escalate every change to the corporate or programme management over and over again.

Even if there is no separate Change Authority, it is advisable to create a separate change budget. This change budget subsequently falls under the responsibility of the Project Board. It stops the operational budget being devoured. Otherwise the contingency sum in particular is often misused for changes, be these wanted or unwanted. Combined with a strict issue and change budget and a good prioritization of changes (MoSCoW), a limited change budget can prevent a torrent of changes.

9.7 Roles and responsibilities

For an overview of the changes, roles&responsibilities for the Change theme, see table 9.1.

Corporate/programme management Provide corporate/programme CMS	Project Manager (PM) • Prepare CMS • Manage CM & CC procedures, assisted by Project Support • Create and maintain Issue Register, assisted by Project Support • Ensure TMs implement CM & CC measures • Implement corrective actions
Executive • Approve CMS: • Set scales for severity & priority • Determine change authority/budget • Respond to request for advice • Take decisions on issues	
	Team Manager (TM) • Implement CM & CC measures • Implement corrective actions
Senior User/ Supplier • Respond to request for advice • Take decisions on Issue Reports	**Project Support** • Maintain Configuration Item Records • Assist the PM to maintain Issue Register • Assist the PM with CM & CC procedures • Produce Product Status Accounts
Project Assurance • Advise on CMS • Advise on examining and solving issues	
• CC = Change Control • CM = Configuration Management • CMS = Configuration Management Strategy	

Table 9.1 Roles and responsibilities relevant to the Change theme

10 Progress

The aim of the Progress theme is to establish mechanisms in order to be able to monitor and compare actual achievements against those planned so that a forecast can be provided on the project objectives to be fulfilled, including the continued viability of the project, and to enable any unacceptable deviations to be controlled.

10.1 Introduction

The periodic monitoring and controlling of progress is one of the critical success factors in managing a project. It is not only important to produce a plan, have it approved and then react to all manner of problems that crop up. It is also important to reflect periodically on what has actually been achieved and the amount of effort that still has to be expended to deliver the project output. This provides the input needed to look ahead and adjust the course of the project proactively. Project Managers are not just firemen that have to put out fires, but also managers looking ahead and anticipating.

The Progress theme contributes directly to the principles of managing by stages, managing by exception and learning from experience.

10.2 Conceptual framework

Progress – The extent to which a plan's objectives are fulfilled. Progress can be measured on the level of the project, the stage and the Work Package.

Tolerance – The permitted deviation above and below a plan's objectives, within which escalation to the next higher management level is not necessary. Within PRINCE2, tolerances have to be agreed for time, money, scope, quality and benefits.

> In view of the fact that many projects in the programme could not be started due to the limited financing options, it had been agreed that if a project were to have more than a certain amount left, this would immediately be reported to the programme management. Due to the fact that in one of the projects the team was able to purchase things much cheaply than had been anticipated and that this was reported straight away, another project was able to start early using the funds that had become available.

Exception – A situation in which it is foreseen that an agreed tolerance will be exceeded. Exceptions must always be escalated to the next higher level of management.

Control mechanisms – Management procedures and products with which a plan's progress can be monitored, controlled and reported to next higher level of management.

Control mechanisms must ensure that for every management level in the project, the next higher management level:
- Is able to monitor the progress;
- Is able to compare the progress with the agreed plan;
- Is able to evaluate plans and options against future developments;
- Is able to record problems and identify risks;
- Is able to implement corrective measures;
- Is able to authorize work.

10.3 Management by exception

The philosophy behind the principle of management by exception is that effective governance can be achieved by allocating unequivocal responsibilities and authority to the respective levels of governance.

The advantage of working with the principle of management by exception if that the next higher level of management is only involved in the governance of the project if there is a reason for this. For the Executive in a project this will only be if there is a risk of agreed tolerances being exceeded, at decision times agreed in advance and if advice and direct intervention is required. The principle provides the Project Manager with room for manoeuvre, limits the number of meetings and prevents the Executive and other members of the Project Board continually looking over their shoulders and getting involved in directing things. A disadvantage is that it can easily create greater distance between the Executive/Project Board and the Project Manager and the project loses the ownership of the Executive. The principle of management by exception also requires a good degree of job-maturity both from those directing and those implementing the project.

An alternative is to manage the project on the basis of management by objectives (MBO). Management by objectives places significant emphasis on teamwork, openness and communication between management and workers. In this regard it is important that the objectives are set up together with the workers and that regular feedback on the state of affairs is provided - not in the form of progress reports but in the form of coaching and resolution of problems. Objectives within MBO are not used as an assessment tool but as an opportunity for development. In this regard, creating a win-win situation and paying attention to the workers' personal and/or career wishes is very important. MBO leads to regular discussion between the parties involved. This is not an PRINCE2 approach.

Within a PRINCE2 project the principle of management by exception is leant support by forming agreements on the following things:
- The Project Board will only meet at decision times agreed in advance and if interim advice and interim direction is needed.
- The Project Board will delegate the responsibility for assurance that the project is being implemented in accordance with the agreements and that the project objectives are being fulfilled to a separate Project Assurance.
- The Project Board will delegate part of the responsibility for decision-making and off-specifications to a Change Authority.

- The Project Board will delegate the day-to-day leadership of the project to the Project Manager within agreed tolerances and with Highlight Reports at pre-agreed intervals.
- The Project Manager will escalate to the Project Board using an Exception Report when it is anticipated that agreed tolerances will be exceeded.

10.4 Progress, control

In a PRINCE2 project, progress is controlled by:
- Delegating responsibilities *and* authority;
- Dividing the project up into management stages;
- Time-driven and event-driven reports and reviews;
- Raising exceptions.

Delegating responsibilities and authority
The four management levels

Between each of the four management levels in the project management structure, agreements have to be made on responsibilities and authority to be delegated.

PRINCE2 recognizes six performance areas that have to be managed in every project, namely time, money, scope, quality, risks and benefits. For each of these performance areas tolerances have to be agreed upon among the various management levels in the project management structure. Team Manager, Project Manager and Project Board must each report regularly to the next higher management level. If there is a risk of tolerances being exceeded, then this has to be escalated to the next higher management level (see figure 10.1).

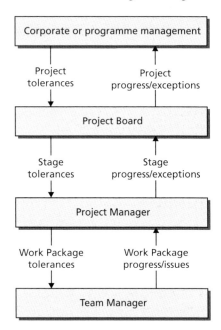

Figure 10.1 Delegating tolerance and reporting actual and forecast progress (Source: Managing Successful Projects with PRINCE2, produced by OGC)

- **The corporate or programme management** is responsible for determining the final project output and the objectives within which the final project output will have to be delivered and also specifies the tolerances linked with the project.
- **The Project Board** is responsible for directing the project as a whole and reports on this to the corporate or programme management. The Project Board specifies the stage tolerances for the Project Manager. If there is a risk of the project tolerances being exceeded, then the Project Board must escalate this to the corporate or programme management.
- **The Project Manager** is responsible for the day-to-day leadership of the project within the authorized stage and reports on this to the Project Board. The Project Manager specifies the Work Package tolerances for the relevant Team Manager. If there is a risk of the stage or project tolerances being exceeded, the Project Manager must escalate this to the Project Board.
- **The Team Manager** is responsible for producing the specialist products and reports on this to the Project Manager. If there is a risk of the Work Package tolerances being exceeded, then the Team Manager must escalate this to the Project Manager.

The six tolerance areas for each level

The various tolerances for time, money, scope, quality, risks and benefits are recorded at project, stage and Work Package level in different management products (see figure 10.2).

Tolerance areas	Project level tolerances	Stage level tolerances	Work Package level tolerances	Product level tolerances
Time	Project Plan	Stage Plan	Work Package	N.A.
Cost	Project Plan	Stage Plan	Work Package	N.A.
Scope	Project Plan	Stage Plan	Work Package	N.A.
Risk	Risk Management Strategy	Stage Plan	Work Package	N.A.
Quality	Project Product Description	N.A.	N.A.	Project Product Description
Benefits	Business Case	N.A.	N.A.	N.A.

Figure 10.2 The six tolerance areas by level (Source: Managing Successful Projects with PRINCE2, produced by OGC)

- **Tolerances in time, money and scope** – Recorded in the Project Plan and in the relevant Stage Plans and Work Packages.
- **Risk tolerances** – Recorded at project level in the Risk Management Strategy. At stage and Work Package level the risk tolerances are recorded in the relevant Stage Plans and Work Packages.
- **Quality tolerances** – Recorded at project level in the Project Product Description. At stage and Work Package level quality tolerances are recorded in the relevant Product Descriptions.
- **Benefit tolerances** – In PRINCE2, only recorded at project level and in the Business Case.

Time, money and scope are the primary tolerance areas. From the perspective of PRINCE2 the tolerances in quality must be handled with the utmost restraint.

Control mechanisms

The Project Board's most important control mechanisms are:

- **Authorizations** – For the initiation, start and implementation of the project, the subsequent stages and ultimately the closure of the project, the accompanying stage tolerances and approval of the documents present for these.
- **Progress updates** – The Highlight Reports, the End Stage Reports and the End Project Reports.
- **Changes and exceptions** – The Issue Reports and the Exception Reports.

The Project Manager's most important control mechanisms are:

- **Authorizations** – For the individual Work Packages and the Work Package tolerances.
- **Progress updates** – The Checkpoint Reports, the team meetings and the Product Status Accounts.
- **Changes and exceptions** – Issues and risks that are reported/identified and the various records and logs such as the Issue Register, the Risk Register and the Quality Register and the Lessons Log.

Dividing the project up into management stages

Management stages – Comprise temporary divisions in time, linked to go/no go decisions pertaining to continuation of the project. There are at least two management stages in every project - the initiation stage and the implementation stage. The implementation stage can be further divided into several individual management stages, all depending on the complexity and the context of the project. The decision as to whether the implementation stage will be divided up into management stages (and, if so, how many) is made during the initiation stage when setting up the project controls and is confirmed on approval of the Project Initiation Documentation when the Project Board authorizes the project.

Technical stages – Stages characterized by the application of a set of techniques or specialist work. Technical stages often include design stage, production stage and roll-out stage. Technical stages can overlap one another. There are usually more technical stages than management stages.

The management stages, **number** depends on:

- How far in advance can plans reasonably be made;
- Where the decision times are in the project;
- The number of risks surrounding the project;
- The desired extent of project control: too many short stages as opposed to too few long stages;
- Confidence of Project Board and Project Manager that the project will be continued.

A large number of short stages offer a lot of control, but also take a lot of time and constantly cause interruptions to the implementation. This is particularly undesirable if there is a risk of team members being put to work elsewhere and then no longer being available for the project. In a management stage it is always a matter of a decision on whether or not to continue with the project. Updating the Business Case takes time. In such cases, it is not possible to press on with the work, or a short, temporary task has to be assigned specially. With long stages, on the other hand, there is another, lower level of control. It is possible to press on with projects unnoticed, whereas in actual fact the business justification of the project in its present form has long since disappeared.

The management stages, **duration** depends on:
- The planning horizon in which plans can still be made with sufficient accuracy;
- The technical stages in the project;
- Harmony with the corporate or programme activities;
- The overall risk level in the project.

The end of the financial year or the end of a programme stage can necessitate a go/no go decision for a project, thereby establishing the end of a management stage.

If a go/no go decision has to be made in the middle of a technical stage, then the technical stage will have to be split up so that the first part of the technical stage can be delivered prior to the time of the decision (see figure 10.3).

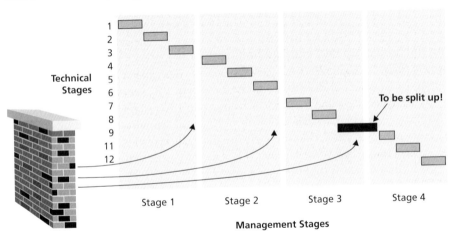

Figure 10.3 Management and technical stages

Time-driven and event-driven reports and reviews
PRINCE2 has time-driven and event-driven reports:
- **Time-driven reports** – These are done at a set point in time or in a fixed time-based cycle, such as the Checkpoint Reports and Highlight Reports.
- **Event-driven reports** – These are done at the end of a stage (End Stage Report), or at the end of a project (End Project Report), or if there is a risk of tolerances being exceeded (Exception Report).

Baselines for managing progress are:
- **Project Plan** – Used by the Project Board to monitor and steer the project stage by stage.
- **Stage Plan** – Used by the Project Manager for the day-to-day leadership of the project during a stage.

- **Exception Plan** – Used for the direction of the work required to correct the effects of (any risk of) the tolerances being exceeded. Both a Project Exception Plan and a Stage Exception Plan can be prepared.
- **Work Package** – Used by the Project Manager to assign work in a stage to a Team Manager.

Control mechanisms for reviewing progress are:
- **Daily Log** – The Project Manager's personal log. This can be used to record actions and issues that can be dealt with informally.
- **Issue Register and Issue Report** – To record change requests, off-specifications and other formal issues.
- **Product Status Account** – To record the status of the configuration items. This is desirable if the Project Manager wishes to check the status and the versions of the configuration items.
- **Quality Register** – To record all planned and implemented quality activities and as a reference for all quality and approval files.
- **Risk Register** – To record all risks that have to be managed formally, including the respective risk responses.

Recording and reporting lessons:
- **Lessons Log** – To record lessons from previous projects that could be used in the project at hand and to record the lessons in one's own project during implementation of the project itself.
- **Lessons Report** – To report lessons to the corporate or programme management through the Project Board for other current and future projects. Lessons Reports can be prepared during the various stage transitions. A Lessons Report must be produced when closing the project.

Formal records can be set down in the various registers. Files that can be dealt with informally are recorded in the various logs, such as the Daily Log and the Lessons Log.

Reporting on progress:
- **Highlight Report** – Prepared by the Project Manager at agreed times or agreed intervals in order to inform the Project Board of the highlights of the stage's progress and the issues and risks that have arisen. Highlight Reports can also be sent to other stakeholders, if this has been agreed in the Communication Management Strategy.
- **Checkpoint Report** – Prepared by the individual Team Managers at agreed times or agreed intervals in order to inform the Project Manager of the agreed Work Packages' progress and the issues and risks that have arisen in this regard.
- **End Stage Report** – Prepared by the Project Manager at the end of a management stage in order to report to the Project Board on the stage that has just been finished and to enable them to authorize continuation of the project.
- **End Project Report** – Prepared by the Project Manager at the end of the project in order to justify the project to the Project Board and to enable them to authorize closing the project.

Escalating exceptions

If it is anticipated that the agreed tolerances will be exceeded, an exception must be escalated to the next higher level of management:

- **Exception to Work Package tolerances** – If it is anticipated that a Work Package tolerance will be exceeded, then the Team Manager must escalate this to the Project Manager by means of an issue. If the risk of exceeding a Work Package tolerance stays within the stage tolerances, then the Project Manager must take corrective action and authorize one or more new or adapted Work Packages for the relevant Team Managers.
- **Exception to stage tolerances** – If it is anticipated that a stage tolerance will be exceeded, the the Project Manager must escalate this to the Project Board using an Exception Report. The Project Board can decide simply to press ahead with the project or can ask for an Exception Plan. If in doubt, the Project Board can ask for further information and/or can request advice from the corporate or programme management.
- **Exception to project tolerances** – If it is anticipated that a project tolerance will be exceeded, then the Project Manager must also escalate this to the Project Board using an Exception Report, but the Project Board itself must escalate this to the corporate or programme management for a decision. In consultation with the corporate or programme management, the Project Board can decide to still press ahead with the project, request an Exception Plan or decide to end the project prematurely.

For the composition of the various management products for controlling progress, see appendix A.

10.5 Roles and responsibilities

For an overview of the progress, roles and responsibilities for the Progress theme, see table 10.1.

Corporate/ programme management	Project Manager (PM)
• Provide project tolerances in mandate • Approve project Exception Plans **Executive** • Provide stage tolerances • Approve stage Exception Plans • Ensure that progress towards the outcome remains consistent from the business perspective • Recommend future actions in project Exception Plans **Senior User** • Ensure that progress towards the outcome remains consistent from the user perspective **Senior Supplier** • Ensure that progress towards the outcome remains consistent from the supplier perspective **Project Assurance** • Monitor changes to the Project Plan in terms of impact on the Business Case • Confirm stage and project progress against agreed tolerances	• Authorize Work Packages • Monitor progress against Stage Plan • Produce Highlight Reports • Produce End Stage and End Project Reports • Produce Exception Reports • Maintain project's registers and logs **Team Manager (TM)** • Agree Work Package with PM • Produce Team Plan if applicable • Inform Project Support about quality checks • Produce Checkpoint Reports • Notify PM about forecast deviation from tolerances **Project Support** • Assist with compilation of reports • Contribute with specialist expertise • Maintain Issue, Risk and Quality Register on behalf of the PM

Table 10.1 Roles and responsibilities relevant to the Progress theme

Part II Processes

II Introduction to processes

II.1 Why a process-based approach?

In order to manage a project, it is reasonable to approach it like a process. A process aims at reaching a specific goal by means of a structured set of activities. A process approach provides the opportunity for adjusting the course of the project in changing circumstances. The process-based approach is followed by all modern project management methods.

II.2 Four management levels

According to PRINCE2, project management is based on the presence of four management levels: three management levels in the project itself and corporate or programme management. Each management level has its own specific role:

- **Governing** – This is the responsibility of corporate or programme management. The corporate or programme management itself is not part of the project, but does define the project objectives and the deliverables. Corporate or programme management also uses the project output to be able to implement the planned corporate activities and to achieve the anticipated benefits.
- **Directing** – This is the responsibility of the Project Board. The Project Board is chaired by the Executive. The Executive is the representative of the customer's corporate or programme management in the project and is accountable for project fulfillment in accordance with said corporate or programme management. The Project Board makes all the important decisions in the project and lends direction and leadership to the project as a whole.
- **Managing** – This is one of the Project Manager's responsibilities. The Project Manager is responsible for the day-to-day leadership of the project, for leading the Team Managers and for assisting the Project Board's decision-making, e.g. by providing information and updates on the project. The Project Manager is responsible for the project within the framework set by the Project Board.
- **Delivery** – This is the responsibility of the Team Manager. The team members are responsible for the ultimate production of the deliverables. The Team Manager leads the team leaders.

For successful organization, implementation and closure of a project it is important that the various management levels communicate properly with one another.

PRINCE2 can be tailored and so different roles/levels can be combined in a small project: the Project Manager, for example, can take on the role of Project Support and Team Manager. This is not relevant to the PRINCE2 methodology. In such cases, different activities can be combined for the individual projects. In chapter 19 we will look at the management of small and/or informal projects.

II.3 The management processes

In order to manage a project seven processes are distinguished, namely:

- Starting up a Project (SU);
- Directing a Project (DP);
- Initiating a Project (IP);
- Controlling a Stage (CS);
- Managing Product Delivery (MP);
- Managing a Stage Boundary (SB);
- Closing a Project (CP).

The processes are broken down based on the activities being performed during the project and those responsible (see figure II.1).

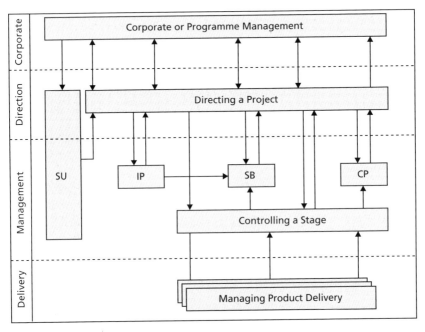

Figure II.1 PRINCE2 process model (Based on OGC PRINCE2 material)

Each process has a number of activities that are/can be performed within that process. Some processes are implemented once within a project, others can be implemented several times.

II.4 PRINCE2 processes in a temporal framework

As a minimum, a project will have an initiation stage ('thinking') and an implementation stage ('doing'). Implementation means the aggregate of specialist work performed in order to produce the project's final products, such as the design, work preparation, fulfillment and implementation. The implementation stage can be subdivided into several management stages. Before the project can be started, however, a number of things do have to be arranged.

Thus the following project lifecycle is adhered to:

- **Pre-project preparation** – Here the project organization is established and the Project Brief and the plan for the Initiation Stage are prepared. These activities are performed in the Starting up a Project (SU) process. Key to this is the question as to whether the project is viable.
- **Initiation stage** – After the decision has been made to start the project, all information describing how the project will be carried out must be gathered and a plan made as to how and when the results of the project will be delivered. In the initiation stage the Initiating a Project (IP) and Managing a Stage Boundary (SB) processes take place
- **Delivery stage(s)** – The implementation stages carry into effect what has been agreed in the initiation stage. In the delivery stages the Controlling a Stage (CS), Managing Product Delivery (MP) and Managing a Stage Boundary (SB) processes are performed.
- **Final delivery stage** – Once all products have been delivered, transferred and accepted, the Project Manager will complete the project. In the final delivery stage the processes of Controlling Stage (CS), Managing Product Delivery (MP) and Closing a Project (CP) are performed. Completing a project is undertaken in Closing a Project (CP).

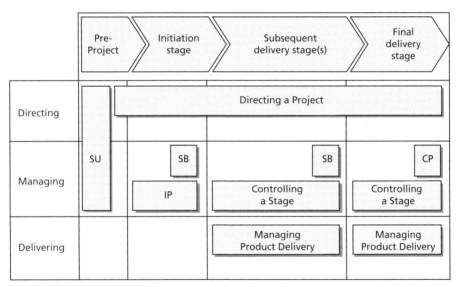

Figure II.2 Key to process diagrams (Source: Managing Successful Projects with PRINCE2, produced by OGC)

The Directing a Project (DP) process describes the Project Board's tasks and responsibilities. This process begins on completion of the Starting up a Project process and runs throughout the lifecycle of the project.

II.5   The structure of the process descriptions
Each process will be described in the following chapters using the following format:
- **Basic principles**
  - What is the aim of the process?
  - Why is the relevant process necessary?
  - What has to be accomplished during the process?

- **Context** – Indicates the relationship between the process and the other processes and with the project's environment.
- **Process description** – Describes how the objectives of the project are fulfilled by means of a set of activities. The activities will be described in an order that is as logical as possible. Usually there is no strict order to the activities, however, and they are performed iteratively.
- **Overview of activities** – Provides an overview of all input and output products and responsibilities for the process activities to be distinguished.

Each project must run through all processes in the process model. However, the extent to which this has to be done will depend on the size, lead-time and complexity of the project. Another important consideration is if the resources to be used are internal or external to the organisation, or if the project is part of a larger project or programme.

It is important to tailor the process for the current project. The question is still how extensively the (sub)processes have to be run through and to what extent the relevant information has to be recorded officially. Small and internal projects can effectively be implemented with little paperwork. In chapter 19 we will look at how the arrangement of a project can be adapted to the circumstances. Managing within different kinds of projects and managing projects within a programme are also explained there.

11 SU, Starting up a Project

The aim of the Starting up a Project (SU) process is to ensure that the prerequisites for initiating a project are present, by answering the question 'Do we have a viable project that is worth the effort?'

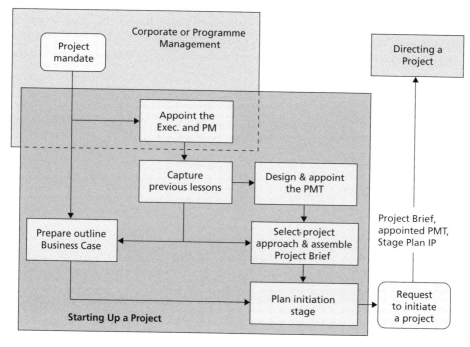

Figure 11.1 Overview of Starting up a Project (Based on OGC PRINCE2 material)

11.1 SU, basic principles

The basic principles for the SU process are:

- There must be a business justification to initiate the project (recorded in the outline Business Case).
- No work can be carried out before responsibilities have been defined and roles filled.
- Sufficient information must be available in order to be able to define and confirm the scope of the project (Project Brief).
- An Initiation Stage Plan must be prepared and approved before a start is made on the work in the initiation stage.
- There must be a shared idea regarding the different solution approaches for the project and a choice of approach before the initiation work can be started.

If there is no business justification to start a project, then one should not be started. If it is unclear why a project is necessary for the organization, then the chances of completing a project successfully are slim. The lack of a good Business Case is one of the most important reasons projects fail.

Certain information is needed to be able to start the initiation stage. It is important that there is a realistic picture of the scope, planning, acceptance criteria and prerequisites. Various parties are already involved in the project in the initiation stage and they are incurring expenses for the project. If it is unclear at the beginning of the initiation stage what the Executive is hoping to achive with the project, then these parties will work on the project from several angles in this stage. This can lead to friction, frustration, ineffective deployment of people and resources, and constitutes a poor basis for implementing the project.

As a minimum, a project requires an Executive and a Project Manager that have agreed to implement the project. The other members of the Project Board should also be appointed in this stage. In general, the people involved in the initiation stage will take also important roles in the project's delivery.

A plan must be prepared for all work. This also goes for the work carried out in the initiation stage. Users and suppliers are already involved in the project in the initiation stage. Agreements need to be made in terms of what will be delivered, by whom, when, how and in what level of detail. It is important to have a controlled start to the project and so a plan should be made and the arrangements for working on the project agreed..

11.2 Context

The Starting up a Project process is not a *part* of the project but constitutes the pre-project work. The project does not start until after the Project Board authorizes the Initiating a Project process based on the results of the SU process. The SU process lasts a relatively short time compared to the overall lead-time of the project.

Receipt of a mandate to start the project sets off the Starting up a Project process. The reasons for the project should be stated in this mandate, as well as what the Executive is hoping to achieve with the project. The project mandate is issued by the customer's corporate or programme management.

The project mandate could be a substantial document, but it could also be a verbal request or a set of drawings on the back of a packet of cigars. If the future project component is from a programme, the project mandate usually encompasses the full content of a Project Brief. In such cases, it falls to the Project Manager to validate the Project Brief, make any amendments and to have the document ratified.

The Starting up a Project process begins with the appointment of the Executive and the Project Manager by the corporate or programme management. They look at the lessons learned from the past and then design the project management team and appoint the individuals for the various roles within the project management team. The Business Case is prepared in outline and the project approach is determined. The Project Brief is produced and finally the Stage Plan for the initiation stage is prepared.

11.3 SU, process description

In order to be able to answer the question as to whether there is a viable project that is worth the effort, a number of aspects have to be sorted out. To this end, activities are performed within the the SU process.

The Starting up a Project process consists of the following activities:
- Appoint Executive and Project Manager;
- Capture previous lessons;
- Design and appoint project management team;
- Prepare outline Business Case;
- Select project approach and assemble Project Brief;
- Plan initiation stage.

Appoint Executive and Project Manager

First of all the Executive and the Project Manager are appointed by the corporate or programme management. Their tasks, responsibilities and authority are established and agreed, as is the required investment of time. It is sensible to have the appointment and the role descriptions confirmed by the corporate or programme management.

When appointing the Executive and the Project Manager, the project mandate is used. It is important that the Executive be able to get behind the project initiative, that the Executive actively wishes to and is able to propagate it and that the Executive is suited to his/her role. Based on what is needed, the Project Manager's role description is produced and the most suitable candidate selected. The Project Manager and the Executive must form a shared idea of the project based on the project mandate. The Project Manager must also be able to get behind the project and want to and be able to provide it with well-reasoned direction. The appointments are ratified within the corporate or programme management.

Whilst carrying out the initial work, the Project Manager also creates the Daily Log for the project. In this log, issues and risks that have been identified are also provisionally recorded providing that no formal Issue and Risk Registers have already been set up.

Capture previous lessons

It could be important to learn from previous experience for the project to be successful. If the strengths and weakness of the organization are known, as well as what approach or techniques work well or not so well, this can affect the choices made with regard to filling roles. The approach and estimates for the Business Case could also benefit from a review of past experiences. It is important to remember that good foundations are more likly to result in successful projects.

The lessons can be captured by looking at Lessons Reports from other relevant projects or programmes, but also by looking at the lessons learned within the company or by external organizations. This forms the start of one's own Lessons Log, which is set up in the SU by the Project Manager under the responsibility of the Executive. The log can be added to in discussions with other people or teams.

Design and appoint project management team

The right man or woman for the job. Sounds simple, but it is not. In addition to having the right knowledge, the people in the project management team also have to have sufficient authority and responsibility to be able to make good decisions within the given period of time. The composition of the project management team should represent the interests of all the stakeholders in a balanced manner. When putting together the project management team, the project mandate, the Lessons Log and the role descriptions for the Executive and the Project Manager are used.

> *The project management team encompasses the Project Board, the Project Manager, the Team Managers, the Change Authority, the Project Support and the Project Assurance.*

The composition of the Project Board in particular is extremely important. Produce a list of the stakeholders, design a possible Project Board and look at whether certain Project Board tasks can be delegated to a separate Project Assurance. Look at whether separate Team Managers and/ or Project Support have to be appointed, prepare role descriptions and select candidates for the individual roles.

It could be the case that the people that are available are not the right people for the specific roles within the project management team. However, in practice it is extremely difficult to leave people out once they have been nominated explicitly. If you are working from the perspective of a project management team concept, and the accompanying role descriptions, these kinds of situations can be prevented.

It is essential that all members of the project management team know what their objective, role and accompanying tasks, responsibilities and authority are and what the communication and reporting lines are. This has to be discussed explicitly and agreed with all members of the project management team and then set down in writing. Ensure that there is no overlap between the different roles. The appointment of the members of the project management team and their role descriptions are confirmed by the corporate or programme management.

Any risks attached to setting up the project management team should be recorded in the Daily Log.

Prepare outline Business Case

The Business Case contains estimates on time and costs, together with a description of the desired outcome and the benefits that are to be delivered with it. In addition to this, the different business options are weighed up and agreements on financing are detailed in the Business Case. It answers the question as to whether the project is worth the effort.

The Executive is responsible for the Business Case and for preparing it. In practice the Project Manager will be responsible for its development and will adopt the Business Case method used. The outline Business Case is based on the information from the project mandate. If the project is part of a programme, there is a possibility that a Business Case has already been prepared.

Usually it is the case that not much information is available yet at this stage of the project. In order to get a good idea of what has to be delivered, the Project Manager prepares the Project Product Description in consultation with the Executive and the Senior User. Here too attention is given to the agreements already made with regard to (service) contracts, quality expectations and acceptance criteria, and the time estimate from the project mandate is validated. During this activity it is also important to set the most important project milestones. Perform a risk analysis and record the risks identified in the Daily Log. Record risks that could endanger the viability of the project in the Business Case.

What is important is that the Business Case provides sufficient clarity for the Project Board to make decisions. It could be necessary to test the draft Business Case with the corporate or programme management. The Business Case will be expanded in more detail in the initiation stage.

Select project approach and assemble Project Brief

Before planning can be prepared in the initiation stage, it has to be established how the project output is to be accomplished. Will the output be purchased or will the work be carried out in-house or outsourced? Will existing products be used or will entirely new products be developed?

Important aspects that could play a role in the choice of project approach include:
- The set prerequisites with regard to time, money and quality;
- The available versus desired deployment and quality of people and resources;
- The applicable corporate and industrial standards;
- The lessons the organization has learned from previous experience;
- The risks associated with the various ways of working;
- The implementation of other projects and programmes.

The project approach is established on the basis of the defined risks, the corporate and industrial standards and best practice. It is important that the Executive and service provider have the same idea with regard to the approach. The project approach is part of the Project Brief.

The Project Brief is an important starting document. It is important that the Project Brief is endorsed by all members of the Project Board and the Project Manager. The members of the Project Board have to be convinced that it is worthwhile commencing the project. The Project Brief is discussed with all stakeholders. This is essential for generating support and for good management of expectations.

The project mandate forms the basis of the Project Brief. It could be that the information as it is described in the project mandate needs revising.

The Project Brief provides the project definition and the framework within which the project has to be implemented. The customer quality expectations and acceptance criteria (functional specifications) should be recorded and prioritized at this stage, as should the most significant risks. These aspects all form part of the Project Brief.

This activity is essential, even if the project is part of a programme and the programme has already defined a complete Project Brief. In this case it could be that parts of the Project Brief need to be modified or developed. In this way, support and commitment are also obtained from the various parties involved. Naturally changes and additions to the Project Brief should be discussed and agreed with the programme management.

Project Brief

Project definition:
- Background: context of the project and the reason for starting the project;
- Project objectives: the targets with regard to the various control aspects;
- Desired outcome: desired changes that the Executive hopes to achieve by means of the output to be delivered;
- Scope: the aggregate of products to be delivered and activities to be performed;
- Exclusion: what does not fall within the scope of the project;
- Project tolerances with regard to the various control aspects;
- Constraints under which the project has to be achieved;
- Assumptions upon which the brief has been based;
- Relationship with other projects: both dependencies with regard to products and the critical deployment of people and resources.

Outline Business Case;
- A description of the project's contribution to the corporate objectives, expressed in measurable units (if possible);
- Why this project has been selected instead of other activities;
- Risks: a list of the most significant risks and the overall risk of achieving the project output and the desired results.

Project management structure:
- Description of the roles and responsibilities;
- Candidate references.

Project Product Description:
- Customer quality expectations (e.g. of Senior User and Executive), both with regard to the process and the project output.
- Acceptance criteria: the requirements the customer is setting on the end product.

Plan initiation stage

During the initiation stage, the Project Initiation Documentation is prepared and the Stage Plan for the first delivery stage is developed. It is important that it is established in advance what exactly needs to be delivered for this purpose and in what level of detail, who has to do what work, how reporting on this will be done, what needs to be ready when and who has to review what for acceptance. Preparing the Project Initiation Documentation and the Stage Plan takes time and effort from both users and the supplier. This renders careful planning of these activities necessary. If this is not determined until after the initiation stage has been authorized by the Project Board then it will be too late. In such cases it is likely that the time required for the people involved will fall short and the work is not completed as planned. This could mean that approval is needed to extend any resource requirements, and may result in delays.

In a programme context the initiation stage should fit within the overall planning of the prorgramme. Sometimes in the Initiation Stage Plan specific implications for the programme can also come to light.

The Initiation Stage Plan is prepared on the basis of what has been recorded in the Project Brief, the defined risks in the Daily Log and the leassons learned captured in the Lessons Log. The Project Manager is responsible for preparing the Initiation Stage Plan. Support is provided by Project Support and Project Assurance, under the overall supervision of the Senior Supplier. The person delegated by the Executive as Project Assurance should indicate how the Business Case will have to be produced and assessed during the initiation stage.

Both the Project Brief and the Initiation Stage Plan are submitted to the Project Board for approval. On the basis of this, the Project Board decides whether the initiation stage (and therefore the project) can be started.

11.4 Overview of SU activities

In table 11.1 the input and output and the responsibilities for all activities for the Starting up a Project process are depicted.

Input Triggers	Input Management Products	Activity	Output Management Products	CP	Ex	PB	PM	TM	PA	PS	Input Triggers
Project mandate		Appoint the Executive and the PM	Executive role description (PBr) (c)	P	P						
			Appointed Executive	P	P						
			PM role description (PBr) (c)	A	P						
			Appointed PM	A	P						
			Daily Log (c)				P				
	Previous Lessons Reports	Capture previous lessons	Lessons Log (c)		R		P				
	Lessons Log; Executive role description (PBr); PM role description (PBr)	Design and appoint PMT	PMT role descriptions (PBr) (c)		A		P				
			PMT structure (PBr) (c)		A		P				
			Appointed PMT	A	P		P				
			Daily Log (u)				P				
Project mandate	Lessons Log	Prepare the outline Business Case	(Outline) Business Case (PBr) (c)	A	P	R	R		R		
			Project Product Description (PBr) (c)		(A)	(A)	P		R		
			Daily Log (u)				P				
	All previous parts of Project Brief; Lessons Log	Select the project approach and assemble the Project Brief	Assembled Project Brief		(A)	(A)	P		R		
			Project approach (PBr) (c)		(A)	(A)	P		R		
			Additional role descriptions (PBr) (c)		(A)	(A)	P		R		
			Daily Log (u)				P				
	Project Brief; Daily Log; Lessons Log	Plan the initiation stage	Stage Plan (c)		(A)	(A)	P		R		*Request to initiate a project*
			Daily Log (u)				P				

Legend:

Input / Output products
CM: Configuration Management
EPR: End Project Report
ESR: End Stage Report
PBr: Project Brief
PID: Project Initiation Documentation
PMT: Project management team
SP: Stage Plan

(a) Approved
(c) Created
(o) Obtained
(u) Updated

Responsibilities
CP: Corporate / Programme Management
Ex: Executive
PB: Project Board
PM: Project Manager
TM: Team Manager
PA: Project Assurance
PS: Project Support

A – Approver
P – Producer
C - Confirmer
R - Reviewer

In addition all input management products are reviewed

Table 11.1 Overview of the activities of Starting up a Project

12 IP, Initiating a Project

The purpose of the Initiating a Project (IP) process is the laying of a good foundation for the project, which enables the organization to become aware of the work that has to be done to deliver the project result, before considerable expenditure is authorized.

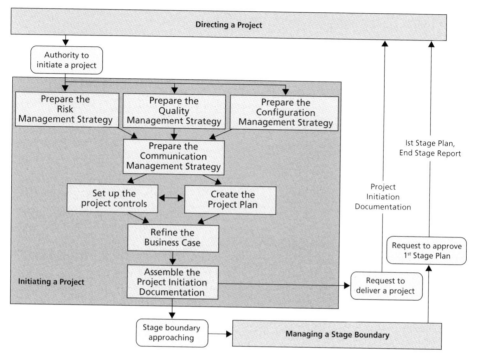

Figure 12.1 Overview of Initiating a Project (based on OGC PRINCE2 material)

12.1 IP, basic principles

For a successful project, the following applies:
* A project is finite with a defined starting and ending point.
* It must clear to all parties what is to be achieved by the project, why the project is necessary, how the results are to be realized and what the responsibilities of all parties involved in this are, before work on the project is started. In this way commitment is created.
* Well-managed projects have a greater chance of success.

Problems develop if it is not clear where the project begins and where it ends. This results in a lack of understanding of where the responsibility of the project and the line organization begins and ends. This leads to mistakes and frustrations and does not do the project any good. The start as well as the end of a project must be defined clearly. In the Starting up a Project process the project is defined along its main lines. In the Initiating a Project process this information is developed further in the Project Initiation Documentation. Where there is a relationship with an external organizations then it is certainly advisable to devote considerable attention to this.

Commitment is one of the most important prerequisites for the realization of a successful project. This should be addressed from the beginning of the project. This clarity is necessary in terms of what is to be achieved, why, by whom and in what manner. It must also become clear who may decide about what, which capital expenditures and risks are involved in the project and how the quality expectations are to be realized. Agreements must be reached about dealing with issues, risks and changes and how progress will be measured and reported.

The basic rule for good project management, 'think first, then do', is essential for a successful project. A comprehensive document for the total project is necessary before work on the project can be started.

12.2 Context

The IP process commences as soon as the Project Board authorize initiation. Once the Project Initiation Documentation is assembled, the Managing a Stage Boundary process is triggered to create the Stage Plan for the (next) delivery stage.

The Initiating a Project process is the second process in the PRINCE2 process model. It is, however, the first process in the project. The first process in the process model is Starting up a Project, but this process happens before the actual start of the project..

The IP process begins with the setting up of strategies for risk management, configuration management, quality management and communication. The Project Plan is produced and the project controls are agreed. The Business Case is tested and specified more narrowly. The Risk Register is organized and the risks are assessed again and improved. Finally the Project Initiation Documentation is assembled and the Managing a Stage Boundary process is triggered to set up the Stage Plan for the first delivery stage and to evaluate the Initiation Stage. The activities have a logical sequence during this time, but can also be partly repetitive.

The Project Board is able to assure by means of the Project Initiation Documentation and the Stage Plan of the first delivery stage that the project is in line with business and programme objectives. The Initiating a Project process also sees to it that the Project Board become the owners of the project. It is important that the Project Manager has regular contact with the Project Board members both individually and collectively during the Initiation of a Project to ensure that the Project Initiation Documentation becomes a document of the Project Board and the Project Manager together and not of the Project Manager alone. The more members of the Project Board take ownership of the project, the more support the Project Manager will experience during the project. On the basis of the Project Initiation Documentation, the Project Board assesses whether the project is viable (go/no go) and authorizes the effort of the people in the undertaking the first delivery stage on the basis of the Stage Plan.

12.3 Process Description

The objective of the Initiating a Project process is to ensure that a basis agreement is made for the entire project in the form of a Project Initiation Documentation. A Stage Plan for the first delivery stage is produced with detailed arrangements about who does what, when and in what way during the first delivery stage.

The Project Initiation Documentation and the Stage Plan can be agreed upon formally as well as informally. However, it is preferable for any decision on the PID to be recorded in writing. Experience has shown that the memory of what has been agreed upon can differ considerably after weeks, and sometimes even after days, especially if circumstances have changed in the meantime.

The Initiating a Project process consists of the following activities:
- Prepare a Risk Management Strategy;
- Prepare a Configuration Management Strategy;
- Prepare a Quality Management Strategy;
- Prepare a Communication Management Strategy;
- Set up Project Controls;
- Create the Project Plan;
- Refine the Business Case;
- Assemble the Project Initiation Documentation.

Prepare the Risk Management Strategy

The Risk Management Strategy describes objectives, procedures, responsibilities and techniques for the application of risk management. It is therefore all about the way in which risk management is applied within the project, providing the framework for risk tolerance and the risk moments when risks must be analysed and reported.

The Risk Management Strategy is formulated by the Project Manager and approved by the Project Board. The Executive is primarily responsible for ensuring the activities of risk management are integral to the project. The point is that risk management is not only a paper exercise; it plays a role in choices that have to be made during the entire project. This links up as far as possible with the standards of business or project management. Following the Risk Management Strategy, the Risk Register is organized and filled in from the Daily Log. This is coordinated with Project Assurance.

Prepare a Configuration Management Strategy

The Configuration Management Strategy provides the project with the ability to control its management and specialist products effectively. What must be controlled under configuration management and at what level of detail differs in every project and is also dependent on the subject and the complexity of the project. In the Configuration Management Strategy the objectives, procedures and techniques for the application of configuration management are specified.

This involves a review of the Project Brief to check whether there are business or programme standards that must be observed. Check the learning points of previous projects and learning points arising out of business and programme management. Review the Risk and Issue Registers and the Daily Log regarding risks and issues that could be important for configuration management and also the agreement on the Configuration Management Strategy.

The Configuration Management Strategy is produced by the Project Manager and approved by the Project Board. At the same time the system of the Configuration Item Records is organized. The Issue Register is also organized and completed from the Daily Log. Any issues and risks that are identified are recorded in the Daily Log or in the Issue and Risk Register, depending on whether they are to be handled formally or informally.

Prepare a Quality Management Strategy

The delivery of accepted project results according to quality expectations is what a project is all about. There needs to be agreement between the customer and supplier on how to manage quality. Just as with other strategies the aims, procedures, responsibilities and techniques for the application of the management aspect concerned are recorded in the Quality Management Strategy. The Quality Management Strategy will state whether the quality system of the customer or supplier is to be used, or a combination of these.

The Project Project Description is reviewed to check what the quality expectations and acceptance criteria of the client are. Review the Project Brief to check whether there are business or programme standards that must be observed. Check the learning points of previous projects and learning points emerging from business and programme management. Review the Risk and Issue Registers and the Daily Log regarding risks and issues that could be important for the management of quality and the agreed Quality Management Strategy.

The Quality Management Strategy is prepared by the Project Manager and approved by the Project Board. The Quality Register is organized for the project as a part of the project's quality management system. Any newly identified issues and risks will be recorded in the Daily Log, Issue Register and Risk Register.

Prepare the Communication Management Strategy

Effective communication within a project is crucial for the connection between the project and its environment. It is all about the project consciously dealing with the communication from and to the different stakeholders. In the Communication Management Strategy the stakeholders are analyzed and it is detailed what the desired cooperation is to be, what the key concepts in the communication are, how often and in what way communication will happen and how the communication documentation will be filled in.

The Communication Management Strategy is co-determined by the Risk Management, Configuration Management and Quality Management Strategies. It can be very beneficial when points that are important for internal and external communication emerge from earlier external communication. A stakeholder analysis should be conducted.

If the project is a part of a programme, attention must also be given to the communication between the project and the programme and the other programme parts. The Communication Management Strategy is formulated by the Project Manager and approved by the Project Board.

Set up project controls

Every decision in the project must be taken in a timely manner and considered carefully. This can only be done if the decision makers have the correct information at their disposal. Control mechanisms help to ensure that every level of the project management team can undertake the following:
- Assess the progress:
- Compare the progress with the plan:
- Test plans and options on the basis of different scenarios:
- Map out problems:
- Take corrective measures and authorize follow-on activities.

The organizing of project control is therefore tailor-made and dependent on the project. For the establishment of the control instruments to be utilised, the Project Brief, the different strategies and the Project Plan are used. It is a repetitive process where the different documents are refined further to form a consistent unit.

The project control not only describes the way in which issues and escalations are dealt with, what the tolerances are for the different levels, but also how responsibilities and authorities are delegated. The responsibility for organizing the project control lies with the Project Board. In practice the execution will be dealt with by the Project Manager.

Create the Project Plan

The Project Plan is an outline plan for the entire delivery stage of the project. The Project Plan states:

- The most important activities;
- The products to be delivered;
- The costs;
- The duration period;
- The required effort of people and resources.

The Project Plan must be established before the project can be started. The Project Plan provides input to the Business Case and forms an important part of the Project Initiation Documentation. The responsibility for creating the Project Plan lies with the Project Board and its realization with the Project Manager.

The Project Manager should not create the plans of the project in isolation, but always together with the project team and consumer representatives. With the drawing up of the Project Plan the management stages in the execution are also defined. If the Project Manager expects that many changes will be implemented during the project, the Project Manager can propose to the Project Board that a separate budget is included for requests for change. In this way it can help to prevent the Executive from having to go back to the corporate or programme management for a supplementary budget, or that the project budget is used to pay for these changes. In addition it may be necessary to include contingency plans and risk budgets to cover anticipated risks.

Prerequisites could be provided for the project by the business and programme management. When drawing up of a Project Plan use must also be made of the Project Brief, the project approach and the different strategies. The Risk and Issue Registers should be reviewed. New issues and identified risks should be recorded regularly in the Issue Register and the Risk Register.

Refine the Business Case

The Business Case describes why the project is necessary and how the project connects with the business objectives of the customer. In addition the Business Case enables the weighing up of the costs, profits and risks of the project. During the project the Business Case must be kept up to date so that important decisions can be taken.

The Business Case is often prepared by corporate or programme management before the start of the project and forms the basis for the providing the project mandate. During the Starting up a Project process the Project Manager includes the outline Business Case in the Project Brief.

During the IP process the Business Case is refined. The validity of the basic assumptions upon which the initial Business Case was based must be tested:

- Are the benefits that the customer expects to realize on the basis of the products to be delivered realistic?
- Are any new benefits expected or do certain benefits expire?
- Have possible dis-benefits been taken into account?
- Are the estimated costs and completion time correct and, if not, what are the consequences for the Business Case?
- What are the risks and do they give cause for adapting the project approach and/or the Project Plan and also the Business Case?

It can happens that the Project Plan must be adapted to achieve a positive Business Case, in order to prevent the project from being stopped. In addition it can be necessary to adapt the Project Product Description. When refining the Business Case the Project Brief, the project approach, the strategies and the Project Plan are used.

In addition to refining the Business Case, the Benefits Review Plan should also be created. How, when and by whom will the expected benefits be assessed? What is the baseline measurement in respect of which the changes will be measured?

The Project Manager is responsible for preparing the Business Case, though this is not always done personally; it is then produced by business analysts from corporate or programme management. It is also important to involve Project Assurance in this. The Executive is responsible for the Business Case and the Benefits Review Plan and must see to it that these are also ratified by the corporate and programme management.

Assemble the Project Initiation Documentation

One base set of documents is needed that contains all relevant information of the project. This is the Project Initiation Documentation This set of documents is assembled by the Project Manager and is necessary to get approval for starting the project. It also serves as reference for the delivery itself. The initial Project Initiation Documentation is then baselined to serve as a benchmark during the entire project.

The Project Initiation Documentation is assembled on the basis of all information that has been produced to date. It is, however, not in itself a one-to-one compilation of all preceding documents. It is advisable to provide for a separate management document for decision taking by the Project Board. It should not be too bulky, otherwise it will not be read by management,which could mean that they do not take ownership of the contents of the document. It is therefore better to assemble a separate text incorporating the main points for the Project Initiation Documentation and to refer to the original documents, rather than to assemble all documents into one document. The Project Initiation Documentation is often forwarded by the Project Board to corporate and programme management.

However, the Project Board cannot approve the start of the first delivery stage on the basis of the Project Initiation Documentation alone. In addition to the Project Initiation Documentation a detailed plan for the first delivery stage is necessary. The Managing a Stage Boundary (SB) process in which the Stage Plan of the first delivery stage is produced, is triggered from the IP process. At the same time the evaluation of the 'performance' during the initiation stage takes place and the End Stage Report for the initiation stage is prepared. If appropriate, the Lessons Log is improved by the experiences from the initiation stage.

12.4 Overview of IP activities

In table 12.1 the input and output and the responsibilities of all activities of the Initiating a Project process are reflected.

Input Triggers	Input Management Products	Activity	Output Management Products	CP	Ex	PB	PM	TM	PA	PS	Input Triggers
Authority to initiate a project	Project Brief Lessons Log Daily Log	Prepare the Risk Management Strategy	Risk Mgt. Strategy (PID) (c) Risk Register (c)		(A) 	(A) 	P A		R R	 P	-
Authority to initiate a project	Project Brief Lessons Log Risk Register Daily Log	Prepare the Configuration Management Strategy	Configuration Mgt. Strategy (PID) (c) PMT structure (PID) (u) Role descriptions (PID) (u) Configuration Item Records (c) Issue Register (c)		(A) (A) (A)	(A) (A) (A)	P P P A A		R R R R R	 P P	-
Authority to initiate a project	Project Product Description (PBr) Lessons Log Risk, Issue Register	Prepare the Quality Management Strategy	Quality Mgt. Strategy (PID) (c) Quality Register (c)		(A) 	(A) 	P A		R R	 P	-
	Project Brief Lessons Log Risk, Issue Register RM, QM, CM Strategy (PID)	Prepare the Communication Management Strategy	Communication Mgt. Strategy (PID) (c)		(A)	(A)	(P)		R		-
	Lessons Log Project Brief All strategies (PID) Project Plan (PID) Risk, Issue Register	Set up the project controls	Project controls (PID) (c) Role descriptions (PID) (u) PMT structure (PID) (u)		(A) (A) (A)	(A) (A) (A)	P P P		R R R		-
	Lessons Log Risk, Issue Register Project approach (PBr) Project Product Description (PBr) All strategies (PID) Project controls (PID)	Create the Project Plan	Project Plan (PID) (c) Product Descriptions (c) Role descriptions (PID) (u) PMT structure (PID) (u) Configuration Item Records (u)		(A) (A) (A) (A)	(A) (A) (A) (A)	P P P P A		R R R R R	 P	-
	(Outline) Business Case (PBr) Project Plan (PID) Risk Register	Refine the Business Case	Benefits Review Plan (c) (Detailed) Business Case (PID) (c)	(C) (C)	(A) (A)	(R) (R)	P P		R R		-
	Project definition (PBr) Project approach (PBr) All previous parts of the PID Tailoring of PRINCE2	Assemble the Project Initiation Documentation (PID)	Assembled PID	(C)	(A)		P		R		*Request to deliver a project Stage boundary approaching*

Table 12.1 Overview of the activities of Initiating a Project

13 DP, Directing a Project

The aim of the Directing a Project process is to make it possible for the Project Board to take responsibility for the success of the project by taking the important decisions themselves, and to control the entire project. The daily management rests with the Project Manager.

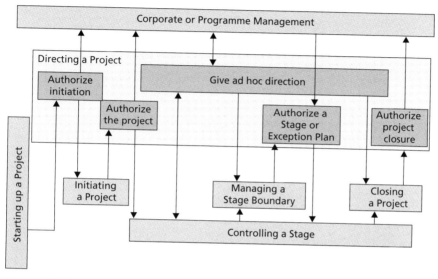

Figure 13.1 Directing a Project (Based on OGC PRINCE2 material)

13.1 DP, basic principles
The objectives of the Directing a Project process are to ensure that:
- Authority has been obtained to commence the initiation of the project.
- Authority has been obtained to initiate the realization of the products to be delivered.
- There is direction and monitoring during the entire life span of the project and that the project remains viable.
- There is an interface between the project and corporate or programme management.
- Authority has been obtained to end the project.
- Plans for assessing the benefits after the closure of the project are developed, assessed and approved.

13.2 Context
The Directing a Project process does not encompass the daily management of the project by the Project Manager, but rather the directing of the project by the Project Board. Here the focus is on managing 'by exception'. The Project Board directs the project by means of a relatively small number of decision points. Regular progress meetings are then unnecessary. The Project Manager informs the Project Board in the interim on the basis of the Highlight Report and escalates only the exceptions to the agreed plan, if these exceptions threaten to compromise the agreed

tolerance boundaries. It is important that the Project Board has an unambiguous vision of the progress of the project. If there is no agreement about this within the Project Board it can be a significant threat to the project.

Communication to and from corporate or programme management and other stakeholders outside the project is an important task of the Project Board that is specified in the Communication Management Strategy.

> If members of the project management team are not very experienced in the execution of their roles or if the project is more complex or risky than usual, it may be advisable to discuss the Highlight Reports verbally and outstanding issues and risks regularly with the Executive and/or the Senior Users.

The Directing a Project process is triggered by the request of the Project Manager for authorization of the initiation stage on the basis of the documentation supplied from the Starting up a Project process. The delivery of the project is authorized and the first delivery stage can commence on the basis of the Project Initiation Documentation and the Stage Plan for the first stage. During the delivery of the project, the Project Board decides on the progress of the project (go/no go), on the basis of the supplied Stage or Exception Plans. Finally the Project Board confirms the closure of the project with the involved parties. During the project the Project Board may provide ad hoc direction to the Project Manager.

13.3 DP, process description

The Directing a Project process consists of the following activities:
• Authorize initiation;
• Authorize the project;
• Authorize a Stage or Exception Plan;
• Give ad hoc direction;
• Authorize project closure.

Authorize initiation

Before execution of the initiation stage can be started, the Project Board:
• What the project entails;
• It is the correct time to start with the project;
• What the activities during the initiation of the project have to be

Authorize project initiation is the first activity of the Directing a Project process. The Project Board must decide whether the decision to authorize initiation can be made. In addition the Project Board must:
• Formally confirm the appointment of the members of the project management team and approve the role descriptions.
• Review, approve and have the Project Brief ratified by corporate or programme management.
• Review and approve the Project Approach.

- Review and approve the Business Case.
- Review and approve the Project Product Description including the quality expectations and the acceptance criteria.
- Review and approve the Initiation Stage Plan.
- Assure the effort required in terms of people and resources on the basis of the Initiation Stage Plan.
- Understand and agree on the risks attached to the chosen execution of the initiation stage.
- Assure that the control mechanisms and reports for the initiation stage are in order.
- Check whether the lessons arising out of earlier projects are appropriately considered in the developed proposals.
- Inform the organization facilitating the execution of the project and other stakeholders of the authorization to commence the initiation of the project.
- Authorize the Project Manager to start with the initiation stage of the project.

The authorize project initiation activity is triggered by the request of the Project Manager that the project may be started and makes use of the Project Brief and Initiation Stage Plan. This activity delivers the formal approval of these documents, the authorization of the project start to the Project Manager and the announcement of the project start to the facilitating organization.

Authorize the project
The costs of the delivery of a project can be considerable. Before the actual execution of the project can be started, it should be ensured that:
- There is an accepted Business Case for the project that indicates that the project is desirable, viable and feasible.
- The Project Plan is suitable for realizing the Business Case.
- The prepared strategies and controls support the execution of the Project Plan.
- The mechanisms to assess and review the envisaged benefits are set up and planned.

The authorize the project activity is triggered by the request of the Project Manager to start with the execution of the project and makes use of the Project Initiation Documentation and the Benefit Review Plan produced during the Initiating a Project process, and of the Lessons Log.

In the authorize the project activity the Project Initiation Documentation and the Benefits Review Plan are approved and the execution of the project authorized. It must be checked whether the lessons learnt and the strategies have been considered in the plans and if everyone knows and accepts their role. The Project Initiation Documentation will usually be ratified by corporate or programme management before the Project Board can approve the documents and authorize the execution of the first stage. The (remaining) corporate or programme management and other stakeholders are informed about the fact that the execution of the project has been authorized.

The Project Board may decide to delegate a part of the assessment tasks to Project Assurance. If the project does not have a sound Business Case, the Project Board cannot authorize the execution of the project and the project must be stopped (no go).

At the same time as the authorize the project activity, the assessment of the Stage Plan for the first delivery stage and the assessment of the End Stage Report of the initiation stage are undertaken.

The Stage Plan and the End Stage Report have been prepared in the Managing a Stage Boundary process, which was triggered by the Initiating a Project process.

Authorize a Stage or Exception Plan

It is important that the activities within a stage only start when the Project Board has explicitly authorized it. To make this possible the Project Board, at the end of every intervening management stage, once again assesses the desirability, viability and feasibility of the project and reviews the Stage Plan of the following stage before it authorizes the next stage. The Project Board can decide to delegate a part of the assessment tasks to Project Assurance.

This activity is also carried out if the project or stage tolerances threaten to be exceeded during the execution of a stage and the Project Manager has produced an Exception Plan via the Managing a Stage Boundary process as requested by the Project Board. The Project Board then assesses the Exception Plan, to ensure the ongoing viability of the project and, if appropriate, to authorize it. If project tolerances are likely to be exceeded, then the Project Board must bring this to the attention of corporate or programme management.

The activity, authorize a Stage or Exception Plan, is triggered by the request of the Project Manager to authorize the next Stage Plan or an Exception Plan. In this activity, the Project Board use the inputs of the Stage Plan for the next stage or the Exception Plan, the End Stage Report for the current stage, the Benefits Review Plan and the Project Initiation Documentation.

The End Stage Report is assessed and approved. The Project Board review of the stage just completed will be to ensure that it was is executed in accordance with the plan and within the agreed frameworks of time, money and quality. In the case of exceptions the Project Manager is asked for an explanation of the cause of the problem and any solutions, and the future consequences are considered. Upon agreement, authorization to proceed is given to the Project Manager.

The update of the Project Plan, the Business Case and the most important risks are reviewed. A possible Lessons Report is assessed and approved and it is decided to whom the report will be sent.

A phased delivery ensures that the products are delivered according to the Configuration Management Strategy. Where appropriate, any products handed over to business operations would need to have been accepted so they may take over control and maintenance, and any recommendations for follow-on actions should have been prepared and should be adequate.

The Stage Plan for the next stage is assessed and approved. The Stage Plan is assessed on feasibility and linking with the Project Plan, the strategies and project control. The Product Descriptions are approved. The required effort of people and resources is ensured. Changes in the project management team are authorized. The updates of the Project Initiation Documentation, including the stage tolerances, are reviewed and confirmed.

The update of the Benefits Review Plan is reviewed and approved. It should be ensured that the Benefits Review Plan is consistent with the updated Business Case. At the same time it is ensured that benefits that will possibly be realized in the following stage will be assessed and reviewed.

The Project Board informs the corporate or programme management and other stakeholders about the progress of the project, in agreement with what has been specified in the Communication Management Strategy.

If the project is no longer viable, the Project Board gives the Project Manager the instruction to end the project prematurely.

Give ad hoc direction

Even when the execution of a project goes according to plan, agreement must take place throughout between the Project Manager and the members of Project Board, for example on:
- Reactions to Highlight Reports received;
- Reactions to informal requests for advice and direction;
- Reactions to Issue Reports received;
- Reactions to advice and decisions of the corporate or programme management;
- Reactions to Exception Reports.

As a result of the Highlight Report being received, the Project Board should review the progress of the project, gaining assurance that the project is running according to plan and remains focused on the Business Case and, if necessary, take corrective action. If the Project Board feel there is an exception situation they can ask the Project Manager to produce an Exception Report. The Project Board informs the corporate or programme management and other stakeholders of the progress of the project, as directed in the Communication Management Strategy. In practice the Project Manager will assemble the progress information and send it off on behalf of the members of the Project Board.

In response to informal requests for advice and direction, the Project Board should advise or instruct the Project Manager. The Project Board can request the Project Manager to produce an Issue or Exception Report. If necessary the Project Board can liaise with the corporate or programme management.

In response to an Issue Report received, the Project Board must decide how the issue concerned is to be dealt with. The Project Board can approve or reject a Request for Change. The Project Board can accept (concession) or reject an off-specification. As a result of a problem or a point of concern the Project Board can take action, advise or instruct the Project Manager. In all cases the Project Board can decide to postpone the decision, ask for more information, request the Project Manager to produce an Exception Plan or even request that the project be concluded prematurely. The Project Board may wish to ask the corporate or programme management for advice.

In response to the advice and decisions of the corporate or programme management the Project Board must inform the project management team of changes that can have an impact on the project. In this matter the Project Board can report an issue to the Project Manager, request the Project Manager to produce an Exception Plan or even request the project to be concluded prematurely.

As a result of an Exception Report received, the Project Board must determine whether or not the project should continue and if so, how the remaining part of the stage and/or the project is to be completed. The Project Board can decide to extend the stage tolerances so that the project can be continued. In this way the Project Board can accept (concession) an exception that falls outside the quality tolerances. The Project Board can decide to consider the situation a little longer if it is not clear whether the project is really going to be outside the tolerances or whether the chance of this is slim. The Project Board can decide to continue the project on the basis of one of the scenarios as indicated in the Exception Report. Alternatively the Project Board can decide to end the project prematurely. If the project seems likely to go outside the project tolerances, the Project Board must bring this to the attention of the corporate or programme management.

The activity, give ad hoc direction, can occur at any time during the entire lifecycle of the project.

Authorize project closure

The decision to close a project is just as important as the decision to start it. With closure it should be checked whether the objectives of the project have been realized and to what extent the result deviates from what was originally agreed. It should also be determined that continuation of the project no longer provides any added value for the organization within the agreed Business Case. Without this approach projects will not end and they become part of regular operational management.

The initial and final version of the Project Initiation Documentation should be reviewed to obtain insight into the differences between the original and current points of departure, strategies and control instruments.

The Project Board must further assure that:
- A control and maintenance organization has been set up for the products to be delivered.
- The end users and control and maintenance have formally indicated that all acceptance criteria for the products to be delivered have been satisfied.
- The responsibility and the ownership of the products to be delivered have been formally handed over to the eventual users
- The End Project Report has been produced and approved for distribution to the corporate or programme management and other stakeholders.
- Outstanding action points and lessons of the project are handed over to the relevant corporate sections.
- The Benefits Review Plan is updated and collated for assessment of profits still anticipated and the performance of the products to be delivered.
- The Business Case is updated to serve as basis for the benefits reviews still to be executed.
- An announcement of project closure is given to all parties who provide support to the project, so that all deployed people and resources can be recalled from the project.
- Discharge is given to the Project Manager.

The authorize project closure activity is initiated by the Project Manager from the Closing a Project process. It comprises the closing activities of the Project Board of the project. The Project Board can decide to delegate a part of the assessment tasks associated with it to Project Assurance.

The documents that are delivered in the Closing a Project process are used. These are approved and released to the stakeholder parties concerned. The announcement of closure is sent as a recommendation to the Project Board by the Project Manager, reviewed by them and despatched.

The Project Board makes use of what has been recorded in the Project Initiation Documentation and the Communication Management Strategy. As a final action the Project Board is disbanded.

13.4 Overview of DP activities

In table 13.1 the input and output and the responsibilities of all activities of the Directing a Project process are reflected.

Input Triggers	Input Management Products	Activity	Output Management Products	CP	Ex	PB	PM	TM	PA	PS	Input Triggers
Request to initiate a project	Project Brief; Initiation Stage Plan; Lessons Log	Authorize initiation	Project Brief (a)	C	A	A	(P)		R		*Authority to initiate a project; Initiation notification*
			Initiation Stage Plan (a)		A	A	(P)		R		
Request to deliver a project	Project Initiation Documentation; Benefits Review Plan; Lessons Log	Authorize the project	PID (a)	C	A	A	(P)		R		*Project authorization notification; Premature close*
			Benefits Review Plan (a)	C	A	R	(P)		R		
Request to approve Exception Plan	Specialist products; End Stage Report; Lessons Log; Lessons Report (if required); Follow-on action recomm. (if required) (EPR); Next Stage Plan; Exception Plan; PID; Benefits Review Plan	Authorize a Stage or Exception Plan	Specialist products (c)		C	C	(R)	(P)	(R)		*Stage authorization; Exception Plan authorization; Premature close*
Request to approve next Stage Plan			End Stage Report (a)		A	A	(P)		R		
			Lessons Report (EPR) (a)		A	A	(P)		R		
			Follow-on action recomm. (EPR) (a)		A	A	(P)		R		
			Next Stage Plan (a)		A	A	(P)		R		
			Exception Plan (a)		A	A	(P)		R		
			PID (if updated) (a)	C	A	A	(P)		R		
			Benefits Review Plan (if updated) (a)	C	A	R	(P)		R		
PM request for advice; Exception raised; Corporate advice and decision	Highlight Report; Exception Report; Issue Report	Give ad hoc direction	Advice, new issue	P	P	P					*PB request for advice; PB advice; Exception Plan request; Premature close; New issue*
Closure recommendation	End Project Report; Lessons Report (EPR); Follow-on action recomm. (EPR); Business Case (PID); Benefits Review Plan	Authorize project closure	End Project Report (a)		A	A	(P)		R		*Closure notification*
			Lessons Report (EPR) (a)		A	A	(P)		R		
			Follow-on action recomm. (EPR) (a)		A	A	(P)		R		
			(Updated) Business Case (a)	C	A	R	(P)		R		
			Benefits Review Plan (if updated) (a)	C	A	R	(P)		R		

Table 13.1 Overview of the activities of Directing a Project

14 CS, Controlling a Stage

The aim of the Controlling a Stage (CS) process is the assignment and monitoring of the work to be completed, dealing with issues, reporting on progress to the Project Board and the execution of corrective actions so that the project remains within the agreed tolerances.

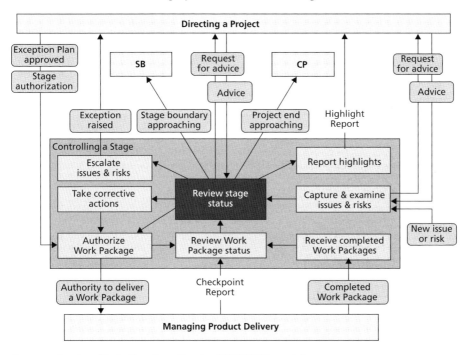

Figure 14.1 Overview of Controlling a Stage (Based on OGC PRINCE2 material)

14.1 CS, basic principles

This process describes the daily management activities of the Project Manager during the different stages of the project. As soon as the decision has been taken to execute the activities in a stage and the required effort of people and resources has been released, the project management team must concentrate on the delivery of the agreed product and services:

- In accordance with the quality requirements determined;
- Within the agreed costs, effort of people, resources and time planning, so as to ensure that the client organization can realize the defined benefits (after closure of the project).

To realize this, the managing of a stage is directed at:

- The delivery of the agreed stage products in accordance with the agreed quality requirements within the agreed tolerances;
- The control of risks and issues;
- Keeping an eye on the agreed Business Case (as well as the benefits);
- The control of the scope so that uncontrolled changes can be prevented.

If changes by parties are desirable, the consequences of the these changes must be examined thoroughly by the Project Manager, and the Project Board must authorize these changes.

14.2 Context

The Controlling a Stage process begins as soon as the Project Board has approved the Stage Plan and the work concerned has been released in the authorize Stage or Exception Plan activity. This activity in turn initiates the authorize a Work Package activity, for the release of the initial Work Package in the stage concerned.

In the process Controlling a Stage, the Project Manager directs the Team Manager whose activities are described in the Managing Product Delivery process. The interfaces between the two processes are specified in the activities, authorize a Work Package, review the Work Package status and receive completed Work Packages.

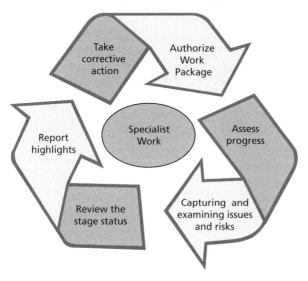

Figure 14.2 Controlling a Stage (Based on OGC PRINCE2 material)

During the activities, capture and examine issues and risks and review the stage status, the Project Manager can request advice from the Project Board. During the reporting of highlights the Project Manager reports periodically to the Project Board by Highlights Reports. If the Project Manager expects the agreed tolerances to be exceeded, the Project Manager reports this in an Exception Report to the Project Board in the escalate issues and risks activity.

The Project Manager initiates the processes, Managing a Stage Boundary (SB) and Closure of a Project (CP) from the review stage status activity.

14.3 CS, process description

The Controlling a Stage process consists of the following activities:

- Authorize Work Packages;
- Review Work Package status;
- Capture and examine issues and risks;
- Review the stage status;
- Take corrective action;
- Report highlights;
- Escalate issues and risks;
- Receive completed Work Packages.

Authorize Work Packages

Chaos develops in a project if everyone starts activities whenever they personally consider them appropriate. Activities, therefore, should only begin if the Project Manager has explicitly agreed this in a Work Package with the appropriate Team Manager.

The Project Manager should check in the Stage Plan which products are to be delivered, at what costs, within what timescale, to which quality and within which tolerances.. The Project Manager should examine the Project Initiation Documentation to understand the arrangements that have been specified for this Work Package in the different strategies and the controls, before a Work Package can be authorized.

A (description of the) Work Package contains among other things the products to be delivered, the quality requirements which must be satisfied, the estimated costs, the required effort of people and resources, the duration of the activities, the relationships with other products and how reporting is to be done in the interim. Separate Product Descriptions of the deliverable products should be made available.

The Project Manager should review the Work Package with the Team Manager to ensure that it is acceptable and work on the Work Package can be authorized to commence. The Project Manager should review the (extract of the) Team Plan with the Team Manager to ensure that the Team Plan links up with the Stage Plan.

As delivery of the project commences it will be necessary to review and update the Stage Plan, as more information is understood about the deliverables or as risks and issues arise. The Project Manager must adapt the Stage Plan accordingly (within the tolerances), or escalate to the Project Board.

In conclusion the Project Manager should adapt the status of the products in the Configuration Item Records, update the planned quality reviews in the Quality Register and update the Risk and Issue Registers as appropriate.

The complimentary activities of the Team Manager as receiving party in this activiy are described in the accept a Work Package activity.

The condition for the transfer of a Work Package to a Team Manager is that the Team Manager has sufficient expertise and authority to take responsibility for the Work Package. If this is not the case then another Team Manager must be found, or the Project Manager should fill the role of Team Manager and assign the individual activities of the Work Package directly to the different team members. This is only recommended for small projects and only if the Project Manager has sufficient expertise and time for the realization of the Work Package concerned. In larger and more complex projects it may not be appropriate as the Project Manager may spend too much time delivering the products and not enough time managing the project. This should be avoided as to do otherwise would be putting the project at risk

The input for this activity is the authorization of the delivery stage, the Stage or Exception Plan including the relevant Product Descriptions and the information from the activity, take corrective action. In addition, the Project Initiation Documentation should be referenced for the appropriate strategies and controls to be considered. As a result of the transfer discussion with the Team Manager, the Stage or Exception Plan, the Risk Register, Issue Register and Quality Register and the Configuration Item Record are updated. The authorize a Work Package activity provides the formal transfer of the Work Package to the Team Manager. Refer to Chapter 15 for the contents of a Work Package.

Review Work Package status

To be able to manage a project the Project Manager should know what the status of the different Work Packages is in relation to the Stage Plan. It could happen that a Project Manager might be focused only on crisis management in one stage, as result of which they might lose sight of what needs to be achieved. A good Progress Assurance should ensure that the focus remains on managing the deliverable products and services of the stage.

The Project Manager monitors the progress of the stage based on the Checkpoint Reports and the progress discussions with the Team Managers. If necessary, confirmation is obtained of the work completed. The Project Manager further makes use of the entries in the Quality Register, the Configuration Item Records and the Issue and Risk Registers.

The Checkpoint Report contains:
• The progress of the activities;
• The costs incurred and the effort of people and resources;
• The quality assessments that have been undertaken;
• The delivered products;
• The time still to be spent, costs to be incurred and the required effort of people and resources;
• The issues that are important for the progress of the stage.

With the help of these particulars, the Stage or Exception Plan is updated.

The Project Manager is responsible for monitoring progress. The Project Manager is primarily helped in this by Project Support. Project Support often records the status of the work and registers the progress of the work in the Stage Plan. If there is a separate configuration librarian, they see to the updating of the configuration database and, if necessary, deliver a Product Status Account to the Project Manager.

Capture and examine issues and risks

Problems, issues and changes can occur in the project at any time. Together these are called 'issues'. All issues should be recorded. Issues can be generated by anyone with an interest in the project, at any time.

Any known issues should not be forgotten, even if no immediate solution or no direct action results from it. If the Project Managers of failed projects or those that have encountered major problems are asked about these, they almost all indicate that there were signs of problems beforehand. However, because nothing could be done about it at that point in time, the problems were placed to one side and not addressed again until it was too late.

Issues that are dealt with informally by the Project Manager must also be registered. These are recorded in the Daily Log. For every formal issue that is registered in the Issue Register, a separate Issue Report is prepared.

Issues are differentiated as:
• Requests for Change;
• Off-specifications;
• Problems/expressions of concern;

Different procedures are agreed for each type of issue. Possible procedures are discussed in the Change theme.

As soon as an issue is registered, an interim impact assessment must be executed. Based on this, the interim priority is determined. Those who have initiated the issue are informed that the issue has been registered and the issue procedure initiated.

Apart from issues, new risks can also be identified. If it is immediately clear that it concerns a new risk, this new risk need not be registered in the Issue Register, but the risk can be entered directly as a new risk in the Risk Register (also refer to the Risk theme).

The capturing of issues and risks is normally done ad hoc. Before a decision can be taken on what must be done as a result of an issue or risk, its impact on the project must first be examined by the Project Manager.

In addition all issues that have not been concluded and risks that are still outstanding, must periodically be examined and actions defined for decision-making. However, this happens during reviewing the stage status and not during capturing and examining issues and risks. A decision on issues and risks can only be taken in the framework of a general assessment of the status of the project. Urgent issues should naturally be tackled directly.

Issues and risks that should be dealt with in the framework of a programme, should be escalated within the project and transferred to the programme by the Project Board.

The Project Manager is responsible for the capturing and reviewing of issues and risks. The assessment can be executed by a third party. The administrative activities can be delegated to

Project Support. Requests for Change should be approved by the Project Board or its designated Change Authority.

New issues and risks are the input to this activity. When the issues are reviewed, use is made of the Stage or Exception Plan, the Communication and Configuration Management Strategy, the Project Plan and the Business Case. In this activity the Issue Register and the Risk Register are updated.

Review the stage status

If the status of the work during a project is not regularly reviewed, the project is not formally under control and hence there is an increased chance of failure. In order to avoid this possibility it is important that a regular assessment is undertaken of the status of the work in respect of the approved plan. Based on this it must be decided whether the next Work Package can be started, whether any corrective action should be taken, whether issues and risks should be escalated and whether the Managing a Stage Boundary or Closing a Project processes should be initiated. If necessary the (individual members of the) Project Board may be asked to give ad-hoc direction.

The status of the stage is reviewed on the basis of the information from the review the Work Package status activity and on the basis of the results from the activity, capture and examine issues and risks.

The activities in review the stage status comprise:
- Review the progress of the work against the Stage Plan;
- Examine whether the activities in the stage are staying inside the tolerances;
- Examine whether the acceptance of the results has been done as agreed in the Product Descriptions;
- Review the effects of the issues in respect of the Stage Plan, the Project Plan and the Business Case, and for Requests for Change also in respect of the Change budget (if present);
- Examine if new risks change actions and/or change existing risks;
- Examine whether the Business Case is still valid and if any realizable benefits are actually being realized;
- Decide if new activities should be started up;
- Decide if corrective actions should be undertaken;
- Decide if the Project Board should be asked for advice, for example about taking decisions on Requests for Change;
- Decide to escalate issues and risks to the Project Board if it is expected that the agreed tolerances will be exceeded;
- Initiate the Managing a Stage Boundary process if it seems that the stage is coming to an end and should be closed;
- Initiate the Closing a Project process if it seems that the project is coming to an end and should be closed.

The Project Manager is responsible for reviewing the status of the stage. The Project Manager can be supported by Project Support, by the configuration librarian, by those who are responsible for the Project Assurance and, if desired, by members of the Project Board.

When reviewing the stage status, the Project Manager makes use of the updated Stage Plan, the Project Plan, the Business Case, the Issue Register and Risk Register, the Quality Register, the Product Status Account and the Configuration Item Records.

The activity supplies information about the status of the stage and leads to decisions about maintaining control in the project and initiating new Work Packages, or the closure of the stage or closure of the project and initiates corresponding processes and activities.

Take corrective actions

Maintaining control of the project and carrying out changes should be done in a structured manner. It lies within the authority of a Project Manager to remain inside the agreed tolerances as appropriate. Taking corrective actions is initiated from the activity, review the stage status. The activity, take corrective action, initiates the activity, authorize a Work Package.

The Project Manager captures the necessary information and selects the most optimal option. The Project Manager adapts the Stage Plan, including the relevant Product Descriptions, and Configuration Item Records accordingly. The Project Manager makes the information available to the stakeholders concerned and then finally initiates the corrective action.

Before actions are started it may be necessary to obtain advice from the Project Board, or if this responsibility has been delegated, from the Change Authority.. If the corrective action originates from an issue or risk that has been recorded earlier, then a number of these steps may already have been taken.

When taking corrective action, the Project Manager makes use of the actual Stage Plan, the Configuration Item Records, the Issue and Risk Registers and the status information from the activity, review the status stage. Entries from the Daily Log can also provide input for taking corrective actions.

This activity provides requests for advice to the Project Board and corrective actions plus an updated Stage Plan, updated Configuration Item Records and an updated Issue and/or Risk Register and ultimately an updated Daily Log.

Report highlights

The Project Manager is responsible for the daily management of the project. An update from the Project Manager to the Project Board and other stakeholders keeps them informed and involved in the project and enables the Project Board to exert its responsibilities.

The Project Manager periodically informs the Project Board on the basis of a Highlight Report. The frequency of the Highlight Report is specified as part of the IP process and is established in the Project Initiation Documentation. The Communication Management Strategy records the information that should be provided to which stakeholder and when.

In this activity the Project Manager makes use of the Checkpoint Reports, the updated Stage Plan, the Issue Register and Risk Register, the Quality Register, the Product Status Account and any preceding Highlight Report. The Project Manager captures the information required, creates a Highlight Report for the current period and ensures distribution in accordance with what has been agreed in the Communication Management Strategy.

Escalate issues and risks

A stage may not exceed any of its agreed tolerances without approval of the Project Board. If one or more agreed tolerances are in danger of being exceeded, the Project Manager must inform the Project Board about this and advise them how to deal with it.

The establishment of tolerances is one of the most important controls of the Project Board. Tolerances should be established for time as well as costs and, if necessary, for scope, quality, benefits and/or risks. If the Project Manager expects that one of the tolerances in a stage will be exceeded, the Project Manager should escalate it as quickly as possible to the Project Board via an Exception Report. As production of an Exception Report takes some time, it is advisable to first inform the Project Board verbally or via e-mail. At the same time consideration should be given as to how and within what timescales the Exception Report should be prepared.

The Project Manager analyses the cause, provides the consequences of the exception for the project, describes the possible options and the consequences of these options, and recommends which option seems to be the most appropriate. With the cause and with each options the consequences for the Stage Plan, the Project Plan and the risks, as well as the consequences for the Business Case are considered. Based on the preceding, the Project Manager prepares the Exception Report and sends it to the Project Board.

With the escalating of issues and risks the Project Manager makes use of the Stage Plan, the Project Plan, the Project Initiation Documentation, the Business Case, the Issue Register and the Risk Register. The activity provides an Exception Report for assessment by the Project Board. The Issue and Risk Registers are updated accordingly.

Receive completed Work Packages

If work is being delivered by external providers it will always be necessary to formally test if the work is completed, accepted and handed over before discharge can be given to the supplier. The same applies to the external delivery of Work Packages to Team Managers.

This activity registers the successful delivery of the Work Package when it is handed over by the Team Manager. This registration is then input for the review the Work Package status activity.

The Project Manager should ensure that:
- All quality assessments of the deliverable products have been executed and that all criteria have been satisfied;
- All deliverable products have been accepted by the responsible persons;
- All entries in the Quality Register have been updated;
- All Configuration Item Records are updated;
- All completed products have been handed over to the configuration management.

After approval of the deliverable products these products cannot easily be adapted further. Changes to approved products must be dealt with through Change Control.

14.4 Overview of CS activities

In table 14.1 the input and output and the responsibilities of all activities of the Controlling a Stage process are reflected.

Input Triggers	Input Management Products	Activity	Output Management Products	Responsibilities							Input Triggers
				CP	Ex	PB	PM	TM	PA	PS	
Corrective action New Work Package Stage authorization Exception Plan approved	Stage Plan Configuration Item Records Product Descriptions (SP) Project controls (PID) QM, Config. Mgt. Strategy (PID) Team Plan	Authorize a Work Package	Updated Stage Plan (u) Work Package(s) (c) Configuration Item Records (u) Quality Register (u) Issue, Risk Register (u)				P P A A P	(R) (A) (R) (R)	R R R R R	P P	Authority to deliver a Work Package
	Stage Plan Configuration Item Records Checkpoint Report(s) Work Package(s) Team Plan(s) Quality Register Issue, Risk Register	Review Work Package status	Stage Plan (u) Configuration Item Records (u) Issue, Risk Register (u)				P A P	(R)	R R R	P	-
New issue New risk	Stage Plan Business Case (PID) Project Plan (PID) CM / Comm. Mgt. Strategy (PID)	Capture and examine issues and risks	Daily Log (u) Issue Report (c) Issue, Risk Register (u)				P P P		R R		Request for advice
Corrective action Project Board advice	Stage Plan Quality, Issue, Risk Register Issue Report Lesson Log Checkpoint Report(s) Business Case (PID) Project Plan (PID) Benefits Review Plan (PID)	Review the stage status	Stage Plan (u) Risk, Issue Register (u) Issue Report (u) Lessons Log (u) Product Status Account (c)				P P P P A		R R R R	P	Corrective action New Work Package Request for advice Tolerance threat Stage boundary approaching Project end approaching

Input Triggers	Input Management Products	Activity	Output Management Products	CP	Ex	PB	PM	TM	PA	PS	Input Triggers
Corrective action	Daily Log Issue Report Issue, Risk Register Stage Plan Configuration Item Records	Take corrective action	Daily Log (u) Issue Report (u) Issue, Risk Register (u) Stage Plan (u) Configuration Item Records (u)				P P P P A	(R)	R R R R	P	*Corrective action* *Request for advice*
	Checkpoint Report(s) Risk, Issue, Quality Register Lessons, Daily Log Product Status Account Stage Plan Highlights Report (previous period) Comm. Mgt. Strategy (PID)	Report highlights	Highlight Report (c)				P		R		-
Tolerance threat	Business Case (PID) Project Plan (PID) Stage Plan Issue Report Issue, Risk Register	Escalate issues and risks	Exception Report (c) Issue Report (u) Issue, Risk Register (u)		(A)	(A)	P P P		R R R		*Exception raised*
Completed Work Packages	Stage Plan Configuration Item Records Quality Register	Receive completed Work Packages	Stage Plan (u) Configuration Item Records (u)				P A	(R)	R R	P	-

Table 14.1 Overview of the activities of Controlling a Stage

15 MP, Managing Product Delivery

The aim of the Managing Product Delivery (MP) process is the control of the relationship between the Project Manager and the Team Manager(s) by setting formal requirements for acceptance, execution and delivery of the project work.

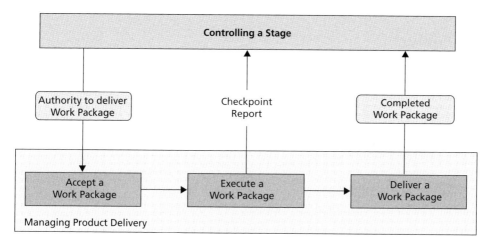

Figure 15.1 Overview of Managing Product Delivery (based on OGC PRINCE2 material)

71

15.1 MP, basic principles

The purpose of the Managing Product Delivery process is to control the way in which the Project Manager assigns activities to the Team Manager on the basis of detailed Work Packages and the way in which these Work Packages are accepted, executed and delivered. The work relationship between the Project Manager and the Team Manager can best be described as a relationship between the Project Manager and a preferred supplier. It does not matter if the Team Manager actually has an entire team carrying out the activities, or if the Team Manager executes the activities personally. Managing Product Delivery is about the delegation of the responsibility from the Project Manager to the Team Manager for the realization of the Work Package within the controls agreed in the Work Package. It also does not matter if the Team Manager is from the internal organization or from an external organization.

Of importance is that:
- The work to be executed is agreed and authorized;
- It is clear to Team Managers what must be delivered, at what costs, with what effort of people and resources and when;
- The planned products are delivered in accordance to the agreed specifications and within the agreed tolerances;
- Accurate progress information is provided to the Project Manager at agreed times to ensure that the expectations are met.

If the Team Manager cannot bear any responsibility for the realization of the Work Package, then the Project Manager can only delegate tasks and the Project Manager remains responsible for the realization of the Work Package. The Team Manager is then actually an ordinary team member and the Project Manager has in fact a double role as Project Manager and Team Manager. It could also happen that the Project Manager directs different Team Managers for the realization of different Work Packages, but that the Project Manager fills the role of Team Manager for one or several Work Packages.

15.2 Context

The Managing Product Delivery process has a direct link with the Controlling a Stage process. The CS process is the responsibility of the Project Manager, while activities of the MP process are the responsibility of the Team Manager.

The Managing Product Delivery process starts with the Project Manager authorizing a Work Package and the Team Manager accepting this. Managing Product Delivery also covers the delivery of the Work Package and subsequently the delivery of the completed product(s) back to the Project Manager. The activities described in this process can also be executed without making use of the PRINCE2 method. The different CS and MP processes allow a controlled division possible between those who do and those who do not work with the PRINCE2 method.

15.3 MP, process description

The Managing Product Delivery process consists of the following activities:
- Accept a Work Package;
- Execute a Work Package;
- Deliver a Work Package.

The Team Manager ensures that the assigned products are realized by the team and delivered to the project by:
- Accepting and verifying the Work Package from the Project Manager;
- Ensuring that the Work Package is authorized by the persons with the authority to do so;
- Setting up and updating the Team Plan for the execution of the work;
- Ensuring that the required activities are executed to realize the Work Package;
- Ensuring that the products are developed according to the methods as they are specified in the Work Package;
- Seeing to it that the interfaces with other products are managed;
- Controlling the progress and reporting on it to the Project Manager;
- Ensuring that the delivered products comply with the specified quality requirements;
- Initiating the quality assessments;
- Obtaining approval and acceptance of the delivered products;
- Delivering and handing over the accepted products to the Project Manager or Project Support in accordance with the procedures specified in the Work Package.

Accept a Work Package

Before execution of the activities can be started there must first be agreement between the Project Manager and the Team Manager about what should be undertaken in the Work Package. The Project Manager cannot simply instruct the Team Manager what to do. The Team Manager has an individual responsibility in respect of the technical and commercial feasibility of the work to be undertaken. The Team Manager is accountable to the Senior Supplier, who has made the agreement /contract agreements with the customer for the realization of the delivered products.

A Work Package comprises:
- Product Description of the deliverable products;
- Interfaces that have to be taken into account during the work;
- Agreed start and delivery date, allocated hours and/or disposable costs;
- Tolerances, prerequisites and assumptions;
- Standards and procedures to be satisfied;
- Method and the contents of reporting, how often and when;
- Changes and escalation procedure;
- Requirements from the configuration management;
- Agreements about the acceptance, delivery and handover of the products.

Product Descriptions detail, amongst other things, the quality requirements with which the product must comply and the manner in which and by whom the product must be tested and accepted.

To be able to accept the Work Package and be accountable for it, the Team Manager should produce a Team Plan and evaluate the associated risks. It may be that the Team Manager has already become involved in the drawing up of the Stage Plan and prepared (the main points of) the Team Plan. In this way maximum account can be taken of the aspects that are important for delivering the Work Package concerned. With the acceptance of the Work Package the Team Manager can then update the Team Plan as required. The Team Manager discusses the Team Plan and the associated risks with the Project Manager.

The input for this activity is the authorized Work Package and the Project Initiation Documentation. During this process the Team Plan is produced/updated and the Work Package approved. The (adapted) data for the quality assessments in the Quality Register is reviewed and approved. New risks are escalated to the Project Manager.

Execute a Work Package

The execute a Work Package activity describes the delegation and managing of the activities that are necessary to be able to execute the Work Package.

The activities of the Team Manager comprise:
- Realizing the deliverable products in accordance with the quality criteria described in the Product Descriptions concerned and in accordance with the agreed processes, procedures and techniques in the Work Package;
- Managing interfaces that have to be taken into account during the work;
- Executing the activities within agreed tolerances of time, money and quality;

- Escalating new issues, risks and lessons to the Project Manager;
- Managing the risks during execution in consultation with the Project Manager;
- Carrying out the agreed changes if necessary;
- Testing the deliverable product and obtaining approval and acceptance of the deliverable products;
- Handing over the quality files to Project Support and the corresponding updating of the Quality Register and the Configuration Item Records by Project Support;
- Monitoring and controlling the progress of the Work Package, updating the Team Plan and coordinating this accordingly with Project Assurance;
- Reporting the progress of the Work Package via the Checkpoint Reports to the Project Manager at the frequency agreed in the Work Package.

The authorized Work Package and associated Product Descriptions, the Quality Register and the Configuration Item Records are used for this. During this activity the Team Manager updates the Team Plan and the Work Package based on the progress of the activities and reports on the progress to the Project Manager through the Checkpoint Reports. Finally the Team Manager escalates the issues, risks and lessons to the Project Manager and hands the quality files over to Project Support.

Deliver a Work Package

The deliver a Work Package activity describes the handing over of the Work Package to the Project Manager and obtaining discharge for the Work Package concerned.

The activities of the Team Manager in the deliver a Work Package activity are:
- Checking if all related actions from the Quality Register have been executed;
- Checking if all deliverable products have been approved and accepted;
- Checking if all quality files have been handed over to Project Support and if the Quality Register and the Configuration Item Records have been updated accordingly;
- Updating the Team Plan to indicate that the Work Package has been completed;
- Handing over the delivered products and informing the Project Manager about this according to the agreements specified in the Work Package;
- Obtaining discharge for the delivered Work Package.

The Team Manager should ensure that the products are accepted by all parties concerned. Acceptance and testing/approving could involve different stakeholders. By involving the concerned parties in the testing of the products during the execution, the Team Manager can ensure that the acceptance of the products by the concerned parties runs smoothly. The concerned parties may be the eventual users of the products, but could also include those who are impacted by the delivered products in the future.

If the Work Package is executed by external workers, then the signing off of the delivered Work Package by the Project Manager is the point at which any financial payments e.g. invoices will be approved and paid.

At the end of this activity the completed Work Package is ready for approval by the Project Manager.

15.4 Overview of MP activities

In table 15.1 the input and output and the responsibilities of all activities of the Managing Product Delivery process are reflected.

Input Triggers	Input Management Products	Activity	Output Management Products	Responsibilities							Input Triggers
				CP	Ex	PB	PM	TM	PA	PS	
Authority to deliver a Work Package	Work Package PID Quality Register	Accept a Work Package	Team Plan (c) Work Package (a)			(A)* (A)*	(A) (P)	P A	R R		New risk
	Work Package Configuration Item Records Team Plan PID	Execute a Work Package	Specialist product(s) (c) Approval records (o) Quality Register (u) Configuration Item Records (u) Team Plan (u) Checkpoint Reports (c)		(A)	(A)	(R) (R) (A) (A) (R) (R)	P P R R P P	R R R R R R	R P P	New risk New issue
	Work Package Quality Register Configuration Item Records	Deliver a Work Package	Work Package (u) Team Plan (u)				(A) (R)	P P	R R		Completed Work Package

* Senior Supplier

Table 15.1 Overview of the activities of Managing Product Delivery

16 SB, Managing a Stage Boundary

The aim of the Managing a Stage Boundary (SB) process is to provide the Project Board with the correct information from the Project Manager so that they can review the success of the current stage, approve the Stage Plan of the next stage, review the revised Project Plan, confirm the justification of the project and accept the risks.

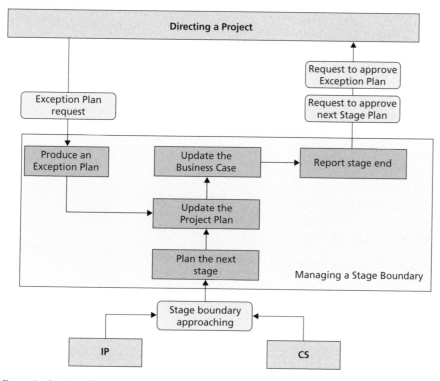

Figure 16.1 Overview of Managing a Stage Boundary (Source: Managing Successful Projects with PRINCE2, produced by OGC)

16.1 SB, basic principles

This process is executed towards the end of a stage, or if it is anticipated that tolerances may be exceeded. It describes the activities of the Project Manager in preparation of the decision taking by the Project Board regarding a go/no go decision at a management stage boundary. During the end stage assessment the Project Board decides whether the project must be stopped or continued and, if it is to be continued, whether it should continue on the same basis or in a changed form.

The objectives of the Managing a Stage Boundary process are:
- Ensuring the Project Board that all products in the previous stage have been delivered according to agreement;
- Preparing the Stage Plan for the next stage, including the agreed tolerances and the required people and resources for the next stage;

- Updating the Project Initiation Documentation and especially the project approach, the Project Plan, the Business Case, the strategies and the project management team with the role descriptions concerned;
- Delivering the information to the Project Board to enable the members to to review the advisability, viability and feasibility of the project, including the most important risks and the aggregated risk level;
- Recording the lessons of the previous stage for the continuation of the project and/or for other projects;
- Requesting authorization from the start of the next management stage.

In the case of a request from the Project Board to produce an Exception Plan, the plan is prepared on the basis of updated information. Following approval by the Project Board, the Exception Plan will replace the Project Plan or the Stage Plan, as appropriate.

16.2 Context

The Managing a Stage Boundary process is based on the principle that there are at least two management stages in a project, namely the initiation stage and one or more delivery stages.

The Managing a Stage Boundary process is initiated from the process, Initiating a Project in the initiation stage and from the Controlling a Stage process for the various delivery stages. The Managing a Stage Boundary process provides the input for the End Stage Assessment of the Project Board in the Directing a Project process.

If the Project Board requests an Exception Plan, the Managing a Stage Boundary process is initiated from the Directing a Project process. The Managing a Stage Boundary process then provides the input for the assessment of the Exception Plan by the Project Board in the give ad hoc direction activity in the Directing a Project process.

The Managing a Stage Boundary process is not activated by the final execution stage, because the Closing a Project process that implicitly also contains the relevant parts of the Managing a Stage Boundary process is then being started.

16.3 SB, process description

The Managing a Stage Boundary process consists of the following activities:
- Plan the next stage;
- Update the Project Plan;
- Update the Business Case;
- Report stage end;
- Produce an Exception Plan.

Plan the next stage

The Stage Plan for the next stage must be sufficiently detailed to serve as basis for the daily management of the stage by the Project Manager. The Stage Plan should contain all specialist and management products to be delivered in the following stage. As part of this planning procedure the Product Descriptions with the quality criteria should be prepared. The Stage Plan should also contain the controls, such as the format, method and frequency of Checkpoint Reports and the Highlight Reports. In conclusion the Stage Plan must contain all tests and other quality activities for the stage, including the effort of people and resources required for this plan.

The Project Manager must coordinate all activities in the quality control framework with Project Assurance. For products to be delivered in the next stage, the Project Manager should work with Project Assurance to establish who needs to be involved in the associated quality control activities in order to achieve acceptance of the products.

In the activity, plan the next stage, the Project Initiation Documentation should be updated and, where appropriate, any adaptations in respect of the quality criteria, strategies and controls should be made. The Stage Plan for the next stage should be developed; the Configuration Item Records for the new products should be prepared and the records for any existing products updated as appropriate. The Quality Register should be updated with the planned quality activities for the next stage. The Issue and Risk Registers should also be updated.

Changes in the staffing of the project management team are ideally made during a management stage boundary. The project management structure and the relevant role descriptions should also be updated as appropriate.

Update the Project Plan

The Project Board uses the Project Plan throughout the entire project to review the progress of the project. It is therefore important that the Project Plan is kept up-to-date, ideally as a minimum at the end of each stage. With an updated Project Plan the members of the Project Board are able to determine what has been achieved so far and what has yet to be realized. The updated Project Plan is also a basis for the updating of the Business Case. An explanation of the possible changes of the Project Plan is included in the End Stage Report.

For the updating of the Project Plan the updated Stage Plan for the current stage, the Stage Plan for the next stage or the Exception Plan, the operative Project Plan, the project approach , the Quality Management Strategy, the Issue Register and the Risk Register are used. This activity produces the updated Project Plan. The updating of the Project Plan can lead to the updating of the project approach, the Product Descriptions, the Quality Management Strategy, the Issue Register and the Risk Register. It may also be necessary to adapt the Stage Plan for the next stage, or the Exception Plan. In a similar situation the update the Project Plan activity or produce an Exception Plan could be started once again.

Update the Business Case

During the entire project a focus on the Business Case is essential. During every management stage boundary the validity of the Business Case is tested once again. Important aspects in this are the updating of the costs, the planning, the dis-benefits and the major risk' of the project. Any external factors which could impact the Business Case should also be considered at this time. With the updating of the Business Case, consideration is given to any known risks and issues and the Risk and Issue Registers may need to be updated and/or reviewed, as appropriate.

A delay in the delivery of the project can have a serious impact on the validity of the Business Case. The implications can include:
- Increase in development costs;
- Shorter production learning curve;
- Loss of a market share;
- Shorter time for recovery of costs;
- Weaker competitive position.

If the Business Case becomes weak, the Project Board should coordinate this with the corporate or programme management. The corporate or programme management will need to determine whether the project is still sufficiently viable to deliver the corporate/programme objectives.

The Project Manager does not own the Business Case, but does have a delegated responsibility for the monitoring of the Business Case. The Project Manager coordinates the changes in the Business Case with the Executive. The Project Manager can be assisted by Project Support and by those from Project Assurance responsible for business assurance on behalf of the Executive. Undertaking the monitoring of the anticipated benefits is the primary responsibility of the Senior User.

The viability of the Business Case is a balance between the risks that are linked to the delivery of the project result and the achievement of the eventual benefits. It is because of this that risks must be regularly assessed and controlled. As part of the Update the Business Case activity a risk analalysis should be performed. With the preparation of the go/no go decision at the management stage boundary it is important that the overall aggregated risk exposure be understood as well as an appreciation of individual risks.

In addition to the Business Case and the Risk Register, the Project Plan, the Benefits Review Plan and the Issue Register provide input for the update the Business Case activity. This activity produces an updated Business Case and Risk Register. It can also lead to the updating of the Benefits Review Plan and the Issue Register. In practice the updating of the Business Case can even lead to having to adapt the Project Plan once more. In such a case the update the Project Plan activity should be repeated.

Report stage end

For each stage, an account must be given to those who have made the effort of people and resources possible and to those who have authorized the execution of the stage. This accountability is presented in the End Stage Report. Ideally this report is best prepared as close as possible to the end of the stage.

In the End Stage Report the actual results of the stage in terms of time, costs and delivered products are reflected in relation to the original Stage Plan and the agreed tolerances. Further, an appraisal of the realizable targets for the next stage and for the entire project is given and a summary is provided of the validity of the updated Business Case and any issues and risks. In this report the team performance is also evaluated and an overview is given of the activities that have been executed within the framework of quality control. The lessons of the past stage are recorded in the End Stage Report: what went well, what can and must be improved, including recommendations for the corporate or programme management. If necessary a separate Lessons Report may already have been prepared for inclusion in an interim Lessons Report to the corporate or programme management.

In the case of benefits that can be realized during the project, any benefits already realized should be included in the review of the Business Case. With a phased-in delivery it should be confirmed by the customer in the End Stage Report that control and maintenance has been arranged so that the delivered products and services can be used. Recommendations for follow-on actions regarding the deliverable products should also be included in the End Stage Report.

The Project Manager sends the End Stage Report with the Stage Plan to the Project Board for assessment and approval. The Project Manager informs the other parties, as is directed in the Communication Management Strategy.

This activity makes use of the current Stage Plan, the updated Project Plan, the Business Case and the Benefits Review Plan, the Issue and Risk Registers, the Communication Management Strategy and the next Stage Exception Plan. This activity produces the End Stage Report and the official request of the Project Manager to start the execution of the next stage. In this activity a Lessons Report and recommendations for follow-on actions are prepared, if necessary.

Produce an Exception Plan

As soon as one or more tolerances of a stage and/or of the entire project are at risk of being exceeded, the Project Manager should escalate this to the Project Board by means of an Exception Report. On the basis of the Exception Report the Project Board decides whether to continue with the project or to stop it. If a valid Business Case still exists then the Project Board in consultation with the programme management can decide to continue with the project in a changed form or not. The Project Board then requests the Project Manager to produce an Exception Plan to support the project going forward. The Exception Plan is produced by the Project Manager via the Managing a Stage Boundary process and is formally approved by the Project Board in the Directing a Project process, via the authorize a Stage or Exception Plan activity.

An Exception Plan is initially produced for the remaining part of the current stage. The Exception Plan replaces the Plan (Project or Stage) that was in trouble; it is about recovery of the project. This replaces the Stage Plan for the next stage. The remaining activities of producing an Exception Plan are equal to the original process, Managing a Stage Boundary. In terms of structure and detail the Exception Plan is equal to the original plan that it replaces, with the addition of the reference to the Exception Report that provides the reason for drawing up the Exception Plan. The Exception Plan is accomplished in cooperation with the project team and members of the Project Board. In the case of an Exception Plan it is even more important to ensure that everybody is involved!

It is important with the preparation of an Exception Plan that the actual status of the Configuration Item Records is checked carefully. It should also be explicitly checked whether the same products are still be delivered and whether the quality expectations and acceptance criteria of the customer have been changed. The outstanding activities of the current stage should be entered in the Exception Plan.

The produce an Exception Plan activity uses the Project Initiation Documentation, the current Stage Plan, the Risk and Issue Registers, the Exception Report and the request of the Project Board to produce an Exception Plan. This activity produces the Exception Plan. The Project Initiation Documentation, the Configuration Item Records and the Issue and Risk Registers as well as the Quality Register must be updated with the particulars of any test to be carried out as recorded in the Exception Plan.

16.4 Overview of SB activities

In table 16.1 the input and output and the responsibilities of all activities of the Managing a Stage Boundary process are reflected.

Input Triggers	Input Management Products	Activity	Output Management Products	CP	Ex	PB	PM	TM	PA	PS	Input Triggers
Stage boundary approaching	Project Plan Lessons Log Configuration Item Records Issue, Risk Register Quality Register PID	Plan the next stage	Next Stage Plan (c)		(A)	(A)	P	(R)	R		-
			Product Descriptions (next Stage Plan) (c/u)		(A)	(A)	P	(R)	R		
			Configuration Item Records (c/u)				A		R	P	
			Risk, Issue Register (u)				P		R	P	
			Quality Register (u)				A		R		
			PID (u)				P		R		
	Project Plan Next Stage Plan Exception Plan Issue, Risk Register PID	Update the Project Plan	Project Plan (PID) (u)	(C)	(A)	(A)	P		R		-
			Issue, Risk Register (u)		(A)	(A)	P		R		
	Business Case (PID) Project Plan (PID) Benefits Review Plan Risk Mngt. Strategy (PID) Risk, Issue Register	Update the Business Case	Business (PID) (u)	C	(A)	(R)	P		R		-
			Benefits Review Plan (u)	C	(A)	(R)	P		R		
			Risk Mngt Strategy (PID) (u)		(A)	(A)	P		R		
			Risk, Issue Register (u)				P		R		
	Current Stage Plan Issue, Risk, Quality Register Lessons Log Business Case (PID) Benefits Review Plan Comm. Mgt. Strategy (PID)	Report stage end	Product Status Account (c)				A		R	P	*Request to approve next Stage Plan* *Request to approve Exception Plan*
			End Stage Report (c)		(A)	(A)	P		R		
			Lessons Report (if required) (EPR) (c)		(A)	(A)	P		R		
			Follow-on action recomm.(if required) (EPR) (c)		(A)	(A)	P		R		
Exception Plan request	Current Stage Plan Exception Report Configuration Item Records Issue, Risk Register Quality Register PID	Produce an Exception Plan	Exception Plan (c)		(A)	(A)	P	(R)	R		-
			Product Descriptions (Exception Plan) (c/u)		(A)	(A)	P		R		
			Configuration Item Records (c/u)				A		R	P	
			Risk, Issue Register (u)				P		R		
			Quality Register (u)				A		R		
			PID (u)	(C)	(A)	(A)	P	(R)	R	P	

Table 16.1 Overview of the activities of Managing a Stage Boundary

17 CP, Closing a Project

The aim of the Closing a Project (CP) process is to create an unambiguous moment when the acceptance of the end result is confirmed and it is established that the objectives according to the original Projection Documentation and the approved changes have been realized, or that the project cannot contribute anything more.

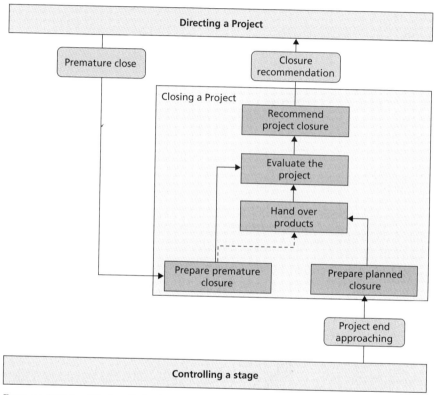

Figure 17.1 Overview of Closing a Project (Based on OGC PRINCE2 material)

17.1 CP, basic principles

A project requires a clear start and end point. Without a definite project closure point a large part of the commitment created through the formal acceptance of the results of the project will be lost. The Closing a Project process describes the activities that must be executed by the Project Manager so that the Project Board can approve the closure of the project. The progress of the project is evaluated against the baseline, ensuring that the project products can be taken into use. Recommendations for follow-on actions are prepared, in . In the case of a phased hand-over it is checked to what extent benefits have already been realized, and the anticipated benefits are updated.

17.2 Context

The Closing a Project (CP) process is generally initiated by the Controlling a Stage (CS) process. If a project no longer has a valid Business Case and is closed prematurely, the CP process is initiated by a direct decision of the Project Board. This can result from the activities, authorize the Project, authorize a Stage or an Exception Plan, or ad hoc direction.

The different activities of the Closing a Project process can be executed in parallel to each other. The activities of the Closing a Project process must be planned separately in the Stage Plan of the final delivery stage.

The Closing a Project process provides the input for the assessment of the project by the Project Board in the activity, authorize project closure.

17.3 CP, process description

The Closing a Project process consists of the following activities:
- Prepare planned closure;
- Prepare premature closure;
- Hand over products;
- Evaluate the project;
- Recommend project closure.

Prepare planned closure

With the closing of a project it is crucial for all information to be available so that the project can be fully completed, leaving no outstanding actions and loose ends. A product status overview prepared by Project Support, can help to check whether all deliverable products comply with the quality criteria, that exceptions have been covered by approved concessions, and whether the delivered products have been accepted by persons with authority. The Project Manager then confirms that all of the delivered products comply with the defined acceptance criteria as specified in the Project Description. The Project Plan is updated with the results of the final stage.

In addition, the project team and the project organization should be dissolved. Approval is requested to inform the parties concerned that the people and resources in service are released and can be deployed elsewhere. A similar instruction is often necessary at quite an early stage in view of contractual agreements made with the suppliers. This, however, contains a risk. It may be that the suppliers are not ready on time and that the instruction is given too soon. It is therefore recommended that the time and the contents of the instruction are carefully coordinated with the different parties, including the Project Board.

Prepare premature closure

A premature closure has a different cause than a planned closure. However, the purpose is the same, namely to create a good basis for the project to be closed. The difference is that the planned closure is initiated by the delivery of all envisaged results, while the premature closure is triggered by the loss of the added value of the project (Business Case).

The Project Manager registers the decision to close the project prematurely in the Issue Register. The Project Plan is updated and the product status overview is requested. From the product status overview it is determined which products have already been accepted by authorized persons, which products are still being developed, which products are covered by approved exceptions and specifications, which products are about to be developed, which products must still be secured or completed within the project or by the corporate or programme management and which products must be transferred to other projects.

This corresponds with the way in which products are handed over to corporate or programme management. Estimates must be prepared for the remainder of the activities. An Exception Plan must be prepared if necessary. Approval is requested to inform the parties concerned that the people and resources in service have been released and can be deployed elsewhere.

Hand over products

The Project Manager should ensure that the project product is accepted by the end users as well as those who will become responsible for the control and maintenance of the project product, and that it is handed over to the customer organization by the supplier. They must ensure that this acceptance and transfer is confirmed. A formal acceptance and handover are essential, especially if products have been developed by external parties.

Statement of acceptance - The Project Manager must provide assurance according to the agreement in the Configuration Management Strategy that the project product complies with the specifications of both parties and that the project product is accepted. It is advisable to have a statement of acceptance signed separately by both parties. The legal handing over of the project product to the customer organization is specified in a separate verbal or recorded process of transfer.

The Project Manager must check beforehand if the necessary control and maintenance organization are present for the project results to be delivered. If that is not the case, the Project Manager must escalate it to the Project Board.

Configuration Item Records - As part of the project product the Configuration Item Records must also be handed over to the customer. They will have to enter the particulars of the delivered products in their configuration management database to enable them to control these products during the period of use.

Recommendations for follow-on actions - Recommendations for follow-on actions must be prepared for all activities not yet executed and for outstanding issues and risks. It is rare for a project to be closed without outstanding actions remaining and/or further recommendations given to the standing organization about how to proceed when the project result has been provided. Requests for exception at the end of a project are typically no longer approved by the Project Board but pushed through to the control stage. Important issues can even provide a reason for starting a new project after completion of the existing project. Many outstanding issues at the end of a project are related to the control stage or to the projects that follow the project currently in hand. These issues should not be lost. If this happens it can lead to a negative experience by the stakeholders in respect of the project. This must be prevented.

Benefits Review Plan - In addition to recommendations for follow-on actions it is important to check whether the existing Benefits Review Plan contains all activities that are required to measure and review the benefits still to be realized after the project has ended. In the case of a phased delivery many benefits will already have been realized during the remaining period of the project. However, most benefits will be realized soon after the project has ended. These benefits can, however, not be measured directly after the project has ended. The project's products will need to have been in operational use for some time before the estimated benefits of the project result can be measured. The measurement and review of these benefits, however, are no longer the responsibility of the project. The plan for similar measurement and assessment must be prepared and agreed upon within the framework of the Project Plan. The Project Manager must update the Benefits Review Plan in this framework accordingly and have it approved.

Project, evaluation

It is important to assesss whether what was agreed has actually been delivered and, if what was originally agreed has changed, how did this happen? How have we directed the project and would we do the same again? Both questions are considered at the end of a project, but each question requires a different line of approach.

End Project Report - The response to the question 'Has what was agreed been delivered and if not, why not?' provides the justification for the project. This justification is recorded in the End Project Report. The End Project Report is prepared by the Project Manager for the Project Board, but is also used by the Project Board for its justification to the corporate or programme management. In the End Project Report the state of affairs at the end of the project is compared to what was originally agreed in the Project Initiation Documentation, and to any changes that have been agreed in the interim. In addition, an assessment of the achievements of the project team is included in an End Project Report and a review is undertaken of the delivered products, the quality assessments undertaken and the registered exceptions to the specifications.

An update is provided of the **Business Case** in the End Project Report. Should any benefits already have been realized on the basis of the delivered products at project closure, then these benefits are also mentioned in the report. If necessary, those benefits that will be realized during the use of the project product are measured later during the post-project benefits review.

In the case of a premature closure of the project the reasons for this closure must also be considered.

People forget very quickly what happened and why things occurred in the way they did. And especially where they were all involved and what they had or had not agreed in the interim. If the Project Manager does not record this personally, then someone else should do it; the worst case is that it does not happen at all. The effect of this can be much more negative than if the Project Manager were to prepare the report personally. It is also advisable to compile the report in such a way that the individual members of the Project Board can use this for reporting to their own corporate or programme management. The End Project Report, in addition to justifying the project for the Project Manager and the Project Board, is an important instrument to retain the commitment built up both during the project and after it as well.

Lessons Report - The response to the question 'How have we directed the project and would we do it the same way again?' provides lessons for corporate or programme management that are important in the preparation and planning of future projects. These lessons are recorded in the Lessons Report. Lessons that are recorded in the Lessons Log are used for compiling the Lessons Report. It is also recommended that another separate lessons evaluation for the entire project is done at the end of the entire project. The lessons of the final management stage should be determined, and then all lessons that have been entered in the Lessons Log to date can be evaluated again. Furthermore new lessons that were not noted before are sometimes identified or it becomes clear that earlier lessons have to be adjusted in the broader context of the entire project. A lessons evaluation at the end of a project is also a good way for the project team to close the project.

As part of the Lessons Report a review is done of what went well and what could have been better in respect of the management and quality control processes, and the methods and techniques. In addition a review is carried out of the specialist activities. It is important that alongside the lessons the particular circumstances of the project are described to ensure that the review is undertaken in this context. Furthermore, the recommendations for following projects are to be explicitly specified. Finally, the calculations of time spent, commitment and costs together with an evaluation of the executed quality reviews are recorded. The lessons can be important to different sections within the corporate organization. It may, therefore, be necessary to divide the lessons for these different sections of organization.

The Lessons Report and the earlier recommendations for follow-on actions can be represented in separate reports, but they can also form a part of the End Project Report.

Recommend project closure

If all preparatory activities, handover and evaluation activities have been undertaken, the Project Manager completes the final activities before going to the Project Board with the recommendation to close the project. The Project Manager closes all logs and registers. The project file is cleared and archived. It is important that this information can be reached easily and remains available for the organization for future audits.

As with the start of the project, communication with the organization and the stakeholders is important, so notification will now have to be given that the project will be closed. The Project Manager informs the Project Board and other stakeholders about the imminent closure of the project, and other matters as specified in the Communication Management Strategy. This communication can be used as a valuable marketing tool. The Project Manager must coordinate this communication with the Project Board beforehand. As a final activity the Project Manager will send the draft project closure notification to the Project Board. Ultimately the Project Board is responsible for all external communication.

In addition to the formal side of the preparation for project closure, the Project Manager must also consider the informal side. Many Project Managers devote significant attention to the building of a team, but forget to pay attention to an effective run-down of the project organization. The run-down is just as important as the building up of a team.

Team members will often not see each other again (at least for a time) after the project, though a bond has been formed. A change of work often leads to uncertainty. These are all reasons for stress. A good closure helps in this respect. A good completion helps team members to close the project successfully for themselves. A good closure is also a good prelude to cooperation in future projects.

The run-down of a project team can, for example, be done by organizing a get-together or a dinner, or by having the project evaluation, or by a celebratory handover of the project product to the customer. In conclusion, ensuring an effective run-down can help team members to leave the project. In this, every project and every person is different.

17.4 Overview of CP activities

In table 17.1 the input and output and the responsibilities of all activities of the Directing a Project process are reflected.

Input Triggers	Input Management Products	Activity	Output Management Products	Responsibilities							Input Triggers
				CP	Ex	PB	PM	TM	PA	PS	
Project end approaching	Project Plan (PID)	Prepare planned closure	Product Status Account (c)				A		R	P	
			Project Plan (PID) (u)				P		R		
Premature close	Project Plan(PID)	Prepare premature close	Product Status Account (c)				A		R	P	
			Project Plan (PID) (u)				P		R		
			Additional Work Estimates (c)		(A)		P		R		
			Issue Register (u)				P		R		
	Issue, Risk Register CM Strategy (PID) Configuration Item Records Benefits Review Plan (PID)	Hand over products	Acceptance records (o)		(A)	(A)	P		R	P	
			Configuration Item Records (u)		(A)	(A)	A		R		
			Follow-on action recommendations (EPR) (c)		(A)	(A)	P		R		
			Benefits Review Plan (u)	(C)	(A)	(R)	P		R		
	PID Issue, Risk, Quality Register Business Case (PID) Follow-on action recomm. (EPR) Lessons Log	Evaluate the project	Business Case (PID) (u)	(C)	(A)	(A)	P				
			End Project Report (c)		(A)	(A)	P				
			Lessons Report (EPR) (c)		(A)	(A)	P				
	Comm. Mgt. Strategy (PID)	Recommend project closure	Issue, Risk, Quality Register (close)				P		R		*Closure recommendation*
			Daily Log (close)				P				
			Lessons Log (close)				P		R		
			Draft Project Closure Notification (c)		(A)	(A)	P		R		

Table 17.1 Overview of the activities of closing a project

18 The Project Environment

Projects can be initiated in completely diverse circumstances: as part of a line organization, a programme or within a portfolio of programmes and projects. For unambiguous communication it is important to reach agreement on the meaning of the different terms that we encounter in the practice of project management. In this chapter we will therefore examine the following concepts:

- What is the difference between a project and a programme?
- What is a multi-project?
- What is a portfolio?

18.1 Project versus programme

In the first chapter of this book the following definition of a project is given:

> *A temporary organization that is created for the purpose of delivering one or more business products according to an agreed-upon Business Case.*

The Executive is accountable for exploiting the end result or product and obtaining benefits. Except for a phased delivery, the benefits start to be realized after the project has been closed. A programme on the other hand is more than the delivery of project results alone. With a programme there is also the responsibility to realize (a part of) the benefits within the completion period of the programme. A programme is defined as:

> *A temporary flexible organization structure created to coordinate, direct and oversee the implementation of a set of related projects and activities in order to deliver outcomes and benefits related to the organization's strategic objectives.*

A programme is a temporary management structure across the entirety of projects and between the projects and the corporate organization, to ensure that specific corporate objectives are realized by means of changes.

In general the results of a number of connected projects are necessary to realize specific objectives. The completion period of a programme therefore is longer than the completion period of the individual projects.

A programme must be deliberately stopped as realizing an organization's strategic objectives and benefits can last for ever. With a programme the pros and cons will have to be weighed in terms of whether the investment in the change and the resultant benefits still justify the continued existence of a separate programme organization. In practice there will come a time when it is no longer necessary to manage the changes in a separate programme, but rather as part of business-as-usual in the line organization. The programme is then dissolved and the programme organization is discharged by the Programme Director. The end of a programme should therefore be self-determined and should not depend directly on an individual output or result determined, as with a project where the delivery of the end result usually marks the end of the project.

In terms of the corporate objectives of an organization, the benefits are defined that must be realized by the programme. Therefore, in addition to undertaking a number of projects, a programme will also have to develop a number of activities through which to exploit the results. The organization must be prepared to carry out the changes. The results of the projects must be implemented in the organization, which must start working with new skills, and care must be taken that the new manner of working becomes 'business as usual' so that the planned-for corporate objectives can actually be achieved.

18.2 Multi-project management

Multi-project management is the management of a group of projects that do not have any mutual coherence other than the optimal use of the same people and resources in the projects.

Projects emanate from a customer-supplier environment. The provider of project services realizes the actual results of the project for the customer and makes the people and resources available for this.

Within multi-project management some optimization can be realized through the directing of the people and resources in these - loose standing - projects. The following matters are important:

- The development of a common reporting structure and of common methods and techniques can lead to a better coordination between the projects and the corporate organization.
- Bundling project-related activities within a corporate unit can ensure that other units can continue to focus on their primary responsibilities.
- Joint purchasing of products and services and/or the joint hiring of staff can lead to an 'economy of scales', and a professional and consistent approach to purchasing and hiring.
- The implementation of a common project management office can lead to a better support of projects, quantitatively as well as qualitatively.
- The use of 'pools' can improve the allocation of staff.

In a supplier organization the projects often have a relationship that goes beyond the use of the same people and resources. Several projects can be undertaken for the same customer. Projects can be developed for a specific market or out of a specific competence that the supplier wants to develop further. These relationships should also be managed by multi-project management.

18.3 Managing a project portfolio

Portfolio management comprises the management of a group of projects and programmes that collectively provide the new capabilities that are necessary to realize one or more strategic corporate objectives.

Starting with the corporate strategic objectives to be achieved and the improvements required for this on the one hand, and the availability of people and resources on the other, individual projects and programmes can be determined and prioritized, and then collectively managed. Based on the total added value of these projects and programmes the organization can realize its corporate objectives.

Projects that jointly deliver new capabilities are also managed as part of programmes. In effect this is also a kind of portfolio. However, the term 'portfolio management' is generally applied to the concept of managing projects and programmes on a corporate level. The management of a coherent set of projects in a programme is usually referred to as a projects dossier or a projects calendar. "What is in a name!".

19 Tailoring

19.1 Introduction

Tailoring, basis principles

One of the characteristics of a project is that the change is unique, or in any case unique enough not to be managed under a line management function but to be started as a project. This means that, in principle, no project is the same as another. Just think of the different sizes of projects, the varying organizations, and the differences in respect of the types of product. Put alongside this the fact that no Project Manager, Executive or project environment is the same and the basis is established for 'tailoring'.

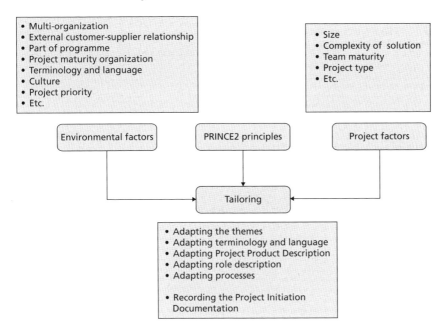

Figure 19.1 Effects of tailoring (Based on OGC PRINCE2 material)

Naturally it is so that a number of types of change, projects and environments can be distinguished to get more insight into all this complexity. This is useful to determine the approach to the project or the selection of the Project Manager who will execute the project. It is important to look at what the project and sometimes even the stage requires. With every project or every stage the Project Manager and the Executive should check what the specific characteristics of the project and the environment are (see figure 19.1). The Project Manager must organize the project accordingly. In this PRINCE2 offers structured guidance to enable the organization of the project to be adapted for every required situation. As such it is a generic method of project management and the method can be used as the start point for organizing and managing all types of projects.

Tailoring a PRINCE2 project is all about making the application of PRINCE2 fit a particular project, so that the correct means of planning, controlling, directing and the use of processes and themes can be adopted.

On the other hand PRINCE2 is embedded with a method for organizing products. This refers to the assurance of the PRINCE2 method throughout the entire organization. The table below indicates all the interim changes and tailoring (see table 19.1).

Embedding	Tailoring
Done by the organization to adopt PRINCE2	Done by the project management team to adapt the method to the context of a specific project
Focus on: • Process responsibilities • Scaling rules / guidance • Standards (templates, definitions) • Training and development • Integration with business processes • Tools • Process assurance	Focus on: • Adapting the themes through the strategies and controls • Incorporating specific terms/language • Revising the Product Descriptions for the management products • Revising the role descriptions for the PRINCE2 project roles • Adjusting the processes to match the above
Guidance in PRINCE2 Maturity Model	Guidance in PRINCE2 method

Table 19.1 Embedding and tailoring (Based on OGC PRINCE2 material)

In tailoring the project organization all aspects of the project must be considered, thus all themes and processes of PRINCE2. What can be used and what not? Can processes be combined (think of Starting up a Project and Initiating a Project in a small project)? How does the terminology link up with the standard corporate terms? Which roles can be combined by one person? How is a link obtained between the programme and the project organization? Which project approach fits which type of project best at the moment? How are the templates and the management products used?

In this chapter an ilustration is given of a number of specific situations and the application of PRINCE2 that can be used. The aim of tailoring the method must always be that what is done is precisely what the project requires to be successful... nothing more and nothing less!

Context

Projects never stand alone and are always executed in conjuction with many factors - whether these are environmental factors or project factors. In figure 19.1 a few examples of such factors have been included. So, tailoring is also about the application of PRINCE2 bearing in mind the external factors.

PRINCE2 has a number of generic principles, themes and processes, but also a few specific topics such as terminology, management products and roles. The principles are universal starting points for project management and in this sense must always be applied in a PRINCE2 project. The themes are the aspects of project management that must be addressed continually and integrally during the entire lifecycle of a project. These aspects must be tailored for the specific project and for the specific circumstances. This often happens in the different project strategies. In a formal organization the risk strategies will, for example, be much more formally structured than in a more visionarily driven organization. Also the way of directing the line organization to the projects will differ in similar organizations and this will have an impact on the plans and strategies.

The PRINCE2 processes consist of connected activities that must be executed at certain times in the lifecycle of the project. It is therefore not advisable to leave these activities out or to skip them. The art is in the application of these process activities, giving each the attention that it deserves. It is thus more a question of how extensively and formally an activity must be executed, or the extent to which activities can be combined, rather than omitting activities altogether.

The same applies for the roles within PRINCE2 (also refer to Appendix B). The starting point is that the correct person must fufill the correct role in terms of the appropriate tasks, repsonsibilities and qualifications, and that everyone is clear what these roles, tasks, responsibilities and qualifications are, and not there is a signed role description available for every party. That can be necessary in critical projects with external parties, but that will more likely work counterproductively in other projects.

The terminology of PRINCE2 is one of the great plus points of using it as standard methodology. By all using the same terms and knowing what they mean, there is much less miscommunication, making the hand-over of work easier. That does not mean that the PRINCE2 terminology must always be insisted on. If everyone in an organization has been used to referring to a project contract instead of a Project Brief and the meaning is the same, then it is probably advizable to continue to use the existing terms.

In principle this also applies to the application of management products. It is sometimes advizable to keep on using existing documents or lay-outs and to enrich these on the basis of the set-up of the management products of PRINCE2, rather than replacing them altogether. One should take care that all aspects are addressed.

> It is always advisable to pay attention to all the parts. Make a conscious choice if it is necessary and, if yes, to what extent it is necessary to describe the part. Avoid bulky plans in which all aspects are described in detail, when this does not contribute to the success of the project. This costs unncessary energy, time and money.
>
> Just think: There are no bureaucratic methods… only the bureaucratic applications of methods. Burocracy is a choice!

The above example ends with the most important starting point in the tailoring of PRINCE2. CHOOSE CONSCIOUSLY!

Whatever an example is given, there will always be a unique situation in a project, so on the basis of that, choices are made for its organization. It is all about the purpose, not the means!

19.2 Projects within programmes

As was indicated earlier, one programme recognizes one or more projects and a number of activities. Think, for example, of an organization that is starting up a warehous as a programme, where all kinds of projects are necessary to bring about its utilization. The aim of the programme is then formulated in terms of profits, stocks, number of customers (per time unit), etc. Examples of projects could be: the organization of the shop, constructing the parking bays, hiring of staff, etc. Nevertheless activities are still required to enable development and to realize benefits, such as the buying and selling of products.

With the tailoring of a project as a part of a programme, a few aspects are adapted: themes, processes and management products. For the programme management aspects reference is made to 'Managing Successful Programmes' (MSP) from the OGC.

With Starting up a Project within a programme there will usually be a good overview in place of what must happen in outline. The project mandate will mainly contain the information that is necessary to enable a Project Brief. Sometimes the complete Project Brief has already been delivered by the programmes. However, this Project Brief must not simply be accepted. It remains important to check again every time whether the delivered particulars are consistent and realistic. That is the responsibility of the Project Manager.

The Business Case of the project is defined on the basis of the standards of the programme. Sometimes the Business Case is provided by the programme or it can be a reduced level of content. The responsibility for realizing and monitoring the benefits of the project lies with the programme. The Benefits Review of the project can be a part of the benefits realization plan of the programme.

The organization structure is about an optimal connection being created between the programme and project organization for an efficient manner of reporting and reviewing. Often the role of Executive will be filled by the programme manager or a direct delegate. In this way coordinated Project Support and Project Assurance is also organized in most cases. This helps enormously with communication in the programme and across projects. In this way the underlying projects will get the necessary information of the programmes much more directly. And vice versa, with information about, for example, a project experiencing scope creep reaching other parties involved in the programme more seamlessly.

Another example of the possible integration of roles is that the change manager(s) in the programme can fill the role of Senior User(s) in the project. The design authority, or the architect of the programme, can also fill the role of Project Assurance or Change Authority in the project (see figure 19.2). What is important is that there is a clear division of responsibilities and that overlap is prevented.

With any project that exceeds the planned level of change, coordination with programme management must take place and, where necessary, programme management will have to take decisions. Here one can for example think of not only changing of the objectives, but also changing the Business Case.

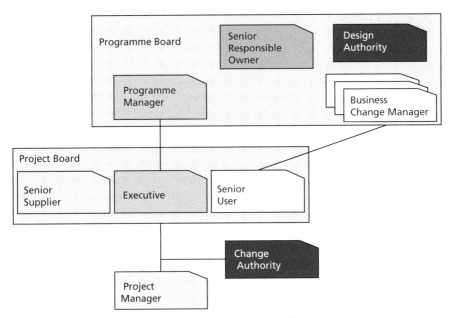

Figure 19.2 Project and programme roles (Based on OGC PRINCE2 material)

Another aspect is that the programme can supply the Quality Management Strategy for the project. In this way the programme can give advice about quality methods and provide help with the execution of quality control and quality assurance activities. With the planning of the project, care must be taken that the standards of the programme monitoring and control are followed. In the Project Plan dependencies with other projects within the programme must be covered.

When determining a project's strategies, the strategies of the programme should form the starting point. It also has consequences for the techniques and classifications to be used,in the project. The issue solution strategy of the programme is used as a guideline for the issue and change procedures of the project.

The information management strategy of the programme will be a guideline for the Configuration Management Strategy of the project. In the same way the monitoring and control strategy of the programme is a guideline for reporting and monitoring activities of the project. In addition the programme determines the project tolerances and the number and length of the stages.

19.3 Project, scale

The scale of a project doesn't only relate to its size, but also the complexity, the risk and the importance of the project. For all PRINCE2 principles it must be established how they can be used instead of not using certain principles (see table 19.2). The use of PRINCE2 can be regarded as the reduction of project failure. If an element of PRINCE2 is taken less seriously, it must be regarded as a risk.

Project scale	Characteristics	Applying PRINCE2

High	• Programme
	  • Business transformation
		• MSP in programme,
		  PRINCE2 in projects

	• Daunting project
	  • High risk, cost, importance, visibility
	  • Multiple organizations
	  • International
		• Multiple delivery stages
		• Extended Project Board
		• Separate TMs and Project Support
		• Individual management products

	• Normal projects
	  • Medium risk, cost, importance, visibility
	  • Multiple site
		• One or more delivery stages
		• Standard Project Board
		• Separate role TM & Project Support optional
		• Some management products combined

	• Simple project
	  • Low risk, cost, importance, visibility
	  • Single organization
	  • Single site
		• Single delivery stage
		• Simple Project Board
		• PM fulfils TM & Project Support role
		• Combined management products

Low	• Task
	  • Simple person Project Board
	  • PM is also carrying out the work
	  • Costs within "business as usual" budget
	  • Straightforward business justification/
	    instruction
		• Work Package delivery

Table 19.2 Examples of projects of different scales (Based on OGC PRINCE2 material)

Large versus small projects

Medium-sized and large projects recognize several delivery stages in addition to the initiation stage. With short-running, non-complex projects with limited risks, the project may only consist of two management stages: the initiation stage and the delivery stage. With small and straightforward projects the Starting up a Project and Initiating a Project processes are sometimes combined (see figure 19.3).

In such cases the two processes can be informally dealt with together in a single discussion. It is advisable in such instances to record the decisions in a discussion memo. For example this could be possible where the project involves a small internal move within one department or something similar.

For small projects the Controlling a Stage process can be summarized in the following activities:
• Allocating work to be executed;
• Monitoring the progress;
• Ensuring that the agreed quality is realized;
• Ensuring that changes are carried out after approval;
• Monitoring risks;
• Reporting the progress of the work;
• Keeping a watchful eye for changes occurring to the plan.

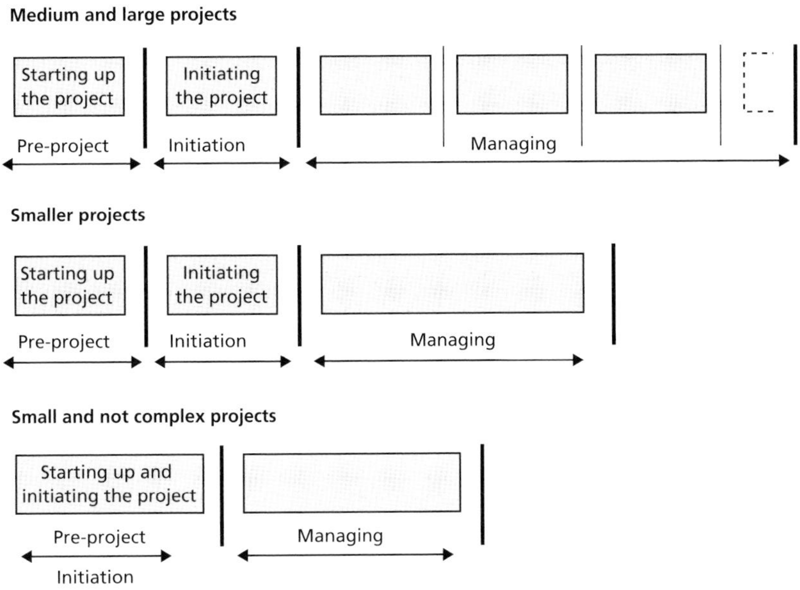

Medium and large projects

Starting up the project	Initiating the project				
Pre-project	Initiation		Managing		

Smaller projects

Starting up the project	Initiating the project	
Pre-project	Initiation	Managing

Small and not complex projects

Starting up and initiating the project	
Pre-project	Managing
Initiation	

Figure 19.3 Phasing projects

These activities must be carried out even in the smallest projects. The question is, however, whether reporting on these activities must always be done by means of bulky reports. In small and informal projects quite simple reports are adequate, or reporting can even be done verbally or via e-mail. However, the project management team must realize that verbal reports have inherent risks. An argument may develop about what had been agreed. And what happens if the Project Manager is temporarily unavailable or leaves the organization? The other themes can also becompleted in a simpler manner, which results in smaller overheads.

For smaller projects and for those projects with only one team that reports directly to the Project Manager, the coordination between the Project Manager and the Team Manager can also be less formal. The Project Manager and the Team Manager may be one and the same person. The work of the Team Manager can be summarized as:

- Setting up agreements on work that must be done;
- Planning the work;
- Supervising the execution;
- Keeping an eye on the progress;
- Reporting the progress;
- Having the products tested;
- Recording the results;
- Keeping up with the changes;
- Ensuring that the products are checked;
- Delivering the products to the Project Manager.

The role of Project Support can also be undertaken by the Project Manager.

For small projects the Closing a Stage process can be summarized in the following activities:
• Checking whether everything has been delivered and accepted;
• Checking that there are no loose ends;
• Recording outstanding points;
• Archiving the project file for later assessments;
• Signing off people and resources.

Small projects and bureaucracy

Sometimes small projects are choked by too much paper and bureaucracy. Most procedures and templates in organizations that are developd to organize and manage projects, are based on large and complex projects. For organistions that have ISO certification, it is applicable for management and specialist activities to be thoroughly undertaken. That requires additional paper work and the accompanying signatures. This is not a PRINCE2 requirement, however.

PRINCE2 can reinforce all of this because the method is complete and is underpinned by a large number of templates. All available PRINCE2 templates are often also used to guarantee a feeling of maximum control over the project. The result is an overkill of documents. This can detract attention from what is really important and can create an aversion to all documents, including instances when a document is in fact important. An overkill of documents in any case costs a lot of time and attention to produce and study. This time and attention can often be better spent on other matters.

All PRINCE2 processes must be adhered to in every project. However, the question is whether all processes in a given project are so important that specific procedures and templates for the execution of these processes are necessary. It is important to use only those procedures and templates in a project that are really important in the given circumstances and provide added value for organizing and managing that project. For small projects certain processes can be gone through and completed quickly and informally.

Project Manager versus Team Manager

Small projects typically use one project team. Only members of the project team itself work on the project, reporting directly to the Project Manager. In addition two situations can arise:

• Separate Work Packagees are to be differentiated, but these Work Packages are still undertaken by one person. This person is then simultaneously a member of the team and Team Manager. In such a case the Project Manager and the Team Manager are separate people.
• The Project Manager does not direct the team member at the level of Work Packages, but at the level of activities. That is also the case if the team member is not yet sufficiently senior to execute the Work Package independently and the Project Manager has sufficient subject content expertise about the work area to be executed. In such a case the Project Manager and Team Manager are one and the same person.

In small projects both situations can occur simultaneously. The second option, however, has the inherent danger that the team member concerned feels insufficiently involved and will sit back, "The Project Manager tells me what to do anyway. It is their project/problem and not my project/problem." This develops especially when a team member (in their own estimation) has sufficient expertise to function as Team Manager, but is not given this responsibility. This is not good for team building and commitment in the team and only reinforces the risk that the Project Manager will still interfere with the content. Too often the Project Manager strongly interferes 'out of habit' with the content of the activities. It could be that the Project Manager is not used to directing on the basis of Work Packages and remains stuck in the old procedure. Coaching by a senior Project Manager is then necessary to avoid similar situations.

Large projects

There is essentially no difference between a 'small' and a 'large' project. A product or service still has to be delivered. A large project, however, is regarded as a project with several project parts where each is directed as a project, for example with its own Executive, Project Board and Project Manager. A Project Board that coordinates all the different Project Boards is responsible for the entire project. The building of the space shuttle is a huge project, just like the building of the Channel Tunnel. However, the result that is delivered is nonetheless still a product. It is for the customer to use the product and to realize their objectives with it. So, it remains a project and not a programme.

The difference between a portfolio of projects and a large project is that in a portfolio of projects the different projects sometimes deliver several results, sometimes solitary and sometimes in clusters, with each being capable of delivering added value for an organization; with a large project, one inextricably bound total result is delivered.

With a large project one can naturally use the same methods and techniques as with multi-project management and with managing a portfolio of projects, and these techiniques are found again in the management of programmes.

19.4 Lifecycle models

PRINCE2 is a project management method; it helps with the management of a project. There are many other methods that address the content approach of a project and the delivery and testing of specialist products. Examples are the waterfall method and agile methods (for example DSDM Atern). Because PRINCE2 stands apart from these aspects, it is possible to connect with these specialist lifecycle models. This is achieved by:

- Enabling the phasing of the management stage to connect with the development lifecycle (for example design, building, testing, handover).
- Using tolerances, such as limited tolerances for time and money and a more generous tolerance for range and quality with the application of an agile model or repetitive models.
- Integrating specialist roles in the Project Management Team. It is often unclear what these roles should be called. This is not a problem. It is only important to be clear about the responsibilities, so that these can be understood by all involved.
- Lifecycle models can also prescribe project management products. In similar cases it is important to avoid double work or breaks in activity. It is also important to make a conscious choice for an unambiguous approach.

19.5 Different kinds of projects

The management of projects is essentially the same, irrespective of the sector in which the project is executed. However, in practice it seems that the approach differs for each sector. So, for example, project management in the IT sector is likely to be different from that for cultural projects. The organization and direction of large and small projects, or single disciplinary and multidisciplinary projects differ. However, in all cases the basic process scheme is the same. The basic scheme can, however, be tailored for each project.

Examples of different kinds of projects are:
- Commercial customer-supplier projects;
- Multi-organization projects;
- Development projects;
- Feasibility projects;
- Projects in the private or public sector.

Commercial customer-supplier projects

If a commercial relationship exists between the customer and the supplier, it is important to realize that there are at least two reasons (one for the customer and one for the supplier) to execute the project, two management systems, two structures and two corporate cultures.

The customer and the supplier also have their own Business Case, commercial customer-supplier projects. If one of the Business Cases no longer applies, the project runs into trouble and will most likely go wrong, even if the Business Case of the other party is still valid. The Business Case of one party is often (partly) not unavailable to the other party.

The appointment of the role of Senior Supplier is a major decision in a commercial relationship. Should the supplier fill this role or leave it to a manager in the customer organization? And what if there is more than one supplier? If there are more than four suppliers, it is recommended that a main accepter be appointed as Senior Supplier. If there is a purchasing stage in the project, an experienced person from the purchasing department can fulfill this role until the supplier has been chosen.

In most cases the Project Manager will be appointed by the customer, while the supplier fills the role of Team Manager. If the project is initiated by the supplier, the corporate representative of the supplier is the Executive, and the head of the department who has to realize the project result is the Senior Supplier. So, who is the Senior User? That is usually the sales manager as they represent the customer within the supplier organization.

It should be indicated in the strategies whether this design emanates from the customer, the supplier or from a combination of the two.

If the project is managed stage by stage, stage assignments can be given, or a contract can be awarded for the entire project with part assignments concluded. The Team Plan of the supplier cannot be made public to the customer. A good Checkpoint Report then forms the basis on which the Project Manager should monitor and control the relevant Work Packages.

The Risk Register can also be confidential, since some risks are relevant to one party only. If a combined Risk Register is kept, then it must be indicated who the owners of the individual risks are.

The change procedure should link up with the purchasing procedures of the customer and the approval procedures of the supplier. The manner in which the progress of the project or the stage is reported, should tie in with the control demands of both organizations.

For the sake of the supplier the processes must be tailored. The Starting up a Project process will take place pre-contract in response to the request of the customer for a tender. Some of the Initiating a Project process will be pre-contract whilst contract negotiations continue. At the end of the initiation stage a contract is subsequently put in place for the delivery. If at the end of SP a contract suddenly has to be placed for the entire project (initiation and delivery), it is advisable that the first stage (the initiation stage) is executed on the basis of hours times price and a definite agreement reached on the contract soon after approval of the Project Initiation Documentation.

The Project Initiation Documentation must fit in with the liabilities and contractual responsibilities. Between the customer and the external supplier a Work Package can be regarded as a legal contract.

Multi-organization projects

It has already been indicated that a project is typically run on the basis of a customer/supplier relationship. However, it can also happen that multiple organizations are involved, such as joint ventures and inter-departmental projects or partnerships. In such a situation the ownership is shared by several organistions. It is advisable to organize similar projects with a programme control as the dominant structure above the actual project and to stick to a single Executive for the project itself.

Development projects

Projects usually start without a rigidly defined output, but with specifications that are developed further during the project. The specifications that have been prepared during the initiation stage are only adequate for making a 'good and agreed' prediction about the business justification of the project. In each stage or with every stage boundary the necessary specifications are defined for the next stage and the specifications of the project products are refined to safeguard the permanent business justification of the project. Similar projects are totally supported by the PRINCE2 method by the drawing up of the Stage Plan and the Business Case at the end of every management stage.

Feasibility projects

A feasibility project or study can be necessary to examine a situation and to develop the options further. A similar study is a project in itself, since such a study is in itself a business product with its own business justification to execute this study (see figure 19.4).

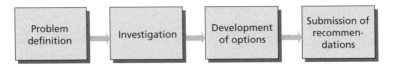

Figure 19.4 An example of a feasibility lifecycle (Source: Managing Successful Projects with PRINCE2, produced by OGC)

A feasibility study produces an advice report containing the recommendation in each case for the future (see figure 19.4). The Project Board can take a decision on the basis of the advice report. Policy projects look like feasibility studies; the output has an immediate value, but contributes to reaching a reliable decision. Executing the decision taken is a project in itself.

Project, private sector or project, public sector

There are different sectors, each with their own dynamics and qualities. However, the characteristics of a project apply whether the organization is in the public sector or the private sector. Despite the fact that there may be differences in the approaches taken to the development of a Business Case, nevertheless the importance of knowing 'what we do it for' is applicable everywhere.

The Business Case, private sector is usually based on a return on investment, even if that is still not the case in some instances. In the public sector the concept of political decision taking often comes up, though the main questions revolve around: what is the added value? Is it realistic and do we want to spend so much money for the proposed solution or are other, less costly solutions available? Even the authorities cannot always get what they want and also their money can only be spent once.

In the public sector as well as the private sector it is notably important that the different stakeholders are involved in the project. The choice of whether to adopt a Project Board depends more on the culture and the scale of the organization and the importance, size and complexity of the project, than on the sector. In the public sector another consultation body is sometimes involved, for which the responsibilities and the competencies are not clear beforehand. Whatever the method, this is a situation to be avoided.

When considering the public responsibility, it is likely that the various reports and decisions are typically recorded more formally in the public sector than in the private sector. In the PRINCE2 method it is entirely up to the customer to complete the necessary documentation.

19.6 Project types

When one looks at the different kinds of projects, the question arises as to whether these projects can be classified and if there are sensible things that can be said about how projects must be approached within each classification. The indications are that some form of classification is certainly possible. Two variables can be identified in each type or kind of project. On the one hand are projects where the 'aim' or 'product' is defined either clearly or obscurely. This is the so called 'product security' of the product. On the other hand the the 'methods of working' or 'processes' can also be clear or obscure.

Turner & Cochrane developed a classification on the basis of methods and clearly defined aims to differentiate between the different types of projects (see figure 19.5).

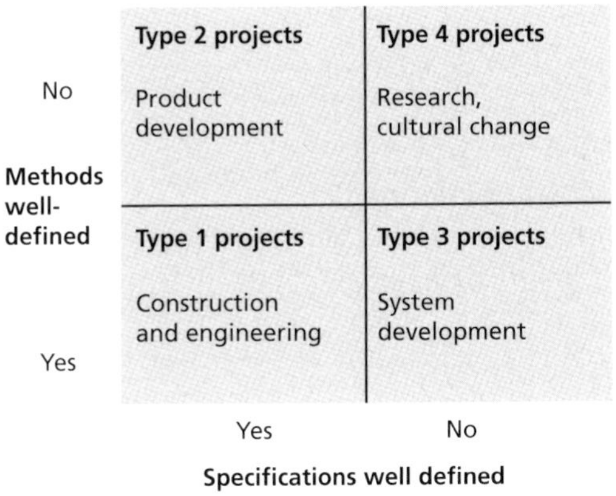

	Yes	No
No	**Type 2 projects** Product development	**Type 4 projects** Research, cultural change
Yes	**Type 1 projects** Construction and engineering	**Type 3 projects** System development

Methods well-defined (vertical axis: No / Yes)

Specifications well defined (horizontal axis: Yes / No)

Figure 19.5 Goals and methods matrix (Source: Turner and Cochrane)

The principle behind this classification is the better the methods and aims are defined, the more chance of success the project has. Equally, it also applies that the weaker the methods and the aims are defined, the lower the chance of success without 'good' management.

Type 1 projects (aims and methods well-defined)
Projects of type 1 are mainly operational projects and are also called classic projects. They are projects with well-known aspects that are structured and executed along fixed lines. For this reason linear phasing is applicable: first analyse, then design, subsequently realize and finally deliver. This phasing is also called the 'waterfall' method.

The compulsory phasing remains necessary to be able to determine decision points with the sponsor or business manager. The projects are in general product-oriented and the project workers have become specialists in the work through repetition. There are, therefore, few uncertainties and, because activities are executed more frequently, there is significant experience which can act as the basis upon which detailed planning can be done. The potential risks are a matter of chance, though the consequences can be estimated well and planned for. As a result of much routine work the Project Manager can concentrate more on work efficiency than with other methods. These projects all have a major chance of success.

An appropriate style of project management is to supervise in the way a manager typically would.

Type 2 projects (aims well-defined, methods not defined)
In this type of project the aim is well defined, but how to achieve that aim is not (yet) clear. Examples include product development projects that are often executed on a multi-disciplinary basis. The completion time is a priority, because the 'time to market' is a determinant for the Business Case and this puts pressure on the project. Because there are many uncertainties about the approach to be adopted, these projects typically start with a preliminary examination stage (feasibility study) which is intended to determine the approach that will lead to the best end result. As a result of this, the project is activity-driven. This subsequently changes into system-directed

or product-directed as soon as the uncertainties have largely been removed. The planning will be undertaken on a detailed basis per stage, and a review will be carried out per stage. It is noticeable that the involvement of users is the greatest at the beginning and at the end of a project. During the project it is minimal.

An appropriate style of project management is to act as a (team) guide.

Type 3 projects (methods well-defined, aims not defined)

These are projects where the requirements and wishes of the user cannot be recorded specifically, or are very difficult to define. These must evolve along with the project. With this type of project the challenge lies particularly in the first project stage. There is a need to change regularly between analyzing and designing the appropriate approach. This approach is also called 'develop phasing' or the 'spiral model'. It can be useful to make use of prototypes, through which the users are quickly confronted with tangible results and, on that basis, to proceed or design a new product. In this manner the requirements evolve during the project.

The projects are tactical or operational and are job-oriented from the start. The more the results become specifically defined, the more they change to being module- or component-directed. With this type of project the involvement of the user is limited to the beginning and the end. The execution is principally in the hands of specialists.

An appropriate style of project management is to act in an advisory style.

Type 4 projects (aims and methods not defined well)

The characteristic of this kind of project is that there are many uncertainties: experience with the activities to be executed is lacking and the consequences of the risks are large. These projects are not easy to plan and therefor they are often worked out and planned in detail stage by stage. The complexity is very high because sometimes ideas that are still vague must deliver concrete results. Given the huge impact for the user, their involvement in the entire project is essential. This is particularly the case in Research & Development projects. The Project Manager and users must work closely together to achieve the desired result. This is called the 'evolutionary project method'. A part of the project is undertaken, completed, learnt from and then implemented in the next stage. By taking small well-organized steps (stages) the users gain an insight into the eventual product and some experience in the manner of working.

An appropriate style of project management would be that of an adventurous explorer who sometimes takes two steps forwards and one back.

Appendices

Appendix A Management products, set-up

In this appendix the set-up of the management products is described, as defined by the PRINCE2 method. The products are described in alphabetical order.

Every management product should be used sensibly and, if necessary, adapted to and tailored to the specific requirements and environment of the project.

The management products are differentiated in terms of baseline products, records and reports (see figure A.1).

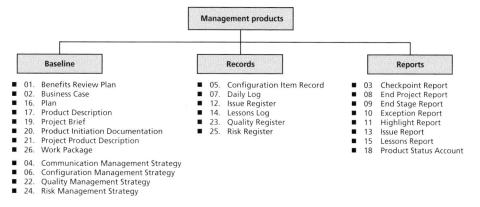

Figure A.1 Overview of management products

Baseline products:
- These management products describe the project and can only be changed after approval and subject to a formal change procedure.

The (presentation) form of these products can differ if this is agreed to. These products are mostly presented in the form of a text document, a spreadsheet or a presentation. Sometimes these products are also presented in the form of a mind map or as a part of a (software) support tool. Sometimes they comprise of separate documents, whilst in other situations it may be preferable to combine them into one document.

Records:
- These are dynamic documents that contain information on the progress of the project.

These products are regularly updated. They are usually reflected in the form of a text document, spreadsheet or according to a specially designed template and printed from a database. The different registers can be used as separate doucuments or be combined. The Daily Log can be a scribbling-pad, but also an electronic agenda or a PDA.

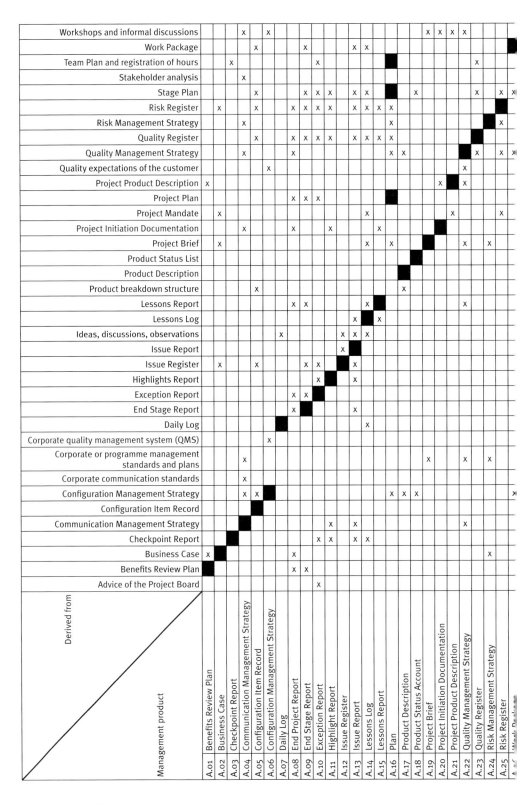

Figure A.2 Relationship between management products

Report:
- This is where the actual status of the diverse aspects of the project is recorded.

There are many (presentation) forms that can be used for the reports. It is important that the reader is informed quickly and clearly about the situation and desired action(s) at that point in time. Reports can be text documents, spreadsheets, or specially designed templates, printed from a database. Often simple signalling functions such as stoplights are used. The reports can also be made verbally during a presentation or meeting, and can also be communicated via e-mail.

The content of the different management products is mostly based on previous management products that have already been prepared, or on information that is made available by corporate or programme management. For an overview of the relationships between the different management products, see figure A2.

A.1   Benefits Review Plan

Aim:

The recording in a structured manner of how and when it will be determined whether the benefits expected by the Executive from the project result have actually been achieved. The Benefits Review Plan is prepared in the Initating a Project process. The Benefits Review Plan is updated at every stage boundary and during the Closing a Project process.

Structure:
- Which benefits should be measured?
- Who is accountable for the anticipated benefits?
- How and when will the anticipated benefits be measured?
- What resources are required to undertake the review of the benefits?
- How will the performance of the delivered products be measured?

Quality criteria:
- Have all benefits mentioned in the Business Case been included?
- Has the baseline situation been determined?
- Are the benefits measureable?
- Has it been detemined which skills or individuals will be required to undertakethe measurements?
- Are the estimated efforts and costs realistic in comparison to the value of the anticipated benefits?
- Has it been considered whether the dis-benefits should also be measured?

A.2   Business Case, aim

Aim:

The Business Case reflects the business justification for the project. The Business Case provides answers to the questions: Why are we doing this project? Which investments are necessary for this? What are the anticipated benefits? The reasons for undertaking the project are indicated in the Project Mandate. In the Starting up a Project process the outline of the Business Case is determined. In the initiation stage the Business Case is refined. The Business Case is used during Controlling a Stage to review the impact of the risks and issues. The Business Case is updated during Managing a Stage Boundary and Closing a Project.

Structure:
- Management summary containing at least the most important benefits and the period to recover costs of the investment;
- Reasons for undertaking the project and how the project contributes to the stategic aims of the organization;
- Possible options considered (doing nothing, doing the minimal or doing something) plus the arguments for not choosing something;
- Expected benefitsthat the project will deliver, both qualitative and quantitative, plus the tolerances for each benefit;
- Anticipated disadvantages, such as higher maintenance and exploitation costs;
- Investment and accompanying assumptions (taken from the Project Plan) plus ongoing operational costs and financing agreements;
- Timescale (taken from Project Plan) and economic life span investment;
- Investment analysis plus manner of financing;
- Most important risks and aggregated risk level with possible countermeasures;
- Advice in respect of business justification and possible actions to be taken.

Quality criteria:
- Are the reasons for undertaking the project in line with the corporate and programme targets?
- Is it clear what the desired option is and why?
- Are the benefits clearly defined and quantified, do they also deliver real financial advantages and is it clear how these benefits will be realized?
- Does the Business Case conform with the Project Plan?
- Is it clear what a successful outcome for the project is?
- Is it clear how the necessary investments are financed?
- Have possible corporate risks been considered, including proposed countermeasures?
- Has the Business Case been prepared according to corporate standards?

A.3   Checkpoint Report

Aim:
The Checkpoint Report is a periodic report from the Team Manager to the Project Manager providing information to the Project Manager on the progress and status of the activities and the interim results of the Work Package to be delivered by the Team Manager. The Checkpoint Reports are prepared in the Managing Product Delivery process.

Structure:
- Release dates;
- Period;
- Follow-on actions of preceding reports;
- Past period:
  –Products being developed;

–Products completed;
–Executed quality activities;
–Identified lessons;
- Next period:
  –Products being developed;
  –Products to be delivered;
  –Quality activities to be undertaken.
- Work Package tolerance status;
- Work Package update on associated issues and risks.

Quality criteria:
- Is the frequency in line with that required by the Project Manager?
- Is the frequency appropriate for the size of the stage and the Work Package?
- Is the information on timely, relevant, accurate and objective?
- Is all the work in hand covered by the report?
- Are all outstanding issues from the preceding report reported?

A.4 Communication Management Strategy

Aim:
Contains a description of the means and frequency of communication to parties both internal and external to the project. It facilitates engagement between stakeholders by establishing a controlled an dbi-directional flow of information.

The Communication Management Strategy is prepared in the Initiating a Project process.

Structure:
- Introduction, including aim, targets and the scope. It also identifies who is responsible for preparing the strategy;
- Communication procedures and possible exceptions to the organization standards;
- Supporting products and resources used;
- Records that are required and how they will be stored;
- Reports prepared, including aim, frequency and the addressees;
- Timing of the diverse communication activities;
- Roles and responsibilities, including those of possible stakeholders from corporate or programme management;
- Stakeholder analysis:
  –Identification of all parties concerned;
  –Current and desired relationships and interfaces;
  –Key messages.
- Information needs of each stakeholder:
  –Information to be delivered by the project;
  –Information to be delivered to the project;
  –Who delivers the information and for whom it is intended;
  –How, how often and in what format does communication take place.
- Description of how execution and effectiveness of the strategy are checked.

Quality criteria:
- Are all stakeholders identified and their communication needs defined?
- Has agreement been reached in respect of the contents, frequency and manner of communication?
- Has a general standard of communication been considered?
- If the project is part of a programme, are the lines of communication structured between project and programme clearly specified?
- Are the different communication resources and frequencies coordinated? Are time, costs and capacity for undertaking the communication activities included and allowed for in the Stage Plans?
- Is an assesment of the efffectiveness of the communication provided?

A.5 Configuration Item Record

Aim:

The Configuration Item Record contains all the necessary information of the associated configuration item (CI) and the mutual relationships with other configuration items. The Configuration Item Record is prepared as a part of the Configuration Management Strategy process. The content of the Configuration Item Records is filled in while creating the relevant plans and updated during the course of the project.

Structure:
- Project identification number;
- CI identification number;
- Current CI version number;
- CI product name;
- CI owner after delivery;
- CI users after delivery;
- Stage when CI is created;
- Source, for example self-produced or supplier;
- CI producer: name of person or group responsible for creating or obtaining the item;
- Release date, for example for production;
- CI status, for example in development, in test;
- Date of last change;
- CI type, for example component, product, release;
- CI category, for example another language;
- CI variants, for example another language;
- Storage site, for example directory or warehouse;
- Copy holders (if applicable);
- Reference to related CIs;
- Reference to relevant issues and risks;
- Reference to relevant correspondence and documentation that defines requirements, design, build, production and verification for the item.

Quality criteria:
- Do the Confguration Items Records reflect the status of the CI's correctly?
- Are all the Configuration Items Records stored correctly in the configuration database and is this sufficiently secure?
- Do the version numbers of the Configuration Items Records conform with the CI's that are in circulation?
- Is the histroy of the CI's recorded?
- Has a process been described where changes of the Configuration Item Records are authorized and are these authorized changes recorded?

A.6 Configuration Management Strategy

Aim:

Recording in an unambiguous manner how the products of the project are to be monitored and safeguarded. The Configuration Management Strategy is prepared during the Initiating a Project process.

Structure:
- Introduction, including the aim, the targets and the scope. It is also specified who is responsible for preparing the strategy;
- Configuration management procedure and possible variances to the organization standards;
- Issue and change procedure and possible variances to the organization standards;
- Supporting tools and techniques used;
- Records used (Issue Register, configuration management database);
- Reports (Issue Report, Product Status Account);
- Planning the configuration management, issue and change control activities;
- Roles and responsibilities, including those of possible stakeholders from the corporate and programme management and the possible Change Authority with the allowed change budget;
- Categories to enable classification of the seriousness and the priority of the issues;
- Coherence with other existing relevant configuration management systems;
- Description of how execution and effectiveness of the strategy are checked.

Quality criteria:
- Are the responsibilities clear to the user as well as the supplier?
- Are the common identification codes indicated?
- Are the agreements for version control and for issues and distribution clear?
- Does the strategy provide the Project Manager with all the necessary product information?
- Are the procedures tested against the corporate and programme standards?
- Is the strategy in proportion to the size and complexity of the project?
- Are the correct people available to manage the chosen configuration management system?
- Has the use of existing management systems been considered?

A.7   Daily Log

Aim:

Recording in a structured manner all relevant information and events in the project that are not covered by other registers and logs. The Daily Log often functions as the personal log for the Project Manager. The Daily Log is organized during the Starting up a Project process.

There may be more than one Daily Log as Team Managers may also decide to have one for their Work Packages.

Structure:

For every registration in the log:
- Date of entry;
- Action/observation/problem/comments;
- Responsible person;
- Target date;
- Results.

Quality criteria:
- Are the entries in the Daily Log legible and unambiguous/understandable should they need to be consulted at a later date?
- Has it been considered who should be given access rights for the Daily Log?
- Are the date, responsible person and target date for being finished consistently filled in?

A.8   End Project Report

Aim:

With this report, the Project Manager gives an account to the Project Board of how the project performed against the version of the Project Initiation Documentation used to authorize it. It also provides the opportunity for passing on lessons that can be applied to other projects, details of any work still to be done, ongoing risks and potential product changes to those who are responsible for future support.

Structure:

Report of the Project Manager about project performance (delivered results, time, money)
- Review of the Business Case;
- Review of the project targets that have been achieved;
- Review of the team performance;
- Review of the products:
  - Quality records;
  - Approval records;
  - Off-specifications;
  - Project product handover;
  - Summary of follow-on action recommendations.
- Lessons Report.

Quality criteria:
- Does the report give a good account of the the course of the project?
- Are all exception situations and their impact described completely?
- Have all issues been concluded or recorded in the follow-on action recommendations?
- Are the recommendations for follow-on actions accompanied with relevant supporting documentation?
- Does everyone responsible for Project Assurance agree with the content of the report?

A.9   End Stage Report

Aim:

The End Stage Report provides a summary of the progress and actual status of the project and is the account of the Project Manager of the past stage. On the basis of this the Project Board can take a well-informed decision on the future of the project (go/no go decision for the next stage) and grant discharge of the past stage of the project. The End Stage Report is prepared in the Managing a Stage Boundary process.

Structure:
- Summary and account by the Project Manager of the past stage;
- Review of the Business Case;
- Benefits already achieved to date;
- Benefits to be achieved later;
- Anticipated net benefits;
- Deviations to the agreed Business Case;
- Aggregated risk level;
- Review of extent to which project targets have been realized;
- Review of extent to which stage targets have been realized;
- Team performance assessment;
- Review of products:
  –Quality records;
  –Approval records;
  –Off-specifications;
  –Phased handover (if relevant);
  –Summary of follow-on action recommendations (if relevant).
- Lessons Report (if relevant);
- Summary of current risks and issues;
- Forecast for project and the next stage against the planned performance targets within the set tolerances for time, cost, quality, scope, benefits and risk.

Quality criteria:
- Does the report give a clear view of the progress against the plan?
- Does the report give a good account of the past stage?
- Are abnmormal situations descibed, including the possible impact upon the project?
- Does everyone responsible for Project Assurance agree with the content of the report?

A.10 Exception Report

Aim:
An Exception Report is prepared by the Project Manager if the agreed tolerances of a Project Plan or Stage Plan have been, or are in danger of being exceeded. The Exception Report gives the Project Board insight into the possible options and recommendations for proceeding. The Exception Report is produced during the Controlling a Stage process.

Structure:
- Title;
- Cause of exception;
- Consequences of the deviation for the project as well as for the corporate and programme management;
- Possible options, including the effect of every option on the Business Case, risks and tolerances;
- Recommendations, icluding reasons;
- Lessons for the current project and future projects.

Quality criteria:
- Is the current status of the progress and expenditure given unambiguously and accurately?
- Is the cause of the deviation given clearly and are its consquences clearly assessed and described?
- Are the effects on the Business Case and the Project Plan included with the description of the consequences?
- Have the options been analyzed and recommendatios made for the most appropriate way to proceed?
- Has the Exception Report been made available in a correctly and imely way?

A.11 Highlights Report

Aim:
The Highlights Report is prepared for the Project Board (and possibly other stakeholders) by the Project Manager to periodically give them an overview of the highlights of the status, the progress and potential problems of the project. The Highlights Report is prepared during the activity, report highlights, in the Controlling a Stage process.

Structure:
- Release date;
- Period;
- Summary of current status;
- Current reporting period:
  - Work Packages (waiting for authorization, in execution, completed);
  - Completed products;
  - Planned products but not started or delivered;
  - Corrective actions taken.
- Next period:
  - Work Packages (to be authorized, in execution, to be delivered);
  - Products to be delivered;
  - Corrective actions to be taken.

- Project and stage tolerance status;
- Status of requests for change (received, approved/denied, current);
- Status of most important issues and risks;
- Lessons report (if relevant).

Quality criteria:
- Does the report correctly reflect the current status of the period?
- Are potential problems adequately exposed?
- Is the information on time, relevant, accurate and objective?
- Are the depth and the frequency of the report correct?

A.12 Issue Register

Aim:

Recording in a structured manner all the reported issues that are being formally managed, so that all issues have a unique reference number, it is known what kind of issue it is and there is a summary of all the issues, including the priority and status of the issues. The Issue Register is organized during the Initiating a Project process and is updated as soon as new issues are recorded or the status of the outstanding issues changes.

Structure:

For every entry in the register:
- Identification number;
- Issue type (request for change, off-specification, problem/concern);
- Submitter;
- Issue Report author;
- Registration date;
- Issue description, the reasons and impact;
- Priority;
- Severity;
- Status;
- Closure date.

Quality criteria:
- Does the status indicate whether action has been taken?
- Does every project issue have a unique reference number?
- Is a process defined for the updating of the Issue Register
- Is access to the Issue Register controlled?
- Is the Issue Register kept in a safe place?

A.13 Issue Report

Aim:

Recording the description, the impact and the decisions regarding requests for change, off-specifications, and problems/points of concern.

The Issue Report is prepared during the capturing and reviewing issues and risks activity in the Controlling a Stage process.

Structure:
- Identification number;
- Issue type (request for change, exception to specification, problem/concern);
- Registration date;
- Submitter;
- Issue Report author;
- Issue description;
- Impact analysis;
- Recommendation;
- Priority;
- Severity;
- Decision;
- Approved by;
- Decision date;
- Closure date.

Quality criteria:
- Is the issue stated clearly?
- Are all consequences included in the assessment of the issue?
- Has the issue been registered correctly in the Issue Register?
- Has the issue been examined for its effect on the tolerances?
- Have the decisions taken been recorded clearly and unambiguously?

A.14 Lessons Log
Aim:

The recording of the lessons in a structured manner during the project. These lessons can be useful for the current project and can also provide input for the Lessons Report, and so prove of value for future projects. The Lessons Log is organized during the Starting up a Project process. The Lessons Log must, as a minimu, be updated at the end of each stage.

Structure:
For every entry in the Lessons Log:
- Type of lesson:
  – Project level, applicable to the project in question;
  – Corporate and/or programme level, to be passed on to corporate and/or programme management;
  – Both project and corporate and/or programme management level.
- Lesson detail (event, impact, cause/trigger, warning indicators, identified as a risk or not);
- Date logged;
- Submitter;
- Priority.

The following questions must always be asked for all lessons: What went well? What can be improved? What are the recommendations?

Quality criteria:
- Does the status indicate whether action has been taken?
- Is there a process in place by which the Lessons Log is updated?
- Are the lessons uniquely identified and is it clear to which product or process they relate?
- Have all lessons been saved correctly and are they secure?

A.15 Lessons Report
Aim:

Recording in a structured manner all of the relevant lessons from the project, so that the lessons can be applied to other projects. The Lessons Report is prepared as a part of the Managing a Stage Boundary and Closing a Project processes. If relevant, a Lessons Report can be created at any time in the project and should not necessarily wait until the end.

Structure:
- Executive summary;
- Scope of the report (stage or project);
- Assessment of what went well and what can/must improve;
  - Project management method (including tailoring PRINCE2);
  - Specialist methods used;
  - Project strategies;
  - Project controls, including the effectiveness of any tailoring.
- Review of the captured data, for example:
  - Amount of effort to create the products;
  - Statistic data of quality activities;
  - Statistic data of issues and risks.

For specific lessons it could be necessary to provide additional details, such as event, impact, cause/triggers, warning indicators and whether the triggered event had been identified as a risk or not.

Quality criteria:
- Are all controls included in the review?
- Is a statistic evaluation of the quality controls included in the review: how many faults have been established after products were approved?
- Have post-calculation data for the delivery of all production, quality and management products been included and recorded?
- Are unexpected risks reviewed so that future projects can prepare for them?
- Is the entire project management team involved in the evaluation?
- Is there approval from Project Assurance?

A.16 Plan

Aim:

A plan is a statement of how and when aims will be achieved. It describes the products, activities and resources required for the scope of the plan. PRINCE2 recognizes three levels of plans: Project Plan, Stage Plan and, optionally, Team Plan. The Team Plan can deviate from the other plans as regards structure and content. An Exception Plan replaces the current plan of the same name.

Structure:
- Plan description, including the scope of the plan and the planning approach;
- Prerequisites;
- External depencencies;
- Planning assumptions;
- Lessons included;
- Monitoring and control;
- Time and budget, including provisions for risks and changes;
- Tolerances (time, money, scope and possible risks);
- Product Descriptions;
- Schedule appendix, which may include graphic representations of :
  –Gantt or bar charts;
  –Product breakdown structure;
  –Product flow diagram;
  –Activity network;
  –Summary of the required resources by resource type;
  –Summary of the requested and specific persons assigned.

Quality criteria:
- Is the plan realistic and feasible?
- Are the estimates based on historical data or underpinned by the resources who will undertake the work?
- Does the plan give a good description of the control activities, as agreed in the Project Initiation Documentation?
- Do the Team Managers agree that the plan is achievable?
- Is the plan described to the correct level of detail?
- Does the plan support the diverse strategies and the project approach?
- Does the plan comprise lessons already acquired and possible legal obligations?
- Does the plan comply with corporate and/or programme standards?

A.17 Product Description

Aim:

A Product Description ensures that all stakeholders have the same picture of what is required to deliver a product in terms of the purpose, function and appearance of the product, who will use it, the level of quality required, the activities and skills required to produce, review and approve the product. The Product Description is created as soon as the necessity for the product has been determined and is baselined as soon as the plan, through which the product concerned is to be delivered, is approved.

Structure:
- Identification number;
- Product name;
- Aim of the product;
- Composition, a list of the different part products;
- Source products, such as:
  –Specifications/drawings on the basis of which the product will be made;
  –Materials with which the product will be made;
  –Supplier or other parties from whom a product is obtained.
- Format and presentation: the characteristics with which the product must comply;
- Required skills to manufacture the product;
- Quality criteria;
- Quality tolerances;
- Quality method;
- Quality skills;
- Quality responsibilities:
  –Producer;
  –Reviewer(s);
  –Approver(s).

Quality criteria:
- Is it clear why the product is necessary?
- Is the Product Description sufficiently detailed to enable the drawing up of a plan for the development of the product and for monitoring the progress of the development of the product?
- Is it clear who is responsible for the development of the product and does this conform with the project management structure and the Quality Management Strategy?
- Are the quality criteria unambiguous and measurable and do the criteria correspond with the applicable quality standards and the agreed acceptance criteria?
- Can it be determined whether the types of quality inspection required are able to verify that the quality criteria have been satisfied?
- Has the Senior User confirmed that their requirements of the product are accurately defined?
- Has the Senior Supplier confirmed that the requirements of the product can be achieved?

A.18 Product Status Account

Aim:

A report on the state of products within defined limits. The limits can vary and could cover the entire project, a stage or a Work Package. The report contains information about the current status, the history and the changes carried out. The report is especially suited for checking the correctness of the version numbers in use. It is derived from the Configuration Item Records.

Structure:
- Scope of the account (project, stage, Work Package);
- Date report is prepared;
- Product status, for example:

–Product identification number;
–Version number;
–Status and date of last change;
–Owners, copy holders, location, user(s);
–Producer and date allocated to producer;
–Planned and actual date Product Description was baselined;
–Planned and real date product was baselined;
–Planned date of next baseline;
–List of related items;
–List of relevant issues and risks.

Quality criteria:
- Are the names of all the products the same as in the product breakdown structure and the Configuration Item Records?
- Do the particulars and the data correspond with those in the updated Stage Plan?

A.19 Project Brief

Aim:
The Project Brief enables the Project Board and the corporate and/or programme management to check whether the project is sufficiently viable. This establishes the basis for the Initiating a Project process. The Project Brief is prepared during the Starting up a Project process. During the Initiaiting a Project process the contents of the Project Brief are extended into the Project Initiation Documentation, after which the Project Brief is no longer maintained

Structure:
- Project definition:
  –Background;
  –Project objectives;
  –Desired outcome;
  –Scope and exclusion;
  –Constraints and assumptions;
  –Parties concerned;
  –Interfaces;
  –Constraints and assumptions.
- Outline Business Case;
- Project Product Description;
- Project approach;
- Project management team structure;
- Role descriptions;
- References.

Quality criteria:
- Is the Project Brief short and yet complete?
- Are the project objectives SMART (Specific, Measurable, Acceptable, Realistic and Time-limited)?

- Does the Project Brief conform with the project mandate and with the requirements of the business and the users?
- Does the Project Brief provide management with a firm and complete basis to establish whether the project is valid and to authorize project initiation?
- Have different solutions for delivering the project product been considered?
- Are the aims, project approach and strategies in line with the corporate guidelines in the area of social responsibility?

A.20 Project Initiation Documentation

Aim:

The Project Initiation Documentation defines the project and contains all the information that the Project Board needs to be able to authorize the project. It forms the basis for managing the project and reviewing the project structures. It is to be regarded as a 'contract' for the project between the Project Manager and the Project Board.

The Project Initiation Documentation provides answers to the following questions:
- What should the project achieve?
- Why is it important to achieve this?
- Where is the project carried out?
- Who are involved and what are their responsibilities?
- How and when will activities take place?

The Project Initiation Documentation is assembled as the final activity during the Initiating a Project process.

Structure:
- Project definition:
  –Background;
  –Project objectives and desired outcomes;
  –Scope and exclusions;
  –Constraints and assumptions;
  –Users and other stakeholders;
  –Interfaces.
- Project approach;
- Business Case;
- Project management team structure and role descriptions;
- Management Strategies (Quality, Configuration, Risk and Communication);
- Project Plan;
- Controls;
- 'Tailoring' of PRINCE2.

Quality criteria:
- Does the documentation give a good and complete picture of the project?
- Does the documentation describe a valid and achievable project that conforms with the targets of the the corporate or programme management?

- Has the project management team structure been filled in comletely with names and duties?
- Has the project management organization been validated by names and titles and approved and signed role descriptions?
- Does the project management structure indicate to whom the Project Board reports?
- Do the controls comply with the scope of the project, the corporate risks and the importance of the project for the organization?
- Does the report have a clear reporting and consultation structure and is this adequate for good direction of the project?
- Are the agreed controls adequate for the desired direction by the Project Board, Project Manager and Team Managers?
- Are the agreed controls also sufficient for those who are responsible for the Project Assurance?
- Is it clear who is reponsible for administering each of the controls?
- Are the aims, approach and strategies consistent with the corporate guidelines in the area of social responsibility?
- Is the documentation adequate for the size and complexity of the project? For smaller projects a single document is sufficient. For larger projects a collection of documents is more appropriate. Consider whether 'dynamic' elements can perhaps be better described and maintained separately.

A.21 Project Product Description

Aim:

Recording what the project must deliver in order to be accepted by the customer. It is used to reach agreement about the scope and rquirements of the project and for determining the quality expectations of the customer, including acceptance criteria, methods and responsibilities. The Project Product Description is created during the Starting up a Project process and refined during the Initiating a Project process when the Project Plan is produced. The description is subject to the formal change procedure and is thus tested and if necessary updated during the Managing a Stage Boundary process. During the Closing a Project process, the Project Description is used to check whether the project has delivered what wasa expected of it, and that the acceptance criteria have been met.

Structure:
- Project title;
- Aim of the project product and who is going to use it;
- List of the most important products to be delivered by the project;
- Source products, such as:
  - Project mandate or feasibility study;
  - Specifications/drawings on the basis of which the product must be developed;
  - Exisiting products that must be modified.
- Required skills to manufacture the product;
- Quality expectations of the customer;
- Acceptance criteria;
- Project-level quality tolerances;
- Manner in which acceptance will be determined;
- Who will be reponsible for confirming acceptance.

Quality criteria:
- Is the aim of the project clear?
- Does the Project Product Description contain the entire scope of the project?
- Do the acceptance criteria comply with the wishes of all stakeholders (for example maintenance and control as well)?
- Does the Project Product Description describe how the users and maintenance and control will review the delivered products?
  –All criteria are measurable and in themselves realistic;
  –The criteria in combination are realistic and consistent;
  –All criteria are tested in the project lifecycle.
- Have the following been included in the preparation of the quality expectations of the customer:
  –The characteristics of the key quality requirements;
  –All elements of the customer's quality management system (QMS) to be used;
  –All remaining standards that must be applied;
  –The level of customer satisfaction to be achieved.

A.22 Quality Management Strategy

Aim:

It is used to define how the quality of the products to be delivered is assured, so that the quality expectations of the customer are satisfied. The Quality Management Strategy is prepared during the Initiating a Project process.

Structure:
- Introduction, including aim, targets and the scope. The person(s) responsible for preparing the strategy is also stated;
- Quality management procedures and possible exceptions to organization standards:
  - Quality planning;
  - Quality control:
    - Quality standards that apply;
    - Templates and forms to be used;
    - Definitions of the type of quality method (for example inspection, review, audit);
    - Metrics to be used in support of quality control.
  - Quality assurance:
    - Quality responsibilities of the members of the Project Board;
    - Compliance audits;
    - Corporate and/or programme management reviews.
- Supporting tools and techniques used;
- Records used (for example Quality Register);
- Reports, including their aim, frequency and addressees);
- Planning of quality checks and other quality activities;
- Roles and responsibilities, including those of possible stakeholders from corporate or programme management.

Quality criteria:
- Is it clearly defined how the quality expectations of the customer will be satisfied?
- Are the responsibilities for the achievement of the required quality defined unambiguously?
- Are the responsibilities for quality defined beyond the project level and thus independently of the Project Manager?
- Does the strategy conform with the quality policy of the organizations concerned?
- Does the strategy comply with the corporate and/or programme quality standards?
- Is the approach to quality assurance appropaite in the light of the standards to be applied?

A.23 Quality Register

Aim:

The recording in a structured manner of all planned and executed quality activities, so that all quality activities have a unique reference number and there is a pointer to all quality records, together with a summary of the number and type of quality activities undertaken. The Quality Register is created during the Initiating a Project process, updated when the consecutive plans are detemined and brought up-to-date after every quality check activity.

Structure:

For every entry in the Quality Register:
- Identification number;
- Product number and product title;
- Method employed (for example test, review, audit, pilot);
- Responsible staff or person (name, duty), for example for a quality review it may be chair, presenter, reviewers, administrator etc.;
- Planned, forecast and actual dates for:
  –Quality activity;
  –Sign-off.
- Result (for example approved, partly approved, rejected);
- Quality records, these being the references to the inspection documentation (for example test plans or the actions to be executed).

Quality criteria:
- Is there a procedure that assures that all quality checks have actually been included in the Quality Register?
- Has the responsibility for updating the Quality Register been assigned to a specific person?
- Is all input uniquely identified and linked to a product?
- Are all actions to be taken plainly and clearly communicated?
- Has the Quality Register been saved correctly and is it sufficiently secure?
- Are all quality activites at an appropriate level of control?

A.24 Risk Management Strategy

Aim:

Recording in an unambiguous manner the specific risk management techniques and standards to be applied, and the responsibilities for an effective risk management procedure The Risk Management Strategy is created during the Initiating a Project process.

Structure:
- Introduction, including aim, targets and the scope. It is also stated who is responsible for preparing the strategy;
- Risk management procedure and possible variations to corporate or programme management standards The procedure comprises at least:
  - Identification of risks;
  - Assess risks;
  - Plan countermeasures;
  - Implement countermeasures;
  - Communication.
- Supporting tools and techniques used;
- Records used (for example Risk Register);
- Reports, including their aim, frequency and addressees;
- Timing of formal risk management activities;
- Roles and responsibilities, including those of possible stakeholders from corporate or programme management;
- Definition of scales for determining the opportunity and impact of the risk;
- Risk proximity categories (for example imminent, during the project, after the project);
- Risk categories (optional);
- Categories of risk responses;
- Early-warning indicators;
- Risk tolerances (project and possible stage risk tolerances);
- Risk budget (if applicable);
- Description of how the execution and effectiveness of the strategy are checked.

Quality criteria:
- Are the responsibilities clear to the customer as well as the supplier?
- Is the risk management procedure unambiguous and understandable to all parties?
- Are the scales, expected value and proximity definitions clear and unambiguous?
- Are the selected scales suitable for the required control level?
- Are the risk reports clearly recorded?

A.25 Risk Register

Aim:
Recording in a structured manner all identified risks relating to the project, including the status, history and the countermeasures to be taken. The Risk Register is created during the Initiating a Project process and is updated as soon as new risks are recorded or the status of the outstanding risks changes.

Structure:
For every entry in the Risk Register:
- Risk identification;
- Risk author;
- Registration date;
- Risk category;

- Risk description;
- Risk probability;
- Risk impact;
- Expected money value risk;
- Proximity of the risk;
- Risk responses;
- Risk response categories (how the project will treat the risk;
- Risk owner;
- Risk-actionee;
- Actual status of risk.

Quality criteria:
- Does the Risk Register indidate whether actions have been taken?
- Does every risk have a unique reference number, including a reference to the product to which it relates?
- Does every risk have a risk owner and if necessary a risk actionee?
- Has the Risk Register been stored correctly and is it sufficiently secure?

A.26 Work Package

Aim:

A set of information about one or more required products that is collated by the Project Manager in order to hand over the responsibility for the delivery of the product(s) to a Team Manager or a team member. A Work Package is prepared by the Project Manager in the Controlling a Stage process.

Structure:
- Date;
- Team Manager or person authorized
- Description of the Work Package;
- Techniques, processes and procedures to be applied;
- Operations and maintenance interfaces;
- Development interfaces;
- Configuration management requirement;
- Agreed targets in respect of effort, costs and start and end data and the most important milestones of the Work Package;
- Tolerances;
- Constraints;
- Checkpoint Reports (frequency and content);
- Problem handling and escalation procedure;
- Main points of Stage Plan (extract or reference);
- Product Descriptions (extract or reference);
- Approval: who will approve the products to be delivered and how will the Project Manager have to be informed of this and of the completion of the entire Work Package.

Quality criteria:

- Are the objectives of the Work Package SMART?
- Has the Work Package been understood and accepted by the recipient?
- Are the Product Descriptions defined for all important deliverable products in the Work Package, including acceptable quality criteria?
- Are the Product Descriptions and the remaining parts of the Work Package consistent?
- Is there agreement on the standards to be applied?
- Do the standards conform with the applicable standards for similar products?
- Are all the interfaces defined?
- Are there agreements on the Checkpoint Reports?
- Is an escalation procedure for issues and risks included?
- Is there agreement on what exactly should happen?
- Is there agreement on the constraints in terms of the resources, the money to be spent and the time available?
- Do the agreements in the Work Package conform with the Stage Plan?
- Are the requirements for independent quality activities documented and agreed?

Appendix B Roles and responsibilities

B.1 Project Board

The Project Board is accountable to corporate or programme management for the success of the project and has the aurthority to direct the project within the conditions and tolerances as stated in the project mandate. The Project Board should give unambiguous direction to the project and make the required capacities available. The Project Board should visibly support the Project Manager and guarantee delivery of the project result within the agreed tolerances. The Project Board is also responsible for communications between corporate or programme management and other stakeholders.

Project Board members can delegate some Project Assurance tasks to individuals, depending upon the scale, complexity, importance and risk of the project. The Project Board can also delegate the authority to decide on the requests for change and off-specifications to a Change Authority.

The members of the Project Board must support the Executive in the execution of his/her role. The Executive can delegate a part of their tasks, responsibilities and authorities to the remaining members of the Project Board.

As a result of this, the Project Board is responsible for:
Start-up and initiation:
- Confirmation of the project mandate and the project tolerances;
- Approval of the Project Brief and the Stage Plan, and authorization of project initiation;
- Determining the different classifications of issues and risks;
- Appointing the Change Authority and approving the change budget;
- Approving the Project Initiation Documentation and authorizing the start of the project;
- Approving the Stage Plan and the execution of the first delivery stage.

During the project:
- Providing complete direction of the project and ensuring that the project remains viable;
- Determining stage tolerances, approving Stage Plans including the accompanying Product Descriptions and authorizing the next stage;
- Ensuring that risks are managed;
- Approving requests for change;
- Taking decisions in respect of escalated issues;
- Approving Exception Plans when stage-level tolerances are forecast to be exceeded;
- Communicating with stakeholders;
- Approving completed products.

At the end of the project:
- Ensuring that all products are delivered satisfactorily and that all acceptance criteria have been satisfied;
- Confirming the acceptance criteria of the project product;
- Approving the End Project Report;
- Approving the Lessons Report and ensuring that this is passed on to the relevant sections of corporate and programme management;

- Ensuring that actions regarding outstanding issues and risks are included in follow-on action recommendations and that these are passed on to the departments concerned;
- Ensuring that the Benefits Review Plan is updated and handed over to corporate or programme management;
- Authorizing the closure of the project and sending the notification of the project closure to the stakeholders concerned.

Members of the Project Board must:
- Have sufficient authority to be able to take decisions and approve plans;
- Have sufficient authority to release people and resources for the project;
- Be capable of representing the interests of the business, users and suppliers;
- Preferably be available during the entire project.

The core competencies for the members of the Project Board are:
- Decision making;
- Delegation;
- Leadership;
- Negotiation and conflict resolution.

B.2 Executive

The Executive is ultimately accountable for the success of the project, supported by the Senior User(s) and the Senior Supplier(s) in the Project Board. The Executive must ensure that the project result is delivered within the set tolerances and that the project result will achieve the anticipated benefits. The Executive is responsible for the Business Case throughout the project.

Resulting from this, the Executive is responsible for:
- Designing and appointing the project management team;
- Supervising the development of the Project Brief and the Business Case;
- Ensuring that the project conforms with corporate or programme management strategies;
- Ensuring the financing of the project;
- Approving external suppliers in a commercial customer-supplier relationship;
- Initiating and chairing the Project Board meetings;
- Holding the Senior User responsible for realizing the benefits defined in the Business Caseand seeing to it that the benefit reviews are undertaken;
- Holding the Senior Supplier responsibile for the quality and integrity of the specialist approach and specialist activities created for the project;
- Monitoring and controlling the progress of the project on a strategic level and monitoring and ensuring the viablitiy of the project;
- Ensuring that issues and risks that can have an impact on the Business Case are identified, assessed and controlled;
- Taking decisions on issues and risks that are escalated, with a focus on the constant viablity of the project;
- Escalating issues and risks to corporate or programme management if it is anticipated that the project tolerances will be exceeded;
- Handing over the responsibility for the benefits reviews after the delivery of the project to corporate or programme management.

B.3   Senior User

The Senior User represents the interests of all those who will be using the project's products. The Senior User is responsible for ensuring that the specifications with the accompanying acceptance and quality criteria are completely and unambiguously prepared and that the product is fit for use.

The Senior User is responsible for identifying and defining the benefits and is required to demonstrate to corporate or programme management that the anticipated benefits have been realized.

The Senior User is responsible in particular for:
- Ensuring that the desired result is specified and realized;
- Approving the Product Descriptions of products that are important to users;
- Ensuring that the delivered products are assessed on the basis of the requirements of the user and are fit for use;
- Ensuring that the appropriate user resources are available for preparing the specifications and reviewing the completed products;
- Resolving differences of opinon between users over specifications and priorities;
- Taking care to focus on the desired end result from the perspective of the users;
- Undertaking Project Assurance from the perspective of the users;
- Informing and advising user management in respect of all project-related matters;
- Ensuring that the expected benefits are realized;
- Providing a statement of the actual versus forecast benefits during the benefit reviews;
- Maintaining business performance stability during the implementation of the delivered products and carrying through the agreed changes.

B.4   Senior Supplier

The Senior Supplier represents the interests of all those who design, develop, facilitate, produce and implement theproject's products. The Senior Supplier is accountable for the quality of the products to be delivered by suppliers and is responsible for the technical integrity of the project.

The Senior Supplier is in particular responsible for:
- Reviewing and confirming the viability of the project approach;
- Ensuring that the suggestions for design, development, production, support and the implementation are realistic;
- Ensuring that the quality procedures during the execution of the work are applied correctly;
- Providing advice on the choice of design, development and acceptance methods;
- Ensuring that the required supplier resources are available;
- Making decisions on escalated isues, with particular focus on safeguarding the integrity of the complete solution;
- Resolving differences of opinon among suppliers over specifications and priorities;
- Ensuring Project Assurance from the perspective of the suppliers;
- Informing and advising supplier management in respect of all project-related matters.

B.5   Project Manager

The Project Manager is responsible for running the project on a day-to-day basis on behalf of the Project Board. The primary responsibility of the Project Manager is to see to is that the project delivers the required products according to the specifications and within the agreed tolerances. The Project Manager is also responsible for the project achieving the anticipated benefits defined in the Business Case.

The Project Manager is responsible for the Risk Register.

Start up and initiation:
- Preparing the Project Brief, including the Project Product Description;
- Preparing and implementing the different strategies;
- Preparing the Project, Stage and Exception Plans and the accompanying Product Descriptions;
- Preparing and updating the Business Case and the Benefits Review Plan;
- Preparing the (separate parts of the) Project Initiation Documentation;
- Preparing Work Packages;
- Organizing and managing the project controls – monitoring and reporting;
- Organizing and maintaining the different logs and registers;
- Implementing the procedures for issues and configuration management.

During the project:
- Coordinating with Project Assurance and with external suppliers and account managers;
- Directing and motinvating the project team;
- Directing and supervising Project Support (unless undertaking this personally);
- Managing the flow of information between the project team and the Project Board;
- Authorizing the required Work Packages;
- Monitoring and controlling the progress of the project and the effort of people and resources and taking the required corrective actions;
- Coordinating with corporate or programme management so that there are no gaps or overlaps with related projects;
- Escalating the relevant issues and risks;
- Preparing the required End Stage Report and updating the PID.

At the end of the project:
- Ensuring that maintenance and control in the client organization has been organized;
- Ensuring that the project product is delivered and accepted by the end users and by operation and maintenance;
- Completing outstanding issues and risks at the end of the project and entering the actions in the recommendations for follow-on actions;
- Preparing the End Project Report;
- Preparing the recommendations for follow-on actions and the required Lessons Reports and handing over to corporate or programme management;
- Running down the project team and handing over the project file to the corporate or programme management;
- Sending a recommendation for closure to the Executive.

The Project Manager must possess a wide range of different skills and competencies, depending on the scope and context of the project.

The core competencies for a Project Manager are:
- Planning;

* Time management;
* People management;
* Problem solving;
* Attention to detail;
* Communication;
* Negotiation and conflict resolution.

B.6   Team Manager

The Team Manager is primarily responsible for ensuring that the assigned products are delivered according to specifications and within the agreed tolerances. The Team Manager reports to the Project Manager in the project.

The Team Manager is responsible for:
* Assisting with the preparation of Stage and Exception Plans;
* Preparing the Team Plan and agreeing on the Work Package;
* Planning, monitoring and controlling the team's work;
* Monitoring and controlling the progress of the team's work and the effort of people and resources, and taking any required corrective actions;
* Liaising with the Project Assurance and Project Support roles;
* Ensuring that quality reviews are undertaken, that quality documents are handed over to Project Support and that the quality results are entered correctly in the Quality Register;
* Preparing and providing Checkpoint Reports;
* Advising the Project Manager on planning exceptions and making recommendations for corrective actions;
* Identifying and reporting on issues and risks regarding the work;
* Assisting the Project Manager in analyzing the impact of possible measures for issues and risks
* Managing assigned issue and risk responses;
* Handing over to the Project Manager the products that have been completed and approved in line with the agreed Work Package requirements.

The core competencies of a Team Manager are broadly speaking the same as those of the Project Manager. However, the actual requirements may vary from project to project and will be dependent on the type, scope and the context of the the project.

B.7   Project Assurance

The primary responsibility of Project Assurance is to ensure that the project is executed according to agreements and that the interests of the individual members of the Project Board (business, user and supplier) are addressed. The Project Assurance must be independent of the Project Manager and the project team.

The key responsibilities for business assurance are:
* Assisting in the development of the Business Case and the Benefits Review Plan;
* Assisting with the selection of the members of the project management team;
* Advising on the Risk Management Strategy;
* Checking whether the Business Case is compliant with corporate or programme standard;

- Reviewing the Business Case in respect of the progress of the project;
- Checking whether the project remains in line with the corporate and programme management strategy;
- Monitoring the financing of the project;
- Ensuring that solutions are effective and provide value for money;
- Checking whether the invoices of suppliers are approved before payment;
- Ensuring that issues and risks are identified and managed correctly;
- Ensuring that the aggregated project risk remains within the risk tolerance;
- Reviewing issues and risks on the basis of their impact on the Business Case;
- Coordinating with representatives from the users and suppliers;
- Informing the project management team about relevant changes caused by a programme of which the project is part;
- Constraining user and supplier excesses;
- Monitoring stage and project progress with reference to the agreed tolerances.

The key responsibilities for user assurance are:
- Advising on stakeholder engagement;
- Advising on the Communication Management Strategy;
- Ensuring that the correct persons are involved in the preparation of the Product Descriptions and that the user specifications are accurate, complete and unambiguous;
- Assessing whether the chosen solutions address the needs of the users;
- Ensuring that the quality assessments are undertaken correctly;
- Ensuring that the users are properly represented in the quality activities for products at all stages;
- Advising on the impact of potential changes from the user perspective;
- Monitoring risks to the user;
- Ensuring that communication with the users is effective.

The key activities for supplier assurance are:
- Reviewing the Product Descriptions;
- Advising on the Quality Management Strategy and the Configuration Management Strategy;
- Advising on the selction of the development strategy, design and methods;
- Ensuring that supplier and operating standards are defined and followed up correctly;
- Ensuring that no scope-creep occurs;
- Ensuring that the quality procedures are used correctly;
- Advising on the impact of potential changes from a supplier perspective;
- Monitoring the risks in the production aspects of the project.

Project Assurance must be able to represent the interests of the business, the users and the suppliers and should have sufficient standing and knowledge of matters, so that their advice is accepted by the parties concerned, contributing to the success of the project. They should preferably be available for the duration of the project.

The core competencies for Project Assurance are:
- Diplomacy;
- Thoroughness;
- Attention to detail;
- Comunication.

B.8 Change Authority

The primary responsibility of the Change Authority is to review the requests for change and off-specifications on behalf of the Project Board. The Project Manager could act as Change Authority for certain parts of the project.

The Change Authority is responsible for:
- Reviewing and approving or rejecting requests for change and off-specifications within the delegated limits of authority and the change budget agreed with the Project Board;
- Escalating to the Project Board if the delegated limits of authority and/or the change budget is in danger of being exceeded.

The Change Authority must be able to represent the different stakeholders and must have sufficient standing and knowledge of matters, so that their decisions are accepted by the parties concerned and contribute to the success of the project.

The core competencies of the Change Authority are:
- Decision making;
- Planning;
- Attention to detail;
- Problem solving.

B.9 Project Support

Project Support is the responsibility of the Project Manager. This support comprises among other things providing administrative support, advice and guidance in the use of project management procedures and associated tools and techniques. The provision of any Project Support on a formal basis is optional, though the role itself is not. If a separate Project Support is not available, the activities will be undertaken by the Project Manager.

The possible tasks of Project Support are:
- Setting up and maintaining project files and document control procedures;
- Providing expertise in the preparation of plans and budgets;
- Collecting actuals data and forecasts;
- Updating plans;
- Assisting in the drawing up of plans and reports;
- Administering and assisting Project Board meetings;
- Administering and assisting quality reviews and benefit reviews;
- The organizing and maintenance of:
  - Quality Register;
  - Other registers and logs on behalf of the Project Manager;
  - Procedures for configuration management and change control;
  - Configuration Item Records.
- Compiling product control lists and conducting configuration audits.

The Project Support role should incorporate knowledge of specialist project management tools and techniques and of relevant corporate and programme standards. It is also importantto have good administrative and organizational skills.

Appendix C Example of Product-based Planning

Scenario

A householder wants a garden shed at the bottom of his garden. It must provide a storage place for his garden implements and he must also be able to perform some garden chores under shelter, such as repotting plants. The location has been indicated in a drawing by a gardener. In preparation, the site must be prepared for building; the existing shrubs and plants must be removed. The garden shed is a pre-fabricated unit from a garden center. For the work in the garden, some extra tools must be bought. He has provided the specifications. The work will be undertaken by the gardener. The shed will be bought by his cousin, who works at the garden center.

The garden shed should, preferably, be eight square meters, but at least six square meters. It should be of tropical hardwood, though European hardwood would do as well.

To have a clear view of the scope of the project and to be able to plan the work well and convey it to the gardener, the householder has produced a product-based plan. For the purchase of the garden shed, he has pepared a separate Product Description:
- Project Product Description (see table C.1);
- Product breakdown structure (see figure C.1, alternatively table C.2.);
- Product Description of purchased garden shed (see table C.3);
- Product flow diagram (see figure C.2).

Title	Garden shed
Purpose	• Storage of gardening tools • Can work sheltered
Composition	• Site prepared • Garden shed purchased • Garden shed in place • Tools purchased
Sources	• Specifications
Competencies required	• Experienced in constructing garden sheds
Customer quality expectations	• Delivered ready to use • Lighting connected • Possible to work comfortably in it • Environmentally friendly, maintenance free
Acceptance criteria	• All tools in place • Wiring earthed • Garden shed 8m2 • Garden shed of tropical hardwood
Project quality tolerances	• Minimum size 6m2 • At least of European hardwood
Acceptance method	• Visual inspection
Acceptance responsibilities	• House owner

Table C.1 Project Product Description

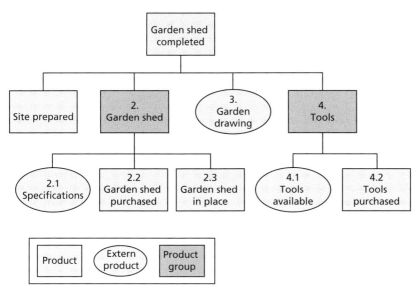

Figure C.1 Product breakdown structure garden shed

Garden shed completed
1. Site prepared
2. Garden shed
    2.1 Specifications
    2.2 Garden shed purchased
    2.3 Garden shed in place
3. Garden drawing
4. Tools
    4.1 Tools available
    4.1 Tools purchased

Table C.2 Alternative product breakdown structure garden shed

Identifier	01
Title	• Garden shed purchased
Purpose	• Garden shed complete for positioning in the garden
Composition	• Building kit of garden shed • Foundation • Lighting plus wiring
Sources	• According to specifications • Available at garden centre
Form and presentation	• Packed and delivered to home address
Quality criteria	• Garden shed of tropical hardwood, wood class FSC • Size of garden shed 8m² • Foundation tiles 30 x 30 x 3cm • Earthed wiring for the lighting
Quality tolerance	• As an alternative European hardwood • Size of garden shed to be at least 6m²
Quality method	• Inspection certificates and documentation • Inspection of materials for numbers and visible defects
Competencies required	• Knowledge of garden shed materials
Quality responsibilities	

Identifier	01
• Producer	• Cousin
• Reviewer(s)	• Gardener
• Approver(s)	• House owners

Table C3. Product Description of purchased garden shed

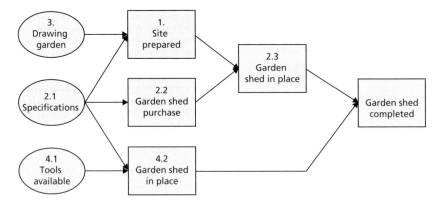

Figure C.2 Product flow diagram

Appendix D Health check

The checklists below can be used in preparation at the start and during a project. They make it easy to 'walk' through the diverse PRINCE2-processes and enable you to check if anything has been forgotten. The lists are not exhaustive, but do give a realistic appraisal of a project that is set up and controlled according to the PRINCE2-method.

D.1 Starting up a Project

#	Question	Yes/No
	Have all roles in the project management team been assigned and accepted?	
	Do the members of the Project Board have sufficient authority, availability and commitment to direct the project?	
	Are all the project's stakeholders sufficiently represented in/by the Project Board?	
	Have role descriptions for all crucial roles in the project been prepared and accepted?	
	Have the lessons from previous comparable projects been recognized and applied?	
	If no comparable projects within the organization have been undertaken, have lessons been sought outside the organization?	
	Have a Daily Log and a Lessons Log been set up?	
	Has a Project Brief been prepared?	
	Is there an outline Business Case?	
	Are the most important risks formulated and included in the Business Case?	
	Has the Project Product Description been prepared?	
	Has the project approach been decided upon?	
	Are the quality expectations and acceptance criteria determined unambiguously?	
	Are the project tolerances for time, money, quality, scope, benefits and risks recorded?	
	Are the interfaces with other projects clearly described?	
	Has a Stage Plan for the initiation stage been produced?	

D.2 Authorizing project initiation

#	Question	Yes/No
	Have the Project Brief and the Initiation Stage Plan been approved by the Project Board?	
	Has the Project Board authorized the start of the initiation stage and designated the required people and resources?	
	Has the Project Board informed corporate or programme management (and other interested parties) that project initiation has been authorized?	

D.3   Initiating a Project

#	Question	Yes/No
	Have lessons from previous similar projects been identified and, where appropriate, have they been applied?	
	Is the Risk Management Strategy defined and documented?	
	Is the Risk Register set up and populated?	
	Is the Configuration Management Strategy defined and documented?	
	Are the initial Configuration Item Records organized and completed?	
	Are the agreements on the change procedure unambiguously recorded?	
	Has a Change Authority been appointed and a change budget prepared?	
	Is the Issue Register set up and populated?	
	Is the Quality Management Strategy defined and doucmented?	
	Is the Quality Register set up and populated?	
	Is the Communication Management Strategy defined and documented?	
	Have the project controls been determined and established?	
	Are the various reports to the Project Board identified and recorded?	
	Has an unambiguous escalation procedure been recorded?	
	Has a Project Plan been created and are its objectives SMART?	
	Is the Project Product Description updated?	
	Has a product breakdown structure been prepared?	
	Are milestones and decision points recorded?	
	Are the most important products to be delivered in the various stages defined?	
	Has a complete and unambiguous programme of requirements been prepared and have Product Descriptions been prepared for the most important products?	
	Have the project tolerances for time, money, scope and quality been refined?	
	Has the project management team structure been updated to reflect any new roles or any changes in responsibilities of existing roles?	
	Has a detailed Business Case been prepared?	
	Has the Senior User identified and quantified the benefits and does the Senior User also take the responsibility for confirming that the predicted benefits have been achieved?	
	Are the benefits financially quantifiable and has it been determined how and by whom the (financial) benefits will be measured?	
	Are possible dis-benefits included in the Business Case and have responsible persons been assigned to control these?	
	Have risks been identified and evaluated and have countermeasures been determined and recorded in the Risk Register?	
	Have risk owners been appointed and has it been determined how the risks will be monitored?	
	Have the risk tolerances been determined?	
	Has a risk budget been included for concluding risks?	
	Are the most important risks formulated and included in the Business Case?	
	Has a Benefits Review Plan been prepared?	
	Has a project file been organized (electronically and physically)?	

	Has the Project Initiation Documentation been assembled?	
	Has a Stage Plan been produced for the first delivery stage?	
	Have tolerances for the first delivery stage been determined and agreed on?	
	Are the quality assessments for the first delivery stage planned and entered in the Quality Register?	
	Has the End Stage Report for the initiation stage been prepared?	
	Has there been regular consultation between the Project Manager and members of the Project Board and other stakeholders during the initiation stage?	
	Is there commitment to the project and the planned-for results among the users and other stakeholders?	
	Has Project Assurance been involved in the preparation of the Project Initiation Documentation and is it agreed?	
	Are the project management processes and procedures tailored for the project and the project environment?	

D.4   Authorize the project

#	Question	Yes/ No
	Has the Project Initiation Documentation been approved by the Project Board?	
	Has it been confirmed that lessons from the previous projects have been reviewed and incorporated?	
	Have the Quality Management Strategy, the Configuration Management Strategy and the Risk Management Strategy been assessed and approved?	
	Has it been determined how the effectiveness of the different strategies will be assessed during the execution of the project?	
	Are the controls are adequate for the project?	
	Is the manner in which the different stakeholders are involved in the project assessed and agreed?	
	Has it been confirmed that the risks have been assessed and the relevant actions planned?	
	Is the validity and achievability of the Project Plan confirmed and approved?	
	Are the milestones, decision points and reports assessed and agreed?	
	Have all of the tolerances been reviewed to ensure they are appropriate and realistic?	
	Are all roles of the project management team confirmed?	
	Has the consistency of the various themes been assessed and approved?	
	Has the viability of the Business Case been assessed and confirmed?	
	Has the Benefits Review Plan been assessed and confirmed?	
	Has the budget required for the execution of the project been agreed?	
	Has the Stage Plan for the first delivery stage been assessed and approved?	
	Has the required effort of people and resources for the first delivery stage been released?	
	Has the End Stage Report for the initiation stage been agreed?	
	Has the Project Board informed the corporate or porgramme management and other stakeholders that the project has been authorized?	

D.5   Controlling a Stage

#	Question	Yes/No
	Have the Work Packages been prepared and issued?	
	Have all Work Packages been agreed with the Team Managers?	
	Have the plans been created to an appropriate level of detail so that work can be delegated and checked?	
	Has every employee been informed about the procedures, standards and work instructions that apply to them?	
	Have Checkpoint Reports been regularly prepared for each issued Work Package and/or progress meetings held with the Team Managers, and are these effective?	
	Was progress (actual and forecast) checked against agreed tolerances?	
	Is the status of the work regularly updated in the Stage Plan?	
	Is the Daily Log updated daily?	
	Is there a change procedure and does this work effectively?	
	If corrective actions were required, were they logged, implemented and tracked?	
	Do Exception Reports exist for all exceptions raised to the Project Board?	
	Is there an unambiguous Change Authority?	
	Is the Issue Register being maintained/adapted?	
	Are there Issue Reports for all formal issues dealt with?	
	Are any unauthorized changes being carried out?	
	Is there any scope creep?	
	Have the relevant Configuration Item Records been created and updated?	
	Is the status of all products documented and are all stakeholdrers informed about this?	
	Has the Risk Register been maintained?	
	Are risk owners appointed for new risks?	
	Are risks regularly assessed and risk responses agreed?	
	Is the effectiveness of the risk management tested regularly?	
	Are the delivered products tested with reference to the Product Descriptions?	
	Are both the users and suppliers involved in quality reviews?	
	Is the Quality Register being maintained/updated?	
	Are the delivered products formally handed over to, and accepted by, the Project Manager before they are released for use?	
	Is progress tested regularly against the agreed tolerances?	
	Are the required people and resources available and does the Senior Supplier assure that this is the case?	
	Is there effective coordination with Project Assurance?	
	Is the Lessons Log updated with new lessons?	
	Is the Business Case regularly checked for viability?	
	Are the Highlight Reports prepared according to the agreed frequency and reporting format?	
	Are tolerances escalated to the Project Board on time and adequately when they are In danger of being exceeded?	
	Are there Exception Reports for all exceptions reported to the Project Board?	

D.6 Managing Product Delivery

#	Question	Yes/ No
	Do the Work Packages and Product Descriptions contain sufficient information, including cross references, so that the Team Manager can produce the products required?	
	Has a Team Plan been created that indicates that the Work Package can be completed within the agreed tolerances?	
	Is the Team Plan updated on the basis of the actual status and a revised forecast?	
	Is progress (actual against budget) checked against the agreed tolerances?	
	If it is forecast that tolerances are to be exceeded, is it escalated to the Project Manager?	
	Are the Checkpoint Reports delivered according to the agreed frequency and the agreed format?	
	Has the Team Manager informed the Project Manager of all issues and risks?	
	Are there approved records of every delivered product?	
	Has the Team Manager informed Project Support about required updates to the Configuation Item Records and the Quality Register?	
	Has the Team Manager informed the Project Manager that all products in the Work Package have been delivered?	

D.7 Give ad hoc direction

#	Question	Yes/ No
	Does the Project Board function properly in practice?	
	Has a separate project assessment been established on the part of the customer as well as on the part of the supplier and do these function properly?	
	Is there good coordination between the Senior User and the different users?	
	Does the Project Board react adequately to the requests of the Project Manager?	
	Does the Project Board take adequate and timely decisionsin relation to issues?	
	Does the Project Board inform the Project Manager in time about external events that might affect the project?	
	Does the Project Board focus on the business justification of the project?	
	Does the Project Board give direction and advice to the Project Manager if necessary?	
	Does the Project Board remain informed and involved in the project?	
	Does the Project Board react quickly when notified that agreed tolerances may be exceeded?	
	Does the Project Board inform corporate or porgramme management (and other interested parties) of the project's progress as specified in the Communication Strategy?	

D.8 Managing a Stage Boundary

#	Question	Yes/No
	Has a Product Status Account been created to check the status of the stage's products?	
	Have all products planned to be completed within the stage actually been delivered and approved?	
	Have the Product Descriptions been created for the next stage's products?	
	Has the Lessons Log been assessed and updated?	
	Are the Issue Register and the Risk Register assessed and updated?	
	Has a risk analysis been done and have risk responses been agreed?	
	Have the Risk Management Strategy, the Configuration Management Strategy and the Communication Management Strategy been reviewed and, if necessary, updated?	
	Have the project controls been reviewed and, if necessary, updated?	
	Have the tolerances for the next stage been updated and agreed?	
	Has the project management team structure been updated to reflect any new roles or any changes to responsibilities of existing roles?	
	Has the Stage Plan for the next stage been produced?	
	Has an Exception Plan been prepared, if requested by the Project Board?	
	Have the quality assessments been planned and entered in the Quality Register?	
	Has the Project Plan been reviewed and, if necessary, updated?	
	Has the Business Case been reviewed and, if necessary, updated?	
	Has the Benefits Review Plan been reviewed and, if necessary, updated?	
	Has the End Stage Report been produced and issued to the Project Board in accordance with the project controls?	
	If necessary, has a Lessons Report been prepared?	
	With phased delivery: have recommendations for follow-on actions been prepared?	

D.9 Authorize a Stage or Exception Plan

#	Question	Yes/No
	Is each stage preceded by a formal 'go' from the Project Board?	
	Has the Project Board approved the delivered products?	
	Has the Project Board assessed the general progress and viability of the project and agreed the basis of the End Stage Report?	
	Is the Project Plan still valid on the basis of the agreed project tolerances?	
	Is the Business Case still desirable, viable and valid?	
	Are the most important risks still acceptable and have appropriate responses been planned?	
	Has the Project Board assessed and confirmed the achieved benefits?	
	Has the Benefits Review Plan been assessed and confirmed?	
	Has the Project Board approved a possible adaptation of the PID?	
	Has the Project Board reviewed the lessons learnt during the stage?	

	Has the Project Board reviewed the Stage or Exception Plan?	
	Has the Project Board authorized the Project Manager to proceed with the submitted plan (Stage Plan or Exception Plan)?	
	Have the possible revisions of the tolerances for the next management stage been assessed and confirmed?	
	Has the Project Board informed the corporate or programme management and other stakeholders that the Stage or Exception Plan has been authorized?	

D.10 Closing a Project

	Question	Yes/ No
	Are all products complete and approved?	
	Has a Product Status Account been created to check the status of all the products?	
	Has the Project Plan been updated?	
	Have all outstanding issues and risks been recorded in recommendations for follow-on actions In preparation for approval by the Project Board?	
	In the case of premature closure, have the necessary resources for repairing or completing the products been approved by the Project Board?	
	Is there an acceptance record for the handover of the project product?	
	Does the acceptance record include operational and maintenance acceptance?	
	Has the Business Case been updated with actuals?	
	Has the Benefits Review Plan been updated with actuals?	
	Has an end evaluation been undertaken with all relevant parties involved?	
	Has the Lessons Log been assessed and has the Lessons Report been prepared?	
	Has an End Project Report been prepared and given to the Project Board?	
	Has the actual status against the planned progress been clearly described in the End Project Report?	
	Has a good account of the course of the project been included in the End Project Report?	
	Have all registers and logs been closed?	
	Has the project documentation been cleared, closed and handed over?	
	Have the Configuration Item Records been updated and handed over?	
	Have all specialist documents been updated and handed over?	
	Has a draft project closure notification been created for Project Board approval and onward distribution?	

D.11 Authorize project closure

#	Question	Yes/No
	Has the Project Board confirmed the handover and acceptance?	
	Has it been ensured that the recommendations for follow-on actions have been included and handed over?	
	Has the Project Board assessed the Lessons Report and determined who should receive it?	
	Has the Project Board approved and handed over the updated Business Case to corporate and programme management?	
	Has the Project Board approved the updated Benefits Review Plan and handed it over to corporate and programme management?	
	Has the Project Board approved the End Project Report?	
	Has the End Project Report been distributed to all stakeholders concerned according to the Communication Management Strategy?	
	Has the Project Board formally issued the project closure notification?	
	Has the Project Board advised those who have provided the support infrastructure and resources for the project that these can now be withdrawn?	
	Has the Project Board released the resources provided to the project?	
	Has the Project Baord provided a closing date for costs being charged to the project?	

Appendix E Glossary

Term	Description
acceptance	The formal confirmation that the project has satisfied the acceptance criteria and with that the requirements of the stakeholders.
acceptance criteria	A list of measurable criteria which the project product must comply with before the stakeholders will accept it.
activity	A process, function or task that is executed during a specific time, usually as a part of a process or plan.
activity network	An activity flow diagram with the time dependences between activities indicated in it.
approval	Formal confirmation that the project product is complete and complies with the criteria specified in the Product Description.
approver	A person or group (for example the Project Board) who is qualified and authorized to approve the project product(s).
assumption	A statement that is taken as true. Plans are based on this. This is necessary when the specific data is not available at that moment.
assurance	Systematic actions necessary to give confidence that requirements will be met and the aims realized.
authority	The right to allocate resources and to take decisions (at project, stage as well as team levels).
authorization	Formal confirmation that the product complies to the the criteria specified in the Product Description.
bar chart	A plan, reflected in a diagram, in which time is set out on the horizontal axis and the activities to be executed ascending on the vertical axis. The time period is indicated for the different activities by means of a thick line (bar), that is correctly placed in respect of the time scale.
baseline	The documented status of a product or situation. A baseline is retained during the planning period and used as reference against which the product is assessed and controlled.
baseline management product	A management product that describes aspects of the project that can only be adapted by means of a formal adaptation process.
benefit	The measurable change that is indicated positively by one or several stakeholders.
Benefits Review Plan	A plan that indicates how, when and by whom the benefits to be realized are measured.
benefits tolerance	The allowed exception to the estimated benefits of the project result to be delivered, in which escalation to the next level above is not necessary.
Business Case	The information that reflects the justification for the setting up and execution of a project. It typically contains the costs, benefits, risks and timescales against which continuing viability is tested.
cause (trigger)	An occasion or decision that initiates the start of a PRINCE2 activity or process.

center of excellence	An organization-wide coordinating function for portfolios, programmes and projects that makes available standards, knowledge management, assurance and training.
Change Authority	A person or group to whom the Project Board has delegated the responsibility of the assessment of a request for change or exception to a specification.
change budget	The budget that is assigned to the Change Authority, intended for approved requests for change.
change control	The procedure that ensures that all changes that can affect the objectivess of the project are identified and assessed, and are approved, rejected or continued.
checkpoint	An assessment of the progress of a project at the team level at predetermined points in time.
Checkpoint Report	A report on the progress of a Work Package that the Team Manager provides to the Project Manager at predetermined times.
closure notification	Advice from the Project Board to all stakeholders that the project is being closed and that the team members and supporting facilities such as office space, equipment and access are no longer required from a specific date. This should also contain an end date until which costs can still be charged to the project.
closure recommendation	A recommendation to the Project Board, prepared by the Project Manager, that the project can be closed, serving as project closure notification if the Project Board agrees with this.
Communication Management Strategy	A description of the means and frequency of all internal and external communication from and to the stakeholders.
concession	An exception to specification that is accepted by the Project Board without any corrective actions.
configuration item (CI)	A product, component of a product or set of part products of which the realization and/or control must be controlled.
Configuration Item Record	A record in which all relevant information of a configuration item is described including the relationship that configuration item has with other configuration items.
configuration management	The management of the configuration items (CIs), comprising planning, identification, control, status justification and verification of the CIs.
Configuration Management Strategy	A description of how and by whom the products in a project are controlled and protected.
configuration management system	A combination of processes and supporting software that is used to control the Configuration Item Records. The systems already in use by either the customer or the supplier organization are generally used.
constraint	A boundary or limit with which the project must comply.
contingency	A budget post for activities that could not reasonably have been foreseen, but which fall within the scope of the project.
controls	A unit of activities, processes and procedures to control a distinguishing aspect.
corporate standard or programme standard	An over-arching standard from the corporate or programme organisation with which the corporate or programme standard must comply.

corrective action	An action or combination of actions that ensures that the threat to a plan's tolerances or a fault in a product is removed.
cost tolerance	The allowed exception to an estimate of the costs made in a plan in which it is not necessary to escalate to the next management level above.
critical path	The series of consecutive activities from the start to delivery of the project that is critical for the realization of delivery as early as possible. The activities on this path have no margin; this means every delay in the execution of these activities results in a delay of the delivery of the project. In a project several critical paths are possible.
customer	The person or group who commissioned the work and who will profit from the end result of the project.
customer's quality expectations	A statement by the customer about the quality to be expected from the project product.
Daily Log	A diary which can be used to note among other things, problems and points of concern which the party involved can conclude informally. Project Managers and Team Managers can all keep a Daily Log up-to-date for themselves.
deliverable	See: 'output'.
dependencies	The relationship between products and/or activities.
dis-benefit	An outcome that is perceived as negative by one or more of the stakeholders of a project.
earned value analysis	The English name for a method to monitor the progress of the project on the basis of the realized added value to date. It indicates whether the investment made is still in line with the delivered (part) results in terms of time and money.
embedding PRINCE2	The total of activities needed by an organization to adopt PRINCE2 as its corporate project management method.
End Project Report	A report given by the Project Manager to the Project Board at the closure of the project. This report confirms the delivery of all products, provides an updated Business Case and gives an account of the course of the project.
end result	The entirety of the products delivered, or a synonym for 'project product'.
end stage assessment	The assessement by the Project Board and the Project Manager of the project in order to decide whether to approve the next Stage Plan.
End Stage Report	A report at the end of every interim management stage that the Project Manager provides to the Project Board with the results of the past stage and the project status at the end of the stage. Before the last stage no separate End Stage Report is prepared.
event-driven control	A control that is triggered by an event, for example a stage boundary, or an event within the organization, such as a year closing.
exception	A situation in which it can be expected that the agreed tolerance levels of a plan will be exceeded.
exception assessment	The assessment by the Project Board and Project Manager to approve (or reject) an Exception Plan.

Exception Plan	A plan that is produced as a result of a threat to the ageed tolerance levels and which normally follows an Exception Report. The Exception Plan replaces the plan in which the exception appears and describes the period from the exception up to the end of the plan.
Exception Report	A report in which an exception is described. The exception, the causes of the exception, the possible counter responses, an analysis of the counter responses and and the advice indicating which counter responses are considered most appropriate are described in an Exception Report.
Executive	The single individual who is accountable for the ensuring that a project meets its targets and delivers the envisaged benefits.
feasibility study	A study to identify an optimal solution for a problem or opportunity. In the study the alternative solutions for the problem or the opportunity are specified, the feasibility of the different solutions examined and recommendations prepared. A feasibility study provides the outline of a Business Case for the different solutions.
follow–on action recommendations	A report of recommended actions in respect of incomplete activities, outstanding issues and risks and other actions that are needed to take the product into the next stage of its product lifecycle.
Gannt chart	A type of bar diagram indicating the required capacity per activity.
governance	The duties (with the accompanying tasks, responsibilities and authorities), processes and procedures that define how an organization is set up and managed.
handover	The transfer of the ownership of the deliverable products to the user(s).
Highlight Report	A time-driven report in outline that the Project Manager supplies to the Project Board on the progress of a stage.
inherent risk	The size of a risk before any responses are taken.
initiation stage	The first stage of a project after approval of the Project Brief in which the Project Plan is specified and the management infrastructure of the project is designed.
issue	A relevant unplanned event that has occurred and requires attention to resolve or conclude.
Issue Register	A register for recording all issues that are being formally managed.
Issue Report	A report containing the description, impact and the decisions regarding issues such as requests for change or problems that are being formally handled.
Lessons Log	An informal log in which the lessons are recorded for the current and future projects.
Lessons Report	A report in which the lessons of the project are recorded for subsequent use by other projects.
logs	Informal recordings of data, managed by the Project Manager, that do not need any approval from superior management as regards lay-out and presentation. PRINCE2 recognizes the Daily Log and the Lessons Log.

management product	A product that is necessary to manage the project and to determine and guarantee the quality. PRINCE2 recognizes three types: baselines, records and reports.
management stage	A division of the project in time with previously defined activities and deliverables that is managed by the Project Manager under the authority of the Project Board.
milestone	A significant event in a plan's schedule (for example the delivery of specific Work Packages, or the end of a technical or management stage).
off-specification	A project product that (as expected) does not comply with the specifications or has not been/is not being delivered. An exception to specification is an issue type.
operational acceptance and maintenance acceptance	An explicit confirmation by those who are actually going to control and maintain the delivered products, that they comply with the acceptance criteria.
opportunity (risks)	An uncertain fact or uncertain circumstances that, if they arise, have positive consequences for the realization of the project targets.
outcome	The result of change that is normally described in terms of the way in which it affects real-world behavior and/circumstances.
output	A specialist product that is delivered to the user(s). It can be a product as well as a service. It should be noted that management products are not outputs but are created for purpose of managing a project.
performance target	A specific target of a plan in respect of time, cost, quality, scope, benefits and risks.
plan	A detailed proposal for achieving a result or an aim which specifies who undertakes what, where, when and in what way. PRINCE2 incorporates the following types of plans: Project Plan, Stage Plan, Team Plan, Exception Plan and Benefits Review Plan.
planning horizon	The time period for which an accurate and reliable plan can be produced.
plan, prerequisite	A fundamental aspect that must be in place before a plan can be taken into operation.
portfolio	The entirety of programmes and independent projects in an organization, a group of organizations, or an organizational unit..
premature closure	The closure of a product sooner than planned when all the products to be delivered have not yet been achieved.
PRINCE2	A method that supports a number of aspects of project management. The acronym stands for PRojects IN a Controlled Environment.
PRINCE2 principles	The mandatory guidelines for good management that form the basis of a project that is managed according to the PRINCE2 method.
PRINCE2 project	A project to which the PRINCE2 principles are applied.
PRINCE2 theme	An aspect of project management that must be applied mandatorily and continuously in combination with PRINCE2-processes.
probability	The likelihood of a risk occurring.

problem/concern	An issue type that is not a request for change or an exception to the specification that the Project Manager needs to resolve or escalate.
procedure	A series of actions that must be executed in sequence for a specific aspect of project management (for example a risk management procedure).
process	A structured set of activities that are designed to accomplish a specific objective.
producer	The person responsible for the realization of a product.
product	An input or output of a process or project, whether tangible or intangible, that can be described in advance, created and tested. PRINCE2 has two types of products, specialist products and management products.
product-based planning	A technique that leads to a comprehendsive plan based on the creation and delivery of required outputs. The technique considers prerequisite products, quality requirements, and the dependence between products.
product breakdown structure	A hierarchic summary of all requirements and the products to be produced during a plan.
product checklist	A list with the most important products of a plan, plus key dates in their delivery.
Product Description	A description of a product. A Product Description comprises among other things the aim, the composition, the origin and the quality requirements of a product. It is produced at the planning time, as soon as possible after the need for the product is identified.
product flow diagram	A diagram with the production sequence and the time sequence dependence of the products which are listed in a product breakdown structure.
product lifecycle	The total time spans of a product from the original idea to create the product up to the replacement or dissolution of the product. During the product lifecycle several projects can be executed, such as a feasibility study, the delivery, an upgrade and the final replacement or dissolution.
Product Status Account	A report of the status of products. The required products can be specified by identifier, or the part of the project in which they were developed.
programme	A temporary flexible organization structure, created to coordinate, direct and monitor a set of related projects and activities in order to deliver outcomes and benefits that contribute to the strategic aims of an organization.
project	A temporary organization that is set up with the aim of delivering one or several business products according to an agreed Business Case.
project approach	A description of the manner in which a project result will be approached; for example, is the work to be outsourced or will it be undertaken in-house.
Project Assurance	The responsibilities of the Project Board to ensure that the project is executed in the correct way. The Project Assurance members each have a specific focus: business assurance for the Executive, user assurance for the Senior User(s), and supplier assurance for the Senior Supplier(s).

project authorization notification	A notice from the Project Board to all stakeholders and to the site where the project activites will be undertaken that the project is about to start, requesting all required services to be made available during the project.
Project Brief	A statement that describes the purpose, cost, time and performance requirements, and constraints for a project. It is used to create the Project Initiation Documentation.
Project Initiation Documentation	The collection of documents that contain the key information needed to start the project on a sound basis and that conveys the information to all concerned with the project.
project initiation notification	A notice from the Project Board to all stakeholders and to the site where the project is to be undertaken that project initiation is to start, requesting all required support services to be made available during the initiation.
project lifecycle	The total time span of a project from the start up to the acceptance of the project product.
project management	All directing tasks which are necessary to achieve the result of the project. Project management comprises the planning, delegating monitoring and control of all aspects of the project and the motivation of all persons involved in the project.
project management team	The total of all persons who fill the management roles in a project. The project management team comprises the roles of the Project Board, Project Manager, Team Manager, Project Support roles and Project Assurance.
project management team structure	An organization chart showing the people assigned to the project management team roles to be used, and their delegation and reporting relationships.
Project Manager	The person responsible for the daily management of the project to deliver the required products according the agreements with the Project Board.
project mandate	An external product generated by the authority commissioning a project that constitutes the trigger for Starting up a Project.
project office	A temporary office that is established to perform certain administrative tasks for one or several projects. It undertakes the responsibility of the Project Support role.
Project Plan	A high level plan that reflects the most important products of the project, the delivery dates and the costs. It is presented as part of the Project Initiation Documentation.
project product	What the project must deliver to be accepted.
Project Product Description	A special type of Product Description that is used to reach agreement from the user on the scope, the quality expectations and the acceptance criteria of the customer.
Project Support	An administrative role in the project management team that supports the Project Manager and the Team Manager in the form of advice and help with project management tools, filing and administration.
quality	The totality of inherent or attributed characteristics of a product, person, process, service and/or system that contributes to the ability to meet particular expectations or satisfy stated needs, requirements or specifications.

quality assurance	An independent check that products comply with requirements and are 'fit for purpose'.
quality control	The process of monitoring specific project results so that they comply with the relevant standards, and of the establishing ways to eliminate causes of non-compliance and unsatisfactory performance.
quality criteria	A description of the quality specifications with which a product must comply, including the quality measurements that will be applied by those inspecting the finished product.
quality inspection	A systematic and structured assessment of a product that is carried out by two or more selected people in a planned, documented and organized fashion.
quality management	The set of coordinated activities for directing and checking an organization with regard to quality.
Quality Management Strategy	A strategy defining the quality techniques and standards to be applied, including the different responsibilities for achieving the required quality levels during a project.
quality management system (QMS)	The complete set of quality standards processes, procedures and responsibilities for a site or organization.
quality records	Evidence kept to indicate that the required quality assurance and quality control activeties have been undertaken.
Quality Register	A summary of all the planned and completed quality activities. The Quality Register is used by the Project Manager and Project Assurance as part of reviewing progress.
quality review	See 'quality inspection'.
quality tolerance	An accepted exception for quality criterion. The quality tolerances are described in the Project Product Description and the Product Descriptions of the relevant products.
records	Dynamic management products that contain information in relation to the progress of the project.
registers	Formal repositories of data managed by the Project Manager that require agreement by the Project Baord on their format, composition and use. PRINCE2 recognizes the Issue Register, the Risk Register and the Quality Register.
release	The specific set of products in a handover. See also 'handover'.
reports	Management products with which the status of certain aspects of the project are recorded.
request for change	A request to change the baseline of a product, process or condition. It is a type of issue.
responsible authority	The person or identity who is authorized to initiate the project and to commit funds.
residual risk	The risk remaining after a risk response has been applied.
reviewer	An independent person or independent group that assesses products on the basis of the criteria specified in the Product Description.
risk	An uncertain event or set of events that, if it arises, has consequences for the achievement of objectives. A risk is measured by a combination of the probability of a perceived threat or opportunity occurring, and the magnitude of its impact on objectives.

risk actionee	A nominated owner of an action to address a risk. Some actions may not be within the remit of the risk owner to control explicitly. In such a situation there should be a nominated owner of the action to address the risk. They will need to keep the risk owner up-to-date with the situation.
risk appetite	The attitude of an organization towards the taking of risks. The risk appetite determines the extent to which risks are acceptable.
risk assessment	The appraisal of the possible likelihood and impact of the individual risks and of the aggregated risk.
risk evaluation	The assesssment of the net impact of the identified opportunities and threats when aggregated together.
risk management	The systematic application of principles, processes and procedures for the identification and assessment of risks, and the planning and implementing of risk responses.
Risk Management Strategy	A description of the goals of applying to risk management, as well as the procedures that will be adopted, roles and responsibilities, risk tolerances, the timing of risk management interventions, the tools and techniques that will be used, and the reporting requirements.
risk owner	A named person who is responsible for the management, monitoring and control of a particular risk assigned to them.
risk profile	A description of the types of risks which an organization faces and its exposure to those risks.
Risk Register	A register of the identified risks, including the corresponding status and history.
risk response	An action that will bring the exposure to risks within acceptable levels for the organization.
risk response, accept	A deliberate decision not to implement any risk responses to a threat on the assumption that taking action will not be effective until the threat actually occurs.
risk response, avoid	A risk response resulting in the fact that a threat cannot occur or will have no longer an impact.
risk response category	A subgroup of risk responses
risk response, enhance	The risk response to increase the probability and/or the impact of an opportunity.
risk response, exploit	A rsik measure ensuring that an opportunity is seized and that the impact will be realized
risk response, fallback	A risk response to reduce the impact materializes. Planning of a risk when it materializes. The response is not deployed until the risk actually occurs or (as the case may be) threatens to occur.
risk, impact	The result of a threat or opportunity if this occurs.
risk, proximity	The time period in which risks can occur. The impact of the risk can vary during the period depending on when it occurs.
risk response, reduce	A proactive risk response to reduce the probability and/ or the impact of a threat.
risk response, reject	A deliberate decision not to implement any responses to an opportunity on the assumption that taking action will not be effective until the opportunity actually occurs

risk response, share	An agreement between two parties to share the positive as well as the negative impacts of risks (a threat or an opportunity) by means of a pain/gain formula.
risk response, transfer	The transfer of the negative (financial) impact of a risk to a third party.
risk tolerance	The threshold levels of risk exposure within which it is not necessary to escalate to the next level of management level in the form of an Exception Report.
risk tolerance line	The line drawn in the summary risk profile dividing the risks which actually can be accepted and those which cannot be accepted and have to be escalated to the next management level for decision.
role description	A description of the tasks, authorities and responsibilities for a specific role.
scope	The sum total of the deliverable products and their requirements for a plan. The scope is described by the product breakdown structure and the accompanying Product Descriptions.
scope tolerance	The permissible deviation to the scope of a plan, within which it is not necessary to escalate to the next management level.
Senior Responsible Owner	The individual responsible for ensuring that a project or programme of change meets its objectives and delivers the projected benefits. The person should be the owner of the overall business change that is being supported by the project. The SRO appoints the project's executive.
Senior Supplier	The role that represents the suppliers on the Project Board. The Senior Supplier must stand up for the supplier interests within the project and provide supplier resources.
Senior User	The role that represents the users on the Project Board. The Senior User must ensure that the user needs are specified correctly and that the solution meets those needs.
specialist product	A product that must be realized as a part of the specifications during the project. This can be a part of the eventual end result of an interim product of which one or several are dependent on subsequent products.
sponsor	This is not a PRINCE2 term, but it is often used in organizations to indicate the driving force behind a project.The sponsor can be the Executive on the Project Board, or the person who has appointed the Executive.
stage	See 'management stage' and 'technical stage'.
Stage Plan	A detailed plan for the Project Manager to use as the basis for project management control throughout a stage within the project. The Stage Plan also provides a basis to the Project Board for authorizing the start of the stage concerned and making available the capacity required.
stakeholder	Any individual, group or organization that can affect, be affected by, or perceives itself to be affected by, an initiative (for example a programme, project, activity or risk).
start-up	The pre-project activities of the Executive and Project Manager to prepare the outline Business Case, the Project Brief and the Initiation Stage Plan.

strategy	An approach or line to take in order to achieve long-term aims. Strategies can exist at different levels – corporate, programme and project. PRINCE2 defines four strategies: Communication Management Strategy, Configuration Management Strategy, Quality Management Strategy and Risk Management Strategy.
supplier	The person or group who is responsible for the delivery of the project's specialist products.
tailoring	The appropriate use of PRINCE2 on any given project, ensuring that there is the correct amount of planning, control, governance and use of the processes and themes.
Team Manager	The person responsible for the production of the specialist products allocated by the Project Manager, according to the agreed Work Package, to an appropriate quality, timescale and at a cost acceptable to the Project Board.
Team Plan	An optional level of plan used by a team responsible for the delivery of a Work Package.
technical stage	A method of grouping work together by the set of techniques used, or the products created. This results in stages covering elements such as design, build and implementation.
theme	An aspect of project management that must be applied mandatorily and continuously, and that requires specific treatement for the PRINCE2 processes to be effective.
time-driven control	A management control that is triggered by a moment in time. PRINCE2 has two key time-driven progress reports: a Highlight Report and a Checkpoint Report.
time tolerance	The permissible deviation to the plan's time, within which it is not necessary to escalate to the next management level.
tolerance	The permissable deviation above and below a plan's target for time and costs without escalating the deviation to the next level of management. Other tolerance levels that can be applied are scope, benefits, risks and quality.
tranche	A term from programme management that describes a group of projects structured around distinct step changes in capability and benefit delivery.
user	The person or group who will use one or more of the project's products.
user acceptance	An explicit confirmation by those who are actually going to use the delivered products in an operational environment that they comply with the acceptance criteria.
variant	A configuration which slightly differs from the original.
version	A specific baseline of a product. Versions commonly use naming conventions that enable the sequence or date of the baseline to be identified.
waterfall method	A developmental method that has a linear sequence, with distinct goals for each phase of development. Once a phase of development is completed, the development moves to the next phase and earlier phases are not revisited.

Work Package

The set of information relevant to the creation of one or more products. It will contain a description of the work, the Product Description(s) and details of any constraints on production. It also includes confirmation of the agreement between the Project Manager and the person or Team Manager who is to implement the Work Package that the work can be done within the constraints.

Appendix G Additional information

G.1 OGC relevant publications

Managing Successful Projects with PRINCE2®, 2009 Edition
This English manual contains the official description of the PRINCE2 method of managing projects:
Author: Organization of Government Commerce
Publisher: The Stationary Office
ISBN: 9780113310593

Directing Successful Projects with PRINCE2®, 2009 Edition
This English manual contains the official description of the PRINCE2 method of directing projects, specifically for Project Board members and senior management:
Author: Organization of Government Commerce
Publisher: The Stationary Office
ISBN: 9780113310609

Management of Risk: guidance for Practitioners
This English manual contains the official description of the M_o_R method of managing risks:
Author: Organization of Government Commerce
Publisher: The Stationary Office
ISBN: 9780113310388

Managing Successful Programmes
This English manual contains the official description of the MSP method of managing programmes:
Author: Organization of Government Commerce
Publisher: The Stationary Office
ISBN: 9780113310401

Portfolio, Programme and Project Offices
This English manual contains the official description of the P3O method of organizing portfolio, programme and project support in organizations:
Author: Organization of Government Commerce
Publisher: The Stationary Office
ISBN: 9780113311248

G.2   Literature

Aken, T. van, *De weg naar projectsucces, 4th impression.* Van Haren Publishing, 2009

Fredriksz H. e.a., *Handboek projectmanagement, de TIPI-Approach*, Thema, 2002

Groote, G. e.a., *Projecten leiden,* Het Spectrum, 2008

Hedeman B, Seegers R., *PRINCE2 - Pocket Guide*, Van Haren Publishing, 2009

Hedeman B., Vis van Heemst G., *Programmamanagement op basis van MSP, MSP Edition 2007*, Van Haren Publishing, 2009

Hedeman B., Vis van Heemst G., Riepma R., *Projectmanagement op basis van NCB version 3*, Van Haren Publishing, 2008

NCB version 3 - Nederlandse Competence Baseline, Van Haren Publishing, 2007

PMBOK Guide, *4th impression- Dutch edition*, Van Haren Publishing, 2009

G.3   Contact addresses

The APM Group
7-8 Queen Square
High Wycombe
Buckinghamshire P11 2BP
United Kingdom
Tel.: +44(0) 1494 452450
Fax: +44(0) 1494 459559
E-mail: info@apmgroup.co.uk
URL: www.apmgroup.co.uk

APMG-Benelux
P.O. Box 303167
1270 EA Huizen
Tel.: 035 523 1845
Fax: 035 523 1021
E-mail: office@apmg-benelux.com
URL: www.apmg-benelux.com

Exin Institute
P.O. Box 19147
3501 DC Utrecht
Tel.: 030 234 4811
Fax: 030 234 4850
E-mail: info@exin.nl
URL: www.exin.nl

Netherlands Prince User Group
P.O. Box 19020
3501 DA Utrecht
Tel.: 06-46522120
Fax: 084-7471441
E-mail: secretariaat@pugnl.nl
URL: www.pugnl.nl

Index

A

acceptance   229
acceptance criteria   6, 48, 114, 229
activity   229
activity network   229
added value   31, 178
Administrator   52
agile methods   179
announcement of project closure   130
approval   229
approver   229
assumption   229
assurance   229
authority   229
authorization   229

B

bar chart   229
baseline   229
baseline management product   229
baseline products   187
benefit   28, 133, 140, 162, 168, 174, 229
Benefits Review Plan   31, 162, 189, 229
benefits tolerance   96, 229
Brainstorming   77
Break-even point   33
bureaucracy   178
Business   36
Business Case   6, 25, 27, 32, 112, 114, 118,
    121, 122, 138, 140, 153, 162, 167, 174,
    189, 229
Business Case content   32
Business Case PRINCE2 approach   29
Business Case risks   81
Business Case roles&responsibilities   33
Business Case type of   28

C

cause   229
Cause-effect diagrams   77
center of excellence   230
Chairperson   52
change   26, 85, 137
Change Authority   40, 91, 138, 139,
    217, 230
change budget   91, 138, 230
change control   230
change control procedures   90
change, roles & responsibilities   92
checkpoint   230
Checkpoint Report   67, 81, 99, 136, 139,
    153, 190, 230
Checkpoint Reports   67, 81, 153
Closing a Project (CP)   159
closure notification   230
closure recommendation   230
Commercial customer-supplier projects   180
Communication Management Strategy   43,
    120, 126, 129, 131, 155, 191, 230
Compulsory projects   28
concern   86
concession   230
Configuratie librarian   138
configuration   86
configuration item   86, 155, 230
Configuration Item Record   87, 140, 161,
    192, 230
configuration librarian   136
configuration management   86, 140,
    147, 230
configuration management database
    (CMDB)   87
configuration management procedures   89
Configuration Management Strategy   86,
    119, 175, 193, 230
configuration management system   230
constraint   230
contingency   230

Contingency Plan   121
Controlling a Stage (CS)   133
controls   140, 230
corporate management   37
coporate or programme management   36,
    105, 122, 126, 154, 162
corrective action   231
cost tolerance   231
critical path   68, 231
customer   35, 105, 113, 120, 121, 122, 147,
    168, 179, 231
customer's quality expectations   114, 231

D

Daily Log   88, 99, 194, 231
delivery   105
Delivery stage   107
Delphi method   69
dependencies   231
Development projects   181
develop phasing   184
directing   105
Directing a Project (DP)   125
dis-benefit   28, 231
DSDM Atern   179

E

earliest possible finish   68
earliest possible start   68
earned value analysis   231
embedding PRINCE2   231
End Project Report   81, 99, 130, 162,
    194, 231
end result   35, 183, 231
end stage assessment   152, 231
End Stage Report   81, 99, 123, 127, 154,
    195, 231
escalating exceptions   100
event-driven control   231
event-driven reports   98
evolutionary project method   184
Evolving projects   28
exception   93, 231
exception assessment   231
Exception Plan 61, 99, 128, 155, 200,
    226, 232

Exception Report   81, 155, 196, 232
Executive   5, 37, 38, 58, 105, 114, 121,
    174, 179, 212, 232
expected financial value   79

F

feasibility lifecycle   182
feasibility projects   181
feasibility study   182, 183, 232
file structure   53
Final delivery stage   107
fishbone diagram   77
follow–on action recommendations   232
follow-on actions   161
follow-on maintenance   53
force field analysis   77
four management levels   105

G

Gannt chart   232
gateway   10
governance   232
governing   105

H

handover   232
Health check   221
Highlight Report   81, 99, 139, 196, 232

I

identify dependencies   68
identifying context   77
identifying risks   77
inherent risk   232
Initiating a Project (IP)   117
Initiation stage   107, 114, 232
Initiation Stage Plan   114, 115, 127
issue   73, 85, 136, 137, 232
issue and change control   85
issue control procedures   90
Issue Register   88, 99, 137, 139, 153, 197
Issue Report   88, 99, 197
ITIL   10

L

large projects   179
latest possible finish   68
latest possible start   68
lead-time   70
Lessons Log   77, 99, 163, 198
Lessons Report   99, 155, 163, 199
Lifecycle models   179

M

maintenance acceptance   233
Management by exception   94
management by objectives (MBO)   94
management processes   106
management products   187, 233
management stages   97, 233
Management Strategy   175
managing   105
Managing a Stage Boundary (SB)   151
Managing Product Delivery (MP)   145
Managing Successful Programmes   174
meeting   52
milestone   233
M_o_R   10
MoSCoW method   48
MSP   10
Multi-organization projects   28, 181
Multi-project management   168

N

Net Present Value   33
Network planning   68
Not-for-profit projects   28

O

off-specification   86, 233
opportunity   74, 233
optimistic estimate   70
organization   25, 35, 117, 127, 130, 161, 168, 178
outcome   28, 233
output   6, 28, 41, 233
overall margin   68

P

P2MM   10
P3M3   10
P3O   10
Pareto analysis   79
Payback period   32
performance target   233
pessimistic estimate   70
PfM   10
Phasing projects   177
plan   200, 233
plan approach   58
plan design   62
planning   25, 57
planning horizon   233
planning levels   59
planning PRINCE2 approach   61
planning, roles&responsibilities   72
portfolio   233
Portfolio management   168
post-project benefits review   162
precedence chart   69
premature closure   233
prepare estimates   69
Pre-project preparation   107
Presenter   52
PRINCE2   7, 9, 106, 178, 233
PRINCE2 benefits   11
PRINCE2 method   9
PRINCE2 principles   19, 233
PRINCE2 project   233
PRINCE2 quality approach   47
PRINCE2 themes   25, 233
probability   233
Probability impact matrix   79
Probability tree   79
problem   86
problem/concern   234
procedure   234
process   7, 106, 108, 118, 134, 138, 146, 152, 178, 234
process descriptions   107
processes   105
producer   234

product   35, 39, 121, 133, 136, 140, 147,
    148, 151, 154, 162, 174, 177, 182, 183,
    213, 234
product-based planning   218, 234
product breakdown structure   63, 77, 234
product checklist   234
product description   49, 66, 139, 147,
    152, 234
product flow diagram   66, 77, 234
product lifecycle   234
product security   182
Product Status Account   87, 99, 136,
    201, 234
programme   108, 137, 167, 168, 179, 234
programme management   37, 96, 155
programme standard   230
Progress   26, 93
progress control   95
progress, roles&responsibilities   101
project   1, 167, 234
project approach   113, 121, 122, 126,
    153, 234
Project Assurance   40, 112, 115, 138, 153,
    154, 174, 215, 234
project authorization notification   235
Project Board   37, 42, 96, 112, 113, 118,
    121, 122, 127, 129, 134, 137, 138, 139,
    152, 155, 160, 161, 162, 179, 211
Project Brief   107, 113, 114, 121, 126, 174,
    202, 235
project closure   163
project controls   120
Project Environment   167
project file   54
Project Initiation Documentation   114, 117,
    118, 122, 126, 127, 131, 139, 153, 156,
    203, 235
Project Initiation Documention   118
project initiation notification   235
Project issue   138, 139, 140
project lifecycle   107, 235
project management   1, 180, 184, 235
Project management structure   36
project management team   37, 120, 126,
    133, 153, 177, 235
Project Management Team (PMT)   37

project management team structure
    38, 235
Project Manager   4, 36, 40, 58, 96, 105,
    112, 115, 118, 121, 125, 126, 127, 128,
    129, 130, 135, 136, 137, 138, 139, 140,
    145, 147, 151, 152, 154, 155, 159, 161,
    162, 171, 174, 177, 178, 183, 184, 235
project managment   171
project mandate   113, 174, 235
project office   235
project organization   7, 37, 160
Project Plan   59, 98, 121, 138, 140,
    153, 235
project portfolio   168
project product   235
project, PRINCE2 definition   2
Project Product Description   48, 63,
    204, 235
Project Support   41, 112, 136, 138, 154,
    174, 217, 235
Projects within programmes   174
project team   5
project tolerances   100
project types   182

Q

quality   25, 45, 140, 176, 235
quality assurance   46, 236
quality audit trail   47
quality control   46, 51, 154, 236
quality criteria   39, 236
quality documents   51
quality file   54
quality inspection   236
quality management   45, 236
Quality Management Strategy   49, 120,
    175, 205, 236
Quality Management System (QMS)
    45, 236
quality methods   51
quality planning   46, 48
quality PRINCE2 approach   47
quality records   236
Quality Register   50, 99, 120, 136, 139,
    140, 156, 206, 236
quality review   52, 236

quality, roles&responsibilities   55
quality tolerance   96, 236

R

records   187, 236
registers   236
release   236
report   189, 236
request for change   86, 236
requirements   184
residual risk   236
responsible authority   236
result   167, 179, 184
Return on investment (ROI)   32
reviewer   52, 236
reviewing checklists   77
Risico Register   122, 136, 139
risk   25, 73, 113, 114, 133, 137, 138, 140,
     147, 153, 154, 176, 183, 184, 236
risk actionee   82, 237
risk analyse   71
risk appetite   76, 237
risk assessment   237
risk budget   82, 121
risk evaluation   237
risk management   237
risk management procedures   76
Risk Management Strategy   75, 119, 237
risk owner   82, 237
risk profile   79, 237
Risk Register   76, 99, 137, 139, 207, 237
risk response   80, 237
risk response category   237
risk, roles&responsibilities   83
risk tolerance   76, 96
risk tolerance line   238
role description   238

S

schedule   70
scope   238
scope tolerance   238
Senior Responsible Owner   238
Senior Supplier   39, 115, 147, 213, 238
Senior User   39, 213, 238
six tolerance areas   96

small projects   176
specialist product   238
specifications   77, 91, 183
spiral model   184
sponsor   183, 238
stage   238
Stage Exception Plan   155
stage file   54
Stage plan   41, 59, 60, 98, 114, 118, 119,
     123, 126, 127, 134, 135, 138, 139, 140,
     147, 152, 154, 155, 238
stages   107, 184
stage tolerances   100
stakeholders   1, 5, 42, 238
Starting up a Project (SU)   109
start-up   238
Statement of acceptance   161
strategy   239
supplier   5, 36, 40, 120, 140, 160, 168, 239

T

tailoring   171, 239
Team Manager   36, 41, 57, 72, 96, 112,
     134, 135, 136, 140, 147, 177, 178,
     215, 239
Team Plan   59, 60, 147, 239
technical stages   97, 239
theme   239
threat   74
time-driven control   239
time-driven reports   98
time tolerance   239
tolerance   38, 93, 96, 135, 138, 140, 151,
     154,155, 239
tranche   239
Turner & Cochrane   183
Type 1 projects   183
Type 2 projects   183
Type 3 projects   184
Type 4 projects   184

U

user   36, 161, 184, 239
user acceptance   239
users   5, 36

V

variant   239
version   239

W

waterfall method   179, 239
WBS dictionary   68
Work breakdown structure (WBS)   67
Work package   41, 99, 134, 136, 140, 146,
    147, 178, 208, 240
Work Package tolerance   100